NEW TESTAMENT TENSIONS
AND THE
CONTEMPORARY CHURCH

NEW TESTAMENT TENSIONS AND THE CONTEMPORARY CHURCH

Carl S. Dudley
and
Earle Hilgert

FORTRESS PRESS   PHILADELPHIA

For
Shirley and Elvire

Library of Congress Cataloging-in-Publication Data

Dudley, Carl S., 1932–
    New Testament tensions and the contemporary churches.

    Bibliography: p.
    Includes index.
    1. Church controversies. 2. Church controversies—Biblical teaching. 3. Bible. N.T.—Criticism, interpretation, etc. I. Hilgert, Earle. II. Title.
    BV652.9.D83   1987   262   86–45914
    ISBN 0–8006–1955–2

2653A87   Printed in the United States of America   1–1955

CONTENTS

PREFACE

This book had its beginning in a course on "New Testament Tensions in Contemporary Settings," which the authors have taught together at McCormick Theological Seminary. In this endeavor we made the happy discovery that a professor whose life is intensely engaged with the problems of Christian congregations today and one who insists on living in the first century could work together with profit to their students. The bridge between the New Testament and the contemporary church that became real in our experience is one we have undertaken to describe and explain in this book.

More colleagues and friends than we can mention here have contributed to this effort. Students who lived through our initial explorations with us were particularly helpful in relating these to their own insights from their church experiences. In the summer of 1986 a group of pastors and laypersons spent several days working through the initial draft of the book. Their criticisms and suggestions were the foundation for an extensive revision. To them we are deeply grateful. Above all we are indebted to a number of faculty and ministerial colleagues who read the manuscript in full with great care and offered extensive written and oral critiques: Edward F. Campbell, Jr., Hugh Halverstadt, Laurence L. Welborn, and Steve Young of McCormick Seminary, Elise Magers, and A. Wayne Benson, F. Andrew Carhartt, Clayton Cook, Jeffrey E. Doane, Edward Pierson, and Janet Van Lear, all pastors of experience and wisdom, and Loren Mead of the Alban Institute. Without their criticism and support our thinking and writing would have been much the poorer.

The administrators of McCormick Seminary, Jack L. Stotts and David Ramage, Jr., presidents past and present, and Dean Lewis S.

Mudge made possible study leaves for both of us during the 1985–86 academic year. For this and their enthusiastic support we are grateful. Dorothy Hampton's skill with a word processor and her good nature when the load was heavy have eased the burden for us.

Davis Perkins, of Fortress Press, has exceeded normal editorial responsibilities by his careful reading and numerous valuable suggestions both as to style and scholarly content. To all these friends and colleagues go our gratitude and thanks, while we, of course, take full responsibility for what finally appears in these pages.

Carl S. Dudley
Earle Hilgert

INTRODUCTION

Tensions in the church are the focus of this book. By tensions we refer to those experiences of stress that arise from external and internal problems that stretch the church to the limits of its possibilities, and accompany decisions that challenge the church and may threaten to destroy its effectiveness. This study examines several significant tensions in the development of the New Testament church, and suggests comparisons and implications for contemporary congregations.

By focusing on the tensions of the New Testament church, the authors assume a rather different way of reading Scripture. In other settings the Bible is used as a source for spiritual nourishment, theological foundations, and ethical considerations of the faith. This book looks at biblical and other ancient material through the lenses of the social sciences to catch glimpses of the organizing decisions and social behavior of Christian gatherings in the first and early second centuries after Christ. The processes of human interaction are sufficiently similar to provide helpful and provocative comparisons despite intervening centuries and radical shifts in culture. From this perspective what is needed to read the New Testament is insight gained not only from historical perspective but also from congregational experience.

This focus on tension accents the social pressures and leadership decisions essential to congregational vitality, then and now. By comparing and contrasting congregational dynamics we can explore several sources of energy that seem evident in the early church, and are often lacking in contemporary congregations. For this, both biblical scholarship and congregational studies are essential: each to better understand the other, and both to interpret and to challenge the church.

The chapters of this book explore tension-related sources of energy in the early church, beginning with the most basic, progressing through the more dramatic, and concluding with the most durable. These tensions are discussed in the order they might be experienced by a new member or an entering pastor.

1. "Community Formation": How the early church, in basic group-building process, used language symbols and group dynamics to establish strong congregations. We begin with basic group process since what the early church did so well is often unknown, ignored, or overlooked in contemporary congregations.
2. "The Energy of Counterculture Christianity": How the early church kept from being coopted by the culture or subverted by its own success. In the face of many sorts of contemporary church "captivity," we note several ways by which the early church struggled to maintain its distinctiveness and sustain its revolutionary vision.
3. "Faith Crisis and Christian Witness": How the early church turned major crises of faith into energy for evangelical zeal. By contrast, established contemporary churches often rationalize faith crises rather than mobilize this energy for appropriate Christian witness.
4. "Using Conflict Constructively": How the early church faced up to conflict and used it constructively. In the contemporary church, by comparison, withdrawal and denial of conflict often immobilizes the congregation and frustrates even its positive impulses.
5. "Rituals of Structure and Mystery": How the early church used ritual, especially in worship, to develop an international movement and to protect the Christian vision in its sacred space. As traditional, even "creative" contemporary worship often becomes repetitious and boring, the energy of early church worship in widely scattered and richly different situations is notable.

There are certain things that this book is not, and these should be made clear at the outset. It is not a sociology of either contemporary or early Christianity in any of the directions such a study might go: it is not a systematic description, history, or analysis of the social worlds of the church. It does not follow a particular school of sociological thought, but draws on a variety of social theories. Further, it is not a program for action, but a way of comparing and learning from the tensions experienced in Christian communities.

Generalized theories from historical studies and social sciences cannot be applied like a cookie cutter to any situation, particularly when that situation lies at a distance from us of nearly two thousand years. Our method, rather, is to use theoretical perspectives as lenses to view old and familiar situations in new light so as to ask fresh questions and hopefully to gain further understandings.[1]

LEARNING FROM HISTORICAL STUDIES

Certain historical and methodological perspectives have contributed to the approach of this book. The problem of how the experiences and written records of past generations or alien cultures can be meaningful to one's current world has occupied thinkers since ancient times. On the one hand, the church has always recognized that the testimony of the Christian communities of the first hundred years, as preserved in the New Testament, plays a role of special significance and authority for subsequent generations, as under God they live their life in the world and seek to understand that life. This is true regardless of how the authority of Scripture may be conceptualized at any given time or place. On the other hand, the church continues to struggle with the question of how that Scripture, ever more remote in time and culture from us, can remain relevant, can make valid claims on us.

This age-old problem of how past and present can be related meaningfully has been intensified in modern times. With the Enlightenment of the eighteenth century a keen sense of the gulf that separates ancient and modern times became clearly felt as a problem. This was not due only to the fact that the culture of the West by that time was vastly different from that of the ancient world but even more to a new consciousness of history.

Over the last two hundred years there have been a variety of attempts using various intellectual disciplines to relate past and present meaningfully. Christians have, understandably, been much occupied with this issue, and have drawn both on theology and on secular fields of thought. Salient as a characteristically theological approach has been that of *Heilsgeschichte*, "the history of salvation." This view takes from Scripture itself the understanding of a continuity in God's dealing with Israel and the church in terms of a divine plan. This is, of course, not immediately obvious from the data of history but is part of the Christian's confession as seen through eyes of faith.[2] An appreciation of this view is basic to a perception of much of the dynamic that moved the early church and moves many Christian communities today, for it offers a self-understanding of great power in the formation and maintenance of community.

Apart from such strictly theological solutions to the question of the relevance of the past, there have also been important efforts based on philosophy and the social sciences. Ultimately the most widely influential of these has been that initiated by G. W. F. Hegel (1770–1831), who taught that there is an impulse, a dynamic "idea" running through history which, by means of a dialectical process of action, reaction, and synthesis, moves humanity to ever higher levels of culture.[3] Hegelian thought exercised a profound influence on biblical scholarship in the nineteenth century (as, for example, in the work of F. C. Baur [1792–1860] and his followers). Its greatest impact, of course, has been through its economic interpretation by Karl Marx. Without subscribing to Hegelian idealism as the metaphysics of history, the authors of this book are nevertheless impressed by the dynamics of social and economic conflict as continuing factors in shaping human experience.

Since World War I, many have been attracted to philosophical existentialism as a way of relating the present to the past. In New Testament studies, Rudolf Bultmann (1884–1976), building on the thought of Martin Heidegger (1889–1976), was particularly prominent in developing such a rationale. He was convinced that throughout history humans have been similar in their sense of being human, their consciousness of the ultimate issues of life and death, the necessity of choice, their self-ishness and self-lessness. If these do not change, they then provide a continuity between past and present. The relevance of Scripture is realized in our identifying with biblical humanity's struggle in faith with these existential issues.[4] While recognizing that the existential perspective is not the sole basis for the relevance of the past, the authors are struck with its cogency particularly at the level of personal religious and psychological experience.

An essentially nonhistorical or synchronic program for relating the past to the present or varying cultures to each other has been offered in recent years by students of structuralism. Analyzing the structures and patterns of a piece of literature or a society, they discern "deep structures" beneath time- and culture-conditioned phenomena, which they recognize as being widely common to humanity. This "deep structural level" thus provides insights into documents from other times and other cultural worlds which can be applied to our time and our world.[5] While we affirm the value of structuralist analysis, we do not employ it in this study in its more specific sense as a methodology for the elucidation of texts. Our thinking has been deeply influenced, however, by structuralism in the broader sense of the enduring significance of social structure for an understanding of community dynamics then and now.

In seeking to reconstruct the history and thinking of the church to approximately the middle of the second century, we work with the methods and tools of critical biblical and historical scholarship. If one is to understand both the movement led by Jesus and the nascent church, it is important to recognize that the Gospels are throughout an interweaving of elements that emerged in the Christian communities across the decades from the days of Jesus to the times in which they were written late in the first century. Each Gospel thus reflects community development and the tensions inherent in that experience. Similarly, while those epistles generally recognized by scholars as authentically from Paul (Romans, 1 and 2 Corinthians, Galatians, Philippians, 1 Thessalonians, Philemon) allow us to hear his voice, those by his followers and admirers, along with the Acts, offer a variety of perspectives not only on his teachings and his churches, but on developments in Christianity covering many decades after his death. As we move into the second century, there is no clear line, historically, between the later books of the New Testament and the Apostolic Fathers; all this literature must be seen as interactive in providing us insights on the social development of the early Christian communities.

LEARNING FROM THE SOCIAL SCIENCES

The various approaches noted above are compatible with insights and challenges to the church that are available through the tools of social science research. For this study of church tensions, dynamic patterns derived from the social sciences provide invaluable resources for relating the experiences of the church in the first century to those of the church today. From the standpoint of the New Testament and the early church, pioneer work in this direction was undertaken in the 1920s, especially at the University of Chicago, by Shirley Jackson Case and his associates. They were concerned to analyze and interpret the early history of Christianity in terms of the social forces that impacted and shaped it. They were working, however, at a time when sociology itself was in a formative state, and they made, in fact, relatively little use of sociological theory.

Only in the last few years have biblical scholars and church historians begun to avail themselves of the more sophisticated resources of sociological analysis and modeling that now are available. These studies are based on the premise that human social groups tend to follow discernible patterns of development, action, and reaction, given analogous circumstances. We can study modern contemporary social and socioreligious groups and discern such patterns. When we find similar patterns of action and reaction given similar conditions in the past, what we have learned about the present throws light on what happened in the past and on forces that were at work to cause it to happen.[6]

This is the hermeneutical angle of vision from which this book undertakes to view the early and the present-day church. In doing so we make no claim that a social science approach is either more or less appropriate to the task than alternative approaches that have been constructed on the basis of other intellectual disciplines. The gulf separating us from the past may be crossed by many bridges.

SOME PITFALLS

At the same time, certain pitfalls must be avoided. Generalizations must be challenged, especially when we are dealing with as narrow a range of sources as are available to us from first-century Christianity. Unfortunately, in historical research, the fewer the available sources, the greater is the temptation to generalize. When unburdened and unconfused by a plethora of apparently divergent facts, the mind of a historian can all too easily soar to heady heights of generalization. Our sources of knowledge regarding the history of Christianity, at least until the middle of the second century, are frustratingly meager and allow us to see at best only a few paths through the forest, leading here and there to clearings into which the sun shines with brilliance; but even these paths frequently disappear and can only be picked up again at a distance.

Another temptation is the facile imposition of modern social and economic categories on a past that was not necessarily structured in the same way as ours and in which the flow of social dynamics often did not follow patterns we may take for granted. For example, without clear evidence from ancient sources, we should not proceed to the assumption that interaction between urban and rural societies was dynamically as we know it in modern America or even as it existed a century ago in Europe; nor can we take it as a foregone conclusion that the nexus between wealth and class status was that with which we are familiar today. In each case we must first establish the situation as fully as data will allow and confess great tentativeness where, as often, the data are sparse.

A third area for caution is signaled by the fact that we must ask questions of ancient texts that their authors did not intentionally answer. In the area of biblical theology, we agree with the warning of Oscar Cullmann against posing "falsely put questions," seeking to derive authoritative answers from the Bible to questions its authors had no intention of raising. But in attempting to reconstruct a social world, the situation is somewhat different. Here the historian is a detective and must be alert to inferences from data as well as to direct statements of fact. We cannot go back to a past world and conduct interviews, distribute questionnaires, or carry out field investigations—in short, use any of the on-site techniques characteristic of the social scientist. Furthermore, much of our data, particularly in the area of religion, are clouded by understandings of causation that mask, if not actually defy, sociological analysis. If we are to derive plausible understandings of the social dynamics of an ancient culture, we must constantly seek to look beyond the obvious but to do so with a clear realization of the risks inherent in such a procedure.[7]

Finally, and perhaps most importantly, there is the pitfall of reductionism, of explaining religious experience, as well as other aspects of human history, in terms of social psychology alone. From the standpoint of the social sciences, religion *is* a human phenomenon, "a human projection, grounded in specific infrastructures of human history."[8] By their very nature, the presuppositions and the methodologies of the social sciences can legitimately go no further than this. Questions raised by the social sciences regarding religion can rightly be answered only on the basis of critical, controlled observation. For the sociologist qua sociologist, the possibility of the transcendent as a factor in human society rightly remains a nonquestion. At the same time, the theologian legitimately works with questions that often cannot be answered empirically. As much as psychology may truthfully say about certain charismatic phenomena, for instance, other dimensions for investigation justly remain to the theologian. Each discipline should observe its limits and respect those of the other. This is particularly true in matters of causation, where the social sciences discern dynamics and track processes, while questions of ultimate causation and meaning lie in the realm of theology.

SOCIAL SCIENCES AND THEOLOGY: A POSITIVE RELATIONSHIP

What we have said, however, does not mean that the social sciences and theology are hermetically sealed against each other. While they should not attempt to answer each other's questions, there can be legitimate interaction between them. This presupposes, of course, a mutual recognition of each other's function; such mutuality implies a willingness on each side to take the other seriously, and to be informed and cautioned by it. For example, in reflecting on the doctrine of forgiveness, the theologian should be instructed by insights of psychology regarding human emotional dynamics, while the social scientist does well to recognize the more imponderable dimensions of human conscience. Such a dialogue needs to be genuinely mutual.[9]

The social science sources we have chosen generally share with us a respect for the church, and a dedication to our common task to understand and interpret human behavior. Such mutual respect is important for understanding—and not misunderstanding—what we seek to say in this book. This is particularly significant in chapter 3, where we discuss structures and dynamics of belief maintenance, and in chapter 5, regarding the sacraments. We treat these in a functionalist way not because we wish to reduce them only to this dimension but because we are dealing with them from the perspective of the social sciences. At the same time we share the conviction that there are dimensions of reality beyond the reach of the social sciences to which one must look for a sense of ultimacy. In this study we seek to identify areas of overlapping interest where each of these perspectives may inform and enrich the other.

ONE

COMMUNITY FORMATION: VISION, INTIMACY, AND ORGANIZATION

Although contemporary churches have a wide variety of cultural symbols that a particular church may use to define its identity, the Christians of the first century had to generate a new reality. They needed a fresh "social world" that was strong enough to carry the meanings they had experienced and bind them together. They had to make their own identity clear.

Christianity entered a highly developed world, a complex, tightly organized society of interlocking political, social, economic, and religious structures. The Roman government held together one empire from Britain to Egypt, from Gibralter to the Euphrates, through a system of law and administration that was, on the whole, intelligently organized and efficiently administered. This was made possible by a network of roads and shipping lanes that also brought to the cities of the Mediterranean basin the trade goods of lands far beyond the bounds of the empire. In the shops of Rome, Antioch, Alexandria, and throughout the empire, Christians saw and could buy products from China, Scandinavia, and central Africa. Trade and travel of such breadth and magnitude was possible only in a world of social, economic, and political sophistication.

At the same time the Roman Empire was composed of a bewildering array of races, languages, cultures, social groups, and religions, a potpourri that only a structure such as that which the Romans provided could have held together. It was a world of men and women sharply divided into a multitude of classes and categories, but firmly united by a network of legal, economic, and political institutions.

This balance between the centrifugal forces of diversity and centripetal power of empire produced a society in which people generally understood their place in life, their *tychē* or "fate," as the Greeks called it. Men and women knew themselves as Gauls, or Greeks, or Jews, or Egyptians; as freepersons, slaves, or freedpersons; as Roman citizens or not, all of which situations were largely beyond their choice or control. In matters of religion there was, of course, greater opportunity for personal decision: one might worship Isis, Mithra, Yahweh, or a host of other deities. But even here, some limitation was in force through the institution of *religiones licitae,* those religions to which the government had given formal recognition. Thus to live in the Roman world was to live in a highly categorized, strictly ordered society which was at the same time one of vast diversity.

Within this variegated network there was, however, no previously prepared place for Christianity. While Christian proclamation answered the longings of many people in the first century, there was no prearranged slot for it in the social and religious scheme of things that would offer an immediate sense of identity to its adherents, that would give them a clear answer to the question, Who are we?

In fact, we have no record that Christians of the earliest period had a name that clearly distinguished them as a self-conscious group. Acts 11:26 reports a tradition from about fifteen years after Easter that the believers were first called "Christians" at Antioch. But the term appears only two other times in the New Testament, in Acts 26:28 (in the mouth of King Agrippa) and in 1 Pet. 4:16 ("If one suffers as a Christian, let him not be ashamed, but under that name let him glorify God"). In each of these cases it is on the lips of unbelievers! Apparently it was considered a term of reproach; Paul never uses it. Throughout the Book of Acts—and it is unique to Acts—Christians are referred to as "that Way," a vague enough term, but one with which Luke apparently was comfortable. The absence in the New Testament of any clearly recognized name for the Christian community is indicative of the problem with which Christians struggled in determining their own identity as a group.

Racial, national, and religious ambiguities complicated the question of identity. Initially Christians were all Jews—and Judaism was a many-faceted society. For the first several decades, probably most Jews who became Christians did not sense themselves to be any the less attached to Judaism; they simply saw themselves as identifying with a new sect within the purview of their multicolored Jewish world. Even converts who were not as "zealous for the law" as those portrayed in Acts 21:20 could still consider themselves good Jews, as did Paul (Phil. 3:4–6; cf. Acts 22:3; 23:6). From Philo, we know that other Jews who also were not strictly observant of the law saw themselves in a similar light.[1]

The real challenge to identity was precipitated, as far as we can tell, by the appearance of gentile believers in the Christian congregations as self-confessed, full-fledged members—Gentiles who had not become Jewish proselytes. From an internal standpoint, this forced both Jewish and gentile Christians to take the question of their identity with new seriousness. On the one hand, Jewish Christians, to the extent they were willing to admit that nonproselyte Gentiles could be Christians, now were forced to define Christian identity no longer simply in terms of their Judaism, but more broadly. On the other, gentile Christians had to justify the legitimacy of their presence in the church. Both groups were brought to reckon with the fact that gentile converts, in rejecting circumcision, together with those Jewish Christians who admitted them, were at best giving second place to the most deeply meaningful token of Jewish heritage.

In addition to these internal pressures, an important external factor was a further force in intensifying Christian need for self-definition: Jews were rejecting Christians. Acts reflects a sporadic but at times intense persecution almost from the outset. The heightening of Jewish self-consciousness after the national disaster of A.D. 70 also intensified the need for Christians more sharply to define themselves, in some quarters at least, as distinct from their Jewish heritage.[2]

Like churches of today, the early church faced competition from a broad array of alternative commitments in the Greco-Roman world, an identity crisis brought to focus by a vigorous nationalism (in their case, their Jewish heritage) in the Christian community. In this situation the early church made two fundamental responses which were (and are) essential for community development: (1) They developed a Christian language from their experience, and from that language shaped a vision which became their Christian theology of the world in which they lived. We emphasize the order: first the experience, then the shared language and vision, and last a coherent theology; the contemporary church is apt to begin with the theology and try to produce the experience. (2) The early church also developed a communal life style that allowed them to be both intimate in their personal relationships and institutional in their organization. In the contemporary church we have often separated and alienated these essential processes. Among the first Christians, they happened early and together. For convenience we begin with the communal experience of language and vision.

CREATING COMMUNITY: LANGUAGE AND VISION

From their experience of God in Christ, early Christians believed that their lives had meaning as part of God's activity in history. From their streams of culture they selected particular words to share their faith. Before these words became baptized as theological concepts, they were the common language of community life. Christians developed, as James Gustafson says, "a process of *communication* in the church through the language and other symbols that give social identity to this community. The church is a community of *language*."[3]

The development of a community language was essential and inevitable, like the language communities which spring up everywhere from the children in the sandbox to the most sophisticated society. Just as a national language gives identity to the citizens of a country, or groups within a country, and technical language provides identity to a profession, so the core identity and boundaries of church participation are established by the language the members share. In the same way each of us has developed a "social self"[4] based on our understanding of our place among others in the society, so the early church had to learn its identity by the words it developed. This new language not only articulated the community's self-understanding, but also allowed the community constantly to hear itself affirming its identity. As Mead points out,[5] we are not made to see our faces but we do hear our voices. What we say has formative impact on how we come to understand ourselves, both as individuals and especially as socially related human beings. We invent a language to communicate with others, and in turn the language invents us. It defines what we can say and channels the concepts through which we think.

Distinctively Christian Language

One measure of leadership is the ability to borrow vocabulary from the culture, then shape it with distinctive and compelling content around which to mobilize a community. Such discernment requires a world view, a "symbolic universe," which gives larger meaning to particular words and which, in turn, is carried by the language it shapes. The process of loading certain terms and developing a larger vision is interrelated: in this discussion we will begin with language and move to symbolic universe, but recognize that both develop at the same time, then and now. These distinctively "Christian words" provide some of our most ancient and durable insights into community formation in the early church.

Jesus and his disciples spoke Aramaic and, like most Palestinians of their time, they doubtless also knew at least some Hebrew and probably some Greek. Aramaic, however, was their language, and Palestinian Jewish Christianity remained Aramaic-speaking; but it left no literature that has survived. We thus lack direct evidence as to how the earliest disciples, or indeed Jesus himself, may have infused specific words and phrases in their mother tongue with newly nuanced, dynamically formative meanings. While on circumstantial evidence it is reasonable to think that they did so, Jewish Christianity was not the Christianity that "succeeded" historically. We suspect one reason for its failure is the very issue we are talking about: it may never have managed to achieve a clarity of language distinct from Judaism. We note in passing the large number of churches today that have borrowed so freely from contemporary culture that they do not have a language that is distinctively their own. Conversely, those "conservative" churches that are attracting members usually have a language that can be identified among members and is often distinctive in the larger society as well. What we learned from the sandbox we have sometimes forgotten in programs of church development: distinctive language is essential for building a sense of community.

The Christianity that succeeded spoke and wrote Greek, the lingua franca of the Roman world. One could go almost anywhere in the known world and find those who spoke it. The Old Testament was translated into Greek by Jews beginning in the third century B.C., reflecting the fact that it had become their standard language outside Palestine, Syria, and Mesopotamia. The Greek vocabulary was rich and flexible, markedly more so than that of the Semitic languages, Hebrew and Aramaic. Across the Mediterranean world, Jews knew Greek, but, except in the eastern provinces, many Jews and Gentiles generally did not know Aramaic. It is no surprise that Greek was the language of the Christianity that spread across the Roman world and that the earliest Christian writings are in Greek.

Thus it is at the primary level of Greek-speaking Christianity that we can discover this first evidence of a Christian "community-language" that articulated a growing, internal self-understanding and public self-definition. This language helped form and in turn reflected and reinforced Christianity's developing "symbolic universe" or "universe of meaning,"[6] that is, it functioned to create a world of the mind and heart in which their existence as a Christian community "made sense." Christians were able to focus on certain key words to which they gave enriched and specifically Christian meanings. Examination of a few such terms that operated dynamically in this process will be instructive.

The Church, the ekklēsia. While we do not know when Christians first applied this term to themselves, it appears initially in the first verse of what is almost certainly the earliest book of the New Testament, Paul's First Letter to the Thessalonians, written about A.D. 50. The term stands chronologically at the very beginning of Christian writing as we have it, and the fact that Paul makes no attempt to explain its meaning in a Christian context tells us that the word was already significantly alive in Christian community experience.

Ekklēsia means, literally, those who are "called out" in the sense of being called out to come together. The word thus had a corporate sense. It was the name of the city council in the Greek city-states, where all male citizens were "called out" to assemble for the business of the community. At Athens one can still see the open area on the top of the Pnyx Hill where the *ekklēsia* met and the stone podium where their leaders presided. The bridge from this secular, political context to the Christian use of the word was provided by the Septuagint, the Greek translation of the Old Testament, which adopted, "proselyted," the word to describe the congregation of Israel in the wilderness. In using *ekklēsia* to designate their communities, Christians thus chose a term that was meaningful both to Jews and Gentiles. Through the Septuagint it asserted a continuity with Judaism, a sense of being God's congregation in a new covenant. But it also evoked images for the Gentile without Jewish roots: citizenship, civic responsibility, a sense of being called by a higher power, and corporate unity. Thus the term *ekklēsia* could work dynamically to bring Jews and Gentiles together into a new sense of common identity.[7]

The Poor, the ptōchoi. The word *ptōchos* (pl. *ptōchoi*) was used in classical Greek for the abjectly destitute, the person who not merely was poor in the sense of having to live hand-to-mouth on meager daily wages but who was totally without resources and therefore dependent on the mercy of others. In this context *ptōchos* was usually a synonym for beggar.[8] The position of such persons in the Greek world was especially desperate because Greek ideals did not consider beneficence toward the poor to be a virtue; even the gods were uninterested in the poor.

When, however, the translators of the Septuagint chose the essentially secular term *ptōchos* to represent the "poor" (Hebrew ʿānî and ʾĕbyôn) in the Old Testament, they cast the word in quite a different light, enriching it from a variety of perspectives. While it continued to carry the classical sense of utter dependence on the grace of another, the poor were now understood to be the object of God's care, and therefore were also to be the concern of their fellow Israelites (e.g., Exod. 23:10–11). The concept of what it meant to be poor was also broadened; not only did it imply economic distress but severe insecurity in general (e.g., Pss. 34:10; 37:14; 86:1, 14). With the exile, when Israel as a whole became "poor," the term *ptōchos* came to refer to the entire nation (Isa. 41:17; cf. Ps. 132:15), despised and oppressed by the world but beloved and ultimately avenged by Yahweh (Ps. 37:14–15).[9]

This concept lived on in the sectarian Judaism of New Testament times, where in numerous instances in the Dead Sea Scrolls the Qumran community refers to itself as "the poor,"[10] who, though now persecuted, will one day possess "the portion of all" and see their oppressor "paid the reward which he himself tendered to the poor."[11]

This rich infusion of meaning into the concept of the poor provided by the Old Testament and carried on in the Dead Sea Scrolls is important for an understanding of the role that the term "poor" played in the early Christian communities. Especially in the writings of Luke, the poor are not simply the economically deprived, although that aspect of the term is never lost from sight. They are also the people of God who find themselves over against the world. These themes will be developed more fully in chapter 2 as they bear both on the early and the contemporary churches.

Faith, pistis. In classical Greek, *pistis* lays emphasis on the sense of trusting. The one who is worthy of *pistis* is "faithful, trustworthy." This is not a specifically religious term. As used in the Septuagint, however, it takes on the richness and dimensions of the relationship between God and Israel. This sense of faith reaches particular heights in Isaiah, where it denotes a level of existence that transcends external threat (Isa. 7:1–9) and internal intrigue and falsehood (Isa. 28:14–17). Faith thus is a way of life rooted in God's covenant promises: the "righteous" person, the one whose existence is grounded in a relationship of faith toward God, "shall live" (Hab. 2:4).[12]

The word *pistis* thus lay ready in their Greek Scriptures for the early Christians to adopt as an expression of their sense of relationship to God. Christians carried over the heritage of the word from both classical Greek and the Septuagint; in their use the word as such acquired no essentially different meaning. What was new was rather their focus on Christ. Whereas Israel's faith in God could be confirmed by his objectively evident acts (Ps. 78:32), Christians' faith centered on God's act in Christ. Here lies the great distinction, for this act defied rationality. It was "a stumbling block to Jews and folly to Gentiles" (1 Cor. 1:23). In chapter 3 we shall discuss further the dynamics of such faith in Christian communities then and now.[13]

Peace, eirēnē. As with the other classical Greek words we have discussed, *eirēnē* has a limited sense as compared with what it means in the Bible. In the classical language it refers principally to peace as respite from or in contrast with war—which all too often seemed to be the natural state of affairs. A striking revolution in the meaning of *eirēnē* occurred, however, when the translators of the Septuagint chose it to represent the Hebrew word *šālôm*, which in its broadest sense implies "well-being." The Old Testament understands *šālôm*, and also *eirēnē*, to be gifts of God and therefore, ideally, the normal state of affairs (cf. Ps. 85:10). It is never, however, a "peace at any price" but a sturdy peace that must be accompanied by righteousness (note how the two concepts are combined in Ps. 85:10 and Isa. 48:18). This becomes clear repeatedly in the history of Israel. When Yahweh promises peace to Israel if they are faithful, this will nevertheless involve struggle with their enemies (Lev. 26:3–13). Jeremiah's and Ezekiel's conflicts with false prophets of safety before and during the exile crystallized in the latter's slogan, "Peace, peace," and the true prophets' bitter rejoinder, "But there is no peace!" (Jer. 6:14; 8:11; Ezek. 13:10; cf. 16). Ultimate peace, *šālôm*, in the Old Testament is a part of messianic expectation.

The richness of meaning that the Septuagint had infused into *eirēnē* by making it the equivalent of *šālôm* carries on into the New Testament. Here it includes peace between Christians in community life because God is a God of *eirēnē* (1 Cor. 14:33); it is peace between Jew and Gentile in the church because of the cross (Eph. 2:14); and, comprehensively, it is salvation (Phil. 4:7; Heb. 13:20–21) which continues through the gift of the Spirit (John 14:25–27). But as in the Old Testament, so in the New, *eirēnē* is never an easily won peace; it is something for which Christians are to strive (Heb. 12:14); and as we shall see in chapter 4, much of the history of early Christianity is the story of such struggle.[14]

Mystery, mystērion. In Greek religious life, especially during the Hellenistic period, the sense of mystery played a prominent role. The "mystery religions" used liturgies, hymns, and other forms of music as well as more exotic and secret rituals to induce states of ecstasy in their devotees during which they sensed themselves to be united with their chosen deities.

Under Platonic influence the term *mystērion* also took on the sense of secret teaching restricted to the understanding of a select group. The Septuagint parallels this sense of mystery and adds an apocalyptic dimension by using *mystērion* as the equivalent of the Aramaic *rāz* (e.g., Dan. 2:18, 27). There it represents God's secret scenario for the world, which is revealed only to his chosen ones. Those who are thus privileged have special insights on history to understand the working out of the divine plan. The Dead Sea Scrolls use *rāz* in a similar manner and understand their leader, the Teacher of Righteousness, to have been accorded unique insight to interpret the Old Testament prophecies in terms of the events of their own community's history (note especially 1QpHab VII. 4–5).

Early Christians also used *mystērion* in an eschatological sense. For Paul the "mystery" is the Gospel, "which was kept secret for long ages but is now disclosed and through the prophetic writings made known to all nations" (Rom. 16:25–26; cf. 1 Cor. 2:7 [literally, "wisdom in a mystery"]; 4:1). The synoptic tradition understands "mystery" in a similar way (Matt. 13:11; Mark 4:11; Luke 8:10). Specific aspects of the history of salvation are also "mysteries" for Paul, such as the attitude of the Jews toward Christ (Rom. 11:25) and the transformation of the righteous at the Parousia (1 Cor. 15:51). Similar understandings of "mystery" appear in Eph. 3:3, 9; 6:19; Col. 1:26, 27; 2:2; and Rev. 10:7. In Eph. 5:32 and Rev. 1:20; 17:5, 7, the sense of an esoteric understanding of a text or a symbol predominates.

In 1 Tim. 3:9 and 16, formalization begins to take place in the setting of the term mystery. This is not surprising in the pastoral epistles, which characteristically are more concerned with community structure than are other New Testament writings. Thus in laying out qualifications for deacons, the writer stipulates that they are to "hold the mystery of the faith with a clear conscience." A few verses later, in a context dealing with "how one should behave in the household of God," we find a major liturgical passage, a hymn under the heading, "Great indeed is the mystery of our religion." Mystery here does not yet refer to a formalized ritual, nor indeed is it a term for the sacraments as it became by the fourth century. But we can sense in this more structured context the beginnings of a liturgical frame of reference.

Raymond E. Brown has shown that "virtually every facet of the NT use of mystery" finds "good parallels in thought and word" in either the Old Testament, the Apocrypha, the Pseudepigrapha, or the literature from Qumran, all of which were current in the Judaism of the New Testament world.[15] The term *mystērion*, when given a Christian orientation, thus evoked for Christians aware of Jewish thought a rich world of faith and expectation which they understood to be fulfilled in Christ. For Christians of purely gentile background the term was also meaningful because of its philosophical heritage, where it portrayed hidden teaching comprehended only by those whose eyes of understanding were open.[16] In chapter 5 we shall consider further the interaction of structure and mystery in the life of the church.

The words we have surveyed here and many others, such as *dikaiosynē* (righteousness), *agapē* (love), *kyrios* (Lord), all demonstrate how the

early Christian communities took originally pagan terms which had
been reoriented by the Septuagint and adapted them further to express
distinctly Christian perceptions. We do not need to exhaust the list
but only to invite the reader to be sensitive to the social function of
such language in the formation of the early Christian community. Such
language is essential in the development of caring communities of faith
in every generation.

SYMBOLIC UNIVERSE AND SALVATION HISTORY

In the development of these terms we recognize relationships between
them which begin to create a whole, a larger "universe" in which the
individual words each contribute their particular meanings and from
which they take a more comprehensive meaning together. Peter Berger
and Thomas Luckmann call this larger framework the community's
"symbolic universe":

> The symbolic universe is conceived of as the matrix of all socially
> objectivated and subjectively real meanings; the entire historic society and
> the entire biography of the individual are seen as events taking place
> within this universe. . . . [It] provides order for the subjective apprehen-
> sion of biographical experience. . . . It puts everything in its right place.[17]

The particular words we have chosen are not isolated elements or
even beads on a string. Neither have we attempted what the New
Testament itself resisted—to organize these words into a single,
comprehensive New Testament theology. Rather we invite the reader
to explore the implications of language formation in community building
in the early church and in our own time. These words, taken together
with others and with the social behavior of the community, form a
compound in which words and actions are organically related and
interdependent. The meaning of *ekklēsia* (church) was defined as much
by community use and practice as it was by its earlier sources. In the
ekklēsia the foundational experience of *pistis* (faith) was conditioned by
association with the *ptōchoi* (the poor), commitment to God's *eirēnē*
(peace), and participation in the *mystērion* (the mysteries of God). Each
of these terms, and others, became stars in the symbolic universe by
which the early church could chart its course.

A symbolic universe not only places words in relation to a more
comprehensive pattern of meaning,[18] it also ranges itself in the flow of
historical experience and events. Paul, for example, understands the
community to be grafted into the root of Israel, claiming the heritage

of Abraham for all believers in Christ. Again, Berger and Luckmann state:

> The symbolic universe also orders history. It locates all collective events in a cohesive unity that includes past, present and future. With regard to the past, it establishes a "memory" that is shared by all the individuals socialized within the collectivity. With regard to the future, it establishes a common frame of reference for the projection of individual actions.[19]

As we move from the earliest decades of Christian identity-formation on through the later first century, we find that the sense of Christians standing within a "history of salvation," already initiated by Paul, is intensified. It is Luke, of course, who develops this theme most fully. This is evident in several of the sermons in Acts attributed to Peter (2:14–36; 3:12–26), Stephen (7:2–53), and Paul (13:16–41), in which the speakers appeal to the prophesies of the Old Testament and the experiences of Israel to legitimate the Christian proclamation. But not only does Luke thus tie Christian identity into the heritage of Israel, he is the first clearly to claim that the experience of the Christian community itself is a continuing part of that same history of salvation. For him the Gospel is incomplete without a second volume, the Acts, for Jesus stands at the midpoint rather than the culmination of this history and thus gives meaning both to what comes before and what follows.[20]

Although Luke's development of the concept of an ongoing history of salvation is commonly understood as an apologetic for the fact that the anticipated return of Christ had not occurred, this was not its only function. The Christian conviction of living in salvation history was also a powerful factor in providing a strengthened sense of church identity. To borrow the words of Berger and Luckmann, it gave the community both a " 'memory' . . . shared by all the individuals socialized within the collectivity" and "a common frame of reference for the projection of individual actions" as they pursued their missionary endeavors.[21]

CONTEMPORARY USE OF "CHRISTIAN LANGUAGE"

In the early church we see the power of a distinctive language, that communities with a particular language and an integrated vision have clearer identity, organizational strength, and, frequently, numerical growth; and that those that lack or ignore their own language suffer a comparable disadvantage. Although leadership and social location are also significant factors in contributing to congregational vitality, a distinctive language and shared symbolic universe are typical for most strong and growing congregations.

Since language is the sea in which we swim, our first concerns in contemporary churches are to become sensitive to different languages and to recognize the values and commitments they imply. One simple exercise in a congregation is to listen to the distinct vocabularies of its subgroups. One language of faith may be current with the women's circle of old friends, and another operative among the young singles of the congregation. The teen-agers may use a very different vocabulary from the trustees. These different terms reflect the strands of language that provide identity in the larger society and are imported into the church by members seeking ways to share their experiences. Sometimes pastors and church leaders must be "multilingual" in order to understand the language used by various members when they talk about their personal crises, communal conflicts, and the common activities of their lives.[22]

In one sense, the early church had an advantage—they shaped their language based on their experience. But like contemporary churches, they had to use what was at hand, to borrow terms from the streams of their cultural springs and accumulate meaning based on their experience. They did not accept the existing religious language until it was grounded in their personal and corporate experience. In using language, the contemporary church must deal with three problems: (1) the language must be grounded in experience, (2) it must be shared in community, and (3) it must remain sufficiently distinctive to retain community identity.

Grounded in Experience

Congregational language is strong only as it is attached to personal and communal experience. It may be the historic language of the church or the functional language of other communities—but its power remains vital when it carries an interpretation of God touching one's life directly or through others in one's life. Often the pastor has a language that is experience-based in the seminary community but has little grounding in the lives of members in the local church. Such imported language may alienate and oppress the continuing members of the congregation. Sometimes active church members, for example, may refuse to pray in public because they are uncomfortable with using the "God talk" they have heard from professional clergy. The language of theology should be grounded in experience.

Strong congregations typically develop a shared language of faith which both reflects and shapes their distinctive communal experience. Thus Denham Grierson observes:

In one community "salvation" is the dominant symbol of their faith, in another "reconciliation," in a third "unity in the love of peace," and in yet another, "sharing." Listening carefully to the language in pulpit and pew, in one congregation one will hear the language of pastoral care and group dynamics. In the next congregation, organizational development and systems language will hold the key. Here is a congregation at home with the language of Canaan interspersed with the cadences of the King James translation of the Bible. There the 1662 prayer book remains the language of faith.[23]

Finding, shaping, and mobilizing the appropriate language of faith is a primary task in congregational development. Recent studies suggest[24] that congregations were more likely to become successfully involved in controversial social issues if they had large and active programs of adult study and fellowship. The specific content of their program was less important than the fact that such an arena existed for the congregation to hear itself develop and use an appropriate language of faith experience. Educationally, what the members said to each other proved to be more important than what was "taught" to them by the authority of the church.[25] Members need such program space to hear themselves and to hear each other practice the articulation of their faith in their common congregational language.

Shared in Community

A common language strengthens congregational leadership and enriches the vocabulary of faith. The creative homilies of black preachers are made possible by a strong community of language. Well-known black preachers have a flare for turning a phrase, using language that is grounded in a traditional ethnic community base. Religious television has sustained a powerful appeal because the presentations have often skillfully woven together dramatic contemporary metaphors with historic strands of Christian piety. Each has drawn from specific faith traditions, and each intentionally builds strong language communities. It may seem ironic that congregations with the most traditional symbolic universe often produce the most imaginative preaching—because they assume a vocabulary that their community "hears" and supports, and they can "play" with those assumptions to mobilize community sentiment.

Common language is more difficult but still accessible in mainline congregations. One exercise by which churches can hear and shape their language has been developed by James F. Hopewell, who specialized in the symbol systems of congregations. Hopewell suggests that congregational language may be understood through categories familiar in literature.[26] He describes how some congregations convey a *comic* interpretation of the world in which they believe that present tensions will be resolved later through understanding: they engage in "possibility thinking." In the "opposite" world view, those of the *tragic* orientation are convinced that flawed humanity is saved in the world beyond by obedience here and now: they choose "the way of the cross." The *romantic* view admits to the reality of evil, but believes in divine (heroic) intervention: they "expect a miracle." The *ironic* world view takes life as it is, seeking neither illusion nor patterns: they want "realism over fantasy." Hopewell's use of literary categories provides a fresh way to understand the relationship between language and the core commitments of a congregation, the symbolic universe that holds it together. Hopewell suggests that such language/identity provides a significant key to patterns of congregational leadership, participation, and recruitment.

Distinctive Identity

Although the vocabulary of this language is often borrowed from the streams of culture that feed the church, its meanings must be sufficiently distinctive to be uniquely significant for the members.

Some congregations borrow their language from the subcultures of their members, such as business or sports; some church leaders use language from the social sciences, such as sociology and psychology; some pastors import a language from the great traditions of the church with little or no connection with the life of a local parish. Churches can borrow language if they limit it to common definitions or transform it to carry their commitments, just as the early church converted language from the sources that nourished its culture. *Ekklēsia,* for example, functionally combined the Jewish sense of continuity with the covenant community of Israel with a sense of public accountability derived from Greek culture. Through its common use in the early church, it took on the meanings of a community-called-in-Christ. Similarly today some congregations claim their language from a phrase in the liturgy, or the way a leading member begins her prayers, "Help us, Jesus . . ."

But a language imposed or unthinkingly absorbed from the surrounding culture denies the church its distinctiveness, and church members are tempted to accept the implicit values and world view of the society whose language they unconsciously embrace. Many mainline congregations do not recognize the power of the language by which they live and do not seek a common base in which to anchor their pluralism. With an emphasis on personal freedom, they resist a common statement of faith. With a priority for symbolic creativity and community diversity, they deemphasize shared experience and an integrating vision. Sometimes they are more united in active mission than in doctrine. More often these congregations reflect the individualism of their members, demoting or denying the common Christian language and symbolic universe which sustains their unity in the midst of their diversity.

In contrast to many churches in our time and in the midst of even more radical social diversity, the early church developed a compelling vision and supporting language. In faith they made it real, and in action it made them strong.

BUILDING COMMUNITY: THE
SOCIAL DYNAMICS

Along with language and vision, the early church built community through social relationships. With Jesus, the disciples were a very human group, and we begin with an emphasis on their humanity. Our scholarship should enhance, not inhibit, our view of the people—like ourselves—who found their calling in company with Jesus. This picture of kindred humanity in the Jesus movement has fueled the faith of the church through the centuries. At the same time the New Testament is more than gospel stories. It also provides an incomparable record of the early church struggling with the tough questions of organization, as it structured its community and spread its truth. Many of the tensions in the early church were created by its effort to combine intimacy of warm relationships with clarity of organizational structures.

As many students of the New Testament have noted, there seems to be a shift of emphasis in the flow of biblical material, from the initial, close relationship with Jesus to the later institutional organization of the church. Thus at the beginning of the New Testament story, we find the picture of an intimate community bound together by an itinerant teacher from Nazareth: the Jesus movement. However, by the end of the first and beginning of the second century we encounter a very different scene, that of a well-organized and structured institution with officers in charge and a tradition to maintain: the First Church of Christ, the Lord. We believe this tension was important to the health of the church, although we reject as biblically inaccurate and socially dysfunctional any idea of a simple progression from one to the other.

The tension between intimate groups and institutional structures has been with the church from the beginning, often like two mules in the same harness pulling in different directions. In contemporary churches we see this tension acted out in the difference between the intimacy of a close-knit prayer group and the efficiency of a church agency or board meeting. We hear it in the chitchat of the Bible study among close friends and in the call for the "scheduled agenda" in the formal meeting of church officers. We feel it in the differing expectations of those members who want church meetings to function "on time" and those who always "take time" to catch up with friends and share their experiences. Frequently we are reminded of the tension between these two perspectives, how each can seem a barrier and a frustration to the other.

Rather than resolving this tension, the New Testament sustains both poles, each essential for its contribution to the whole. Consciously or not, the New Testament begins with the warmth of intimacy and concludes by recognizing the importance of established organization.

THE INTIMATE COMMUNITY

The "Jesus movement," as Gerd Theissen[27] has called the Palestinian community centered around Jesus, exhibited clearly the characteristics of a "primary group." Such groups are characterized by small numbers of participants intimately associated by face-to-face interaction over a relatively long period of time.[28] The prime example is usually the family (an image that had a lasting influence in the growth of the church), but also included are the team, the neighborhood, the school, the village, and any close-knit community. "Primary group" refers to more than size—it reflects a feeling of intimacy and mutual belonging. The central feature of primary groups, according to Charles Cooley's well-known definition, is "that they are fundamental in forming the social nature and ideals of the individual."[29] They are communities in which values are formed.

The primary group provides the kind of intimacy and mutual support in which people grow together. Such groups are often united by the powerful attraction of the leader and a close sense of "family" among the members. In the caring of such a community, nicknames become attached to individuals and in-jokes bind the community together.[30] The cohesion of the group is tested and "proven" more by bickering among members than by official status or ᵊlaborate organization. They belong to one another.

Among the disciples, nicknames, in-jokes, and other "in" language played a cohesive role in binding the members together at a level of intimacy not shared by those outside. All three of the disciples reportedly closest to Jesus, Peter, James, and John, are said to have received nicknames from him: Simon was called "Rock" (*Kêpā* in Aramaic or

Petros in Greek; John 1:42) and James and John, "Sons of Thunder" (*Boanērges*, Mark 3:17). From the portrayals of these disciples in the Gospels it is clear that each of these nicknames reflects a certain sense of humor in regard to their personalities.

The disciples are remembered with a kind of humor often identified with the rabbis of their time. Jakob Jónsson, in an extensive study of humor and irony in the New Testament,[31] has shown how many of the sayings in the gospel tradition are fraught with a humorous view of humanity and its foibles. As a factor in promoting the cohesion of the group, humor worked in two ways. In those instances where it was turned on the opponents of the community, it could offer members a wry sense of warmth and "we-ness." Thus the notion of "the righteousness of the Pharisees" (Matt. 5:20) would strike a Christian mind with the humor of irony, if not outright sarcasm. Similarly, the characterizations of the Pharisees ("hypocrites," cf. Mark 12:15; Luke 12:1) as walking through the streets preceded by trumpeters (Matt. 6:2) or of the Pharisee praying "with himself" in the temple, informing God of his fine qualities and many good deeds, gain their impact from their comic irony, and when told within the circle of the community could hardly fail to enhance a sense of common identity. In this connection one is reminded of jokes that characteristically emerge among oppressed groups: these are told at the expense of their oppressors and serve to bolster morale and a sense of oneness by providing a way of sharing the pressures.

Much of the humor and irony in the Gospels, however, is not directed at opponents but is drawn from the affairs of everyday life. To appreciate the power of this, one has but to think of such sketches as that of the man whose crops are so large that he tears down his barns to build bigger ones, only to die that same night (Luke 12:16–21), or the widow who continually pesters an unscrupulous judge until he finally gives in and renders a just verdict (Luke 18:1–8). In such instances as these, their wryness enhanced a binding force for the community that was inherent in the fact that they carried in-group meanings for those "within the family" (note Luke 12:21; 18:6–8). In their efforts to understand the parables, early Christians sensed that the community had special insights into their meaning that were not available to outsiders: "To you it has been given to know the secret of the kingdom of God, but for those outside everything is in parables" (Mark 4:11; cf. Matt. 13:10–16; Luke 8:9–10).

The recital of personal anecdotes was another form of humor which in memory bound the primary group of disciples together with Jesus. These were of two kinds but functioned similarly to promote a sense of warmth within the group: some recalled the cleverness of Jesus and some recounted weaker moments of Jesus or other members of the community. Stories of Jesus' encounters with scribes, Pharisees, and Sadducees have much in common with the Greek *chreiai*, anecdotes regarding famous figures told to exhibit their mental agility and cleverness in repartee.[32] These stories about Jesus tell how by clever dialectic he could turn a conversation to the disadvantage of his questioners (e.g., Mark 12:13–34; Matt. 22:15–46; Luke 20:20–40; Mark 11:27–33; Matt. 21:23–27; Luke 20:1–8).

In one instance, Jesus himself appears as the object of an agile-minded response. When the Syrophoenician woman begs him to heal her daughter and he replies, "It is not right to take the children's bread and throw it to the dogs," she counters, "Yes, Lord; yet even the dogs under the table eat the children's crumbs" (Mark 7:28; cf. Matt. 15:27). The joke is on Jesus, and he accepts it with the words: "For this saying you may go your way; the devil has left your daughter."[33] Peter's comical attempt to walk on water (Matt. 14:28–31) may be a similar instance. A sense of oneness within the group is strengthened when good-natured, positively oriented jokes and laughable incidents can be recalled about its leaders.[34]

Internal tensions among the disciples were another form of affirmation characteristic of the family or other primary groups.[35] Thus the sons of Zebedee were remembered to have confirmed their nicknames by seeking special positions for themselves in the anticipated kingdom (Mark 10:35–45; Matt. 20:20–28)—those who "knew them well" might expect such behavior.

Such familiarity welded the disciples together and united them with their Lord. In Matt. 10:5–25, they are to go forth without money or baggage to preach the gospel. What sustains them is their relationship to Jesus: "It is enough for the disciple to be as his master, and the servant as his lord" (Matt. 10:25). In the parallel account in Luke 10:1–2, where Jesus sends out seventy disciples to preach, after giving them similar instructions, he declares, "He that hears you hears me; and he that despises you despises me; and he that despises me despises him who sent me" (Luke 10:16; cf. Matt. 10:40). Binding them together is a sense of oneness.

THE INSTITUTIONAL CHURCH

In arresting contrast with the intimate "primary group" that we meet at the outset of the New Testament story stands the institution-alized church of two generations later. In the pastoral epistles, those to Timothy and Titus, we encounter it in its most thoroughgoing institutionalized form. While it is impossible to date the writing of these letters precisely, evidence points strongly to their composition in the late first or early second centuries. This fits well with the picture they reflect of the social and organizational situation of the communities with which they are related.

These letters were addressed to pastors of established congregations presumably in the Aegean area and are concerned largely with order and organization in their congregations. The First Epistle to Timothy takes up these matters: prayers are to be offered for kings and governors, "that we may lead a quiet and peaceable life, godly and respectful in every way" (1 Tim. 2:2); women are to dress modestly, be silent and submissive (1 Tim. 2:9–15); bishops are to be appointed from among men who have been married but once, are respected, and have well-ordered families and good reputations in the non-Christian community (1 Tim. 3:1–7). Deacons are to evince the same qualifications. Widows, if they are young women, should remarry, but if older, with grown children, should be supported by them (1 Tim. 5:11–15); at the same time, there is an organization of even older widowed women who have devoted their energies to good works and are now supported by the church (1 Tim. 5:9–10). Slaves are to be obedient and respectful; if their masters happen to be Christians as well, slaves should work all the harder for them (1 Tim. 6:1–2). The Epistle to Titus recapitulates much of the instruction contained in 1 Timothy. Second Timothy is largely a warning against heresies with a call to remain faithful to the received tradition which, along with inspired Scripture, is normative (2 Tim. 3:14–16). "The faith" is objectified as something to be "kept" (2 Tim. 4:7), quite a different concept as compared with Paul's understanding of faith as a relationship of trust.

Here we see that the type of settled Christian communities established by Paul, which in his day were still characterized by many of the elements of primary groups, have become thoroughly organized and institutionalized. They have officers who exercise much authority over the lives of the members; there is discipline and a high regard for respectability both within and without the Christian community. Marriage is now recommended unqualifiedly (contrast Paul's advice in 1 Cor. 7:8, 25–40); family life is to be stable (contrast Matt. 19:29; 27:55–56; Luke 8:2; 14:26); and women and slaves are to be subservient. There is also much concern over heresy, and it is to be measured against the norms of tradition (from Jesus) and Scripture (Old Testament).

Christian communities did not all reach this stage of development simultaneously. The churches reflected in the three epistles of John, probably written about the same time as the Pastorals, appear to have had a notably lower level of formal organization.[36] However, there is good evidence that the churches depicted in the pastoral epistles were not the only ones who were at this point of social development by the end of the first century. Two of our earliest Christian writings outside the New Testament, the epistles of Clement of Rome and of Ignatius of Antioch, offer comparable evidence of a high level of institutionalization.

The *Epistle of Clement* delineates the apostolic succession of authority. It runs from God to Jesus and then through the apostles to the bishops and deacons, who are thus invested with divine authority. The Epistle then goes on to assert that those whom the bishops appoint as their successors share in this apostolic succession (1 Clement 9:1–23). Authority had now been institutionalized into the doctrine of apostolic succession.

About A.D. 115, Ignatius, bishop of Antioch, wrote a series of letters to Christian churches across Asia Minor, and one to the church at Rome. In these he repeatedly stressed the significance of the officials of the church and the importance of obedience to the bishop. Of many statements, this is typical: "All are to respect the deacons as Jesus Christ and the bishop as a copy of the Father and the presbyters as the council of God and the band of the apostles. For apart from these no group can be called the church" (Trallians 3:1). Thus Ignatius took a further step beyond the *Epistle of Clement*: not only was the apostolic succession rooted in church tradition and Scripture but the officers were now seen as analogous to God, Christ, and the apostles, and they constituted the church.

Here, then, is the structure of the early church as an organization with institutionalized power, recognized scripture, and routinized worship. It does not have the emotional appeal of the gospel picture of intimacy with Jesus, but it is far more objective, rational, and durable. Today there is often a kind of nostalgia about the primary relationship with Jesus (like a childish wish to return to the intimacy of the home) and a distaste for the "cold" structures of the organizational church. Fortunately, the fullness of the New Testament does not resolve the tension so easily.

BLENDING THE INTIMATE AND THE INSTITUTIONAL CHURCH

The New Testament provides a blend of the intimate and the institutional church. Even in the Jesus movement there are traces of nascent institutional structure. In addition to those who wandered with Jesus, there was of course a physically settled population of adherents, of Jesus-sympathizers, who expressed their support not by becoming wanderers but by staying in place and offering moral and financial support. Examples of such persons in the gospel traditions are Mary and Martha and their brother Lazarus (Luke 10:38; John 11:1–44) and Simon the Leper (Mark 14:3). Such settled, income-producing persons were essential to the movement, although they were not in the limelight.

In our earliest New Testament sources from Paul, the interaction between intimacy and organization is clearly evident. Paul was a wanderer and a charismatic (1 Cor. 14:18) but his program differed from that of the apostles in the Gospels in several ways.

From all the evidence we have, Paul worked almost exclusively in urban centers. This stands in sharp contrast to the gospel tradition, which is consistently set in towns, villages, and the countryside. Such a shift implies, among other things, a new socio-economic audience for the gospel: the artisan and middle class of the urban Hellenistic world who in many ways lived under quite different social, economic, and political pressures from those experienced by Jesus' earliest followers in Palestine. It is significant that in this context, Paul did not preach "the kingdom of God," but justification and reconciliation. (The differences between Paul's "theological" gospel and the "ethical" message of Jesus deserve further exploration from this socio-economic point of view.)

In distinction from the earlier apostles, Paul worked for an income instead of depending on gifts (1 Cor. 4:12; 9:4–7), a fact that his detractors raised as a reason for questioning his apostleship (1 Cor. 9:4–7). In response, Paul claimed that he did indeed have the same right to support as that enjoyed by Peter, the other apostles, and the Lord's brothers, who accompanied by their wives were itinerant evangelists at the communities' expense; but that he might "make the gospel free of charge" (1 Cor. 9:18), he chose not to exercise it.[37]

Perhaps the most significant shift in Paul's ministry was that he consciously focused on the establishment of churches over which he continued to exercise pastoral care by visits and letters. On the one hand he had no official office in regard to them, but he clearly sought to exercise an authority which though essentially charismatic (e.g., 1 Cor. 5:4–5; Philemon 17—21) was also much concerned for the inner order and ethical life of the communities: things were to proceed "decently and in order" at Corinth (1 Cor. 14:40); women were to behave with extreme modesty in church (1 Cor. 11:5–7; 14:33–35);[38] marriage was to be honored, but in certain situations the tradition from Jesus forbidding divorce might be modified (1 Cor. 7:1–40); incest was condemned (1 Cor. 5:1). In this sense these churches were his churches; this attitude stands in sharp contrast to his approach to the church at Rome, which he had not founded: in writing to it, he expounds "my gospel" (Rom. 2:16) but avoids mixing in its affairs.

On the one hand, Paul claimed apostleship: he was a wanderer, he was a charismatic, and he claimed to be entitled to support. All this undergirded his claim to status among those who carried on and proclaimed the Jesus tradition in an authoritative way (cf. 1 Cor. 11:23–25; 7:10–13; 15:3–10). On the other hand, he was concerned for organization, which doubtless was related to the settled urban environment of his churches. Thus Gerd Theissen has aptly called Paul a "community organizer."[39] If, as the Book of Acts suggests, in some of the cities where Paul established churches he settled down for significant periods of time and practiced his trade, he thus bridged in his personal life the transition from a wandering ministry to a relatively settled, pastoral one.

In at least some of Paul's churches officers in the form of bishops and deacons (one of whom was a woman, Phoebe of Cenchreae [Rom. 16:1]; see also Phil. 1:1) appear for the first time. Little is known of their functions, but certain analogies are discernible among the officials in the synagogues. Apparently Paul organized his churches following a pattern with which he and many of his converts were already familiar.

The radical shift in social and economic focus that we have observed between the Jesus movement and Paul's churches was not a subject that he was concerned enough to write about.[40] At the time there probably was not yet sufficient historical perspective on the church for the importance of this development to be felt. But this shift began early in the life of the church; within twenty-five years after Easter Paul had established urban Christian communities at many places across Asia Minor and Greece. That he was not alone in this, however, must be recognized from the fact that independently of his initiative congregations had come into being at least in Antioch and Rome within the same period.

The only explicit perspective on this development in the New Testament comes from near the end of the century, long after Paul's death, when the author of Acts offers a theological explanation. He suggests that the shift to an urban focus was initiated by the Risen Lord. Nowhere is the earthly Jesus of Nazareth ever portrayed as implying that his movement was to become urban centered. But in the Lucan view, the Risen Lord commands his disciples, "Stay in the city, until you are clothed with power from on high" (Luke 24:49). In the context of Luke's totally urban-focused narrative in Acts, these words suggest more than simply that the disciples are to stay put. The gospel message is to go forth from Jerusalem throughout Judea to Samaria and thence to the whole world (Luke 24:27; Acts 1:8). What this means for Luke is made clear as the Book of Acts unfolds: the mission detailed there moves from city to city and climaxes in Rome (Acts 28:14). Luke's rationale, then, is that this shift in strategy was part of the divine plan for the spread of the gospel. Though Paul does not say so directly, he implies a similar understanding in Rom. 15:19, where he declares that he has "fully preached the gospel from Jerusalem to Illyricum"—when he had done so in major cities.

Moving on through the Book of Acts, we encounter a series of pictures of the church that are mixed as far as our social models are concerned. A recognition of this is important for understanding the social situations depicted in Acts, for there we find tensions between the Christian communities as primary groups and as organized institutions. On the one hand are the traditions of the early charismatically led communities. On the other hand, we encounter evidence of growing institutionalization: the completion of the Twelve (Acts 1:15–26), the appointment of the Seven (Acts 6), the authority to transmit the Spirit restricted to the apostles (Acts 8:14–15), and the elders at the church at Miletus, who are declared to have been appointed "bishops to shepherd the church of God" (Acts 20:28).

This mixed picture afforded by Acts, which was probably written between A.D. 80 and 90, reflects a good half-century of Christian community development. While many elements of a primary group are evident, indications of institutionalization appear throughout. Those that come early in the story may well be due to a reading back of later situations and attitudes regarding structure and authority into an idealized picture of the earliest community in Jerusalem. At the same time we must beware of becoming doctrinaire in our reconstruction of early Christian history, for there are ample instances of primary groups made up of rootless but highly organized people, such as the early Mormons.

INTIMATE COMMUNITIES
AND ORGANIZATIONAL SOCIETIES

Parish leadership is confronted in every dimension of congregational program with tensions between intimate groups and structured organizations. Should worship be more structured or more informal? How can we help the fellowship hour after worship be less cliquish and more inclusive? Should we begin our programs "on time" (the announced hour) or should we run "on people time" (when all the right people have arrived and we have had a chance to socialize)? Should church groups have officers, keep minutes, and subscribe to a stated purpose, or should we organize more casually around friendship and family lines? Should programs be maintained by "the way we always do it around here," or should we be more purposeful and intentional, and "evaluate our progress as compared to our goals"?

This tension becomes embedded in congregational style and is often reflected in the expectations leaders have of the congregation. What might be natural for some congregations is unthinkable in others. Leaders are often chosen to maintain the assumed style and feel under considerable pressure if they attempt to shift the emphasis. The New Testament, as we suggested above, affirms both. The leadership task is both to recognize the difference and to discern which emphasis is needed in specific situations and by particular people.

One stream of social analysis is particularly helpful in understanding this distinction. The tension between communal intimacy and organizational structure has been a major concern in social theory since Ferdinand Tönnies first published *Gemeinschaft und Gesellschaft (Community and Society)* in 1888. Tönnies, like many New Testament scholars in our time, was primarily interested in conceptual tools to understand the shift from an agrarian to an industrial society and emphasized this dichotomy as a way of thinking rather than as a social process.

Tönnies called one kind of group *Gemeinschaft*, a group held together by feeling, and the other kind of group *Gesellschaft*, a group held together by structure. For Tönnies the primary sources for the former were birth (blood ties), shared space (common land), and friendship (bonds of sacred places and common values and beliefs).[41] Members of such a community share strong family feelings among themselves, develop common language symbols and world views, and retain a relatively fixed place within the life of the community. *Gemeinschaft* provided the model that Charles Cooley used in developing his concept of the primary group. By contrast, *Gesellschaft* is a voluntary (contractual) society composed of individuals who work together for a common goal and for individual compensation.[42] It is a rational organization in which each individual agrees to exchange his or her labor for an agreed price toward a common goal—the foundation and maintenance of the urban, industrial society.

In an analysis of contemporary religious behavior, Bruce Reed of the Grubb Institute has used the same basic dichotomy as a way of interpreting the "dynamics of religion."[43] Reed notes a wide range of social observers who employ a similar division in interpreting human behavior drawn from many cultures and seen from various perspectives. G. H. Mueller has extended the parallels into poetry, architecture, and the arts.[44] For our purpose we note that this dichotomy is not unique to the New Testament. Indeed, it is so pervasive in Western culture and human experience that we must be especially clear in our meanings and wary of reading into the text our own experience and expectations.

For Tönnies, the intimate community (*Gemeinschaft*) and the structured society (*Gesellschaft*) are substantially different in the values they hold and the social dynamics they encourage:

Intimate community:	*Structured society:*
intimate feelings	contractual agreements
family ties	organizational office
communal sharing	individual effort
sacred places	social mobility
loved leaders	skilled professionals
tradition, continuity	change, creativity
past to be enjoyed	future to be achieved
relationships are primary	task is primary

This distinction has been used frequently as a basic tool to interpret and manage the social dynamics of the congregation. (1) It appears as the building block for every sort of program, and sometimes the frustration of expectations within program design and performance. (2) The dichotomy illuminates social dynamics in congregations of different size and location. (3) The concepts involved point up significant sociological differences in the ethnic culture and character of various congregations. (4) The distinction also helps identify differences in the personal needs and leadership styles in the church. (5) Because of the numerous distinctions these concepts generate, both intimate community and structured society are elements essential to the strength of the church. Taken together, they provide the foundation of congregational social dynamics.[45]

Intimate and Organizational Program Dynamics

The appeal of the intimate community is its ability to bind individuals into a group and to shape the values and commitments of their lives. The family is the prototypical intimate group, where members are held together by deep and often preconscious feelings about one another. The emotions can be warm, caring, and mutually supportive; feelings can also be hot, cruel, and petty. But the group is held together by feelings, not rational agreements.

Many church programs take on the characteristics of an extended family and become an intimate or "primary" group. Members have a deep and continuing personal interest in others, share their feelings freely (even in anger), and find their identity in the life of the group. Bible study and prayer groups often become significant for participants directly in proportion to the intimacy of the group. Church school classes (e.g., the older adults, the teen-agers, or parents with children of a similar age), church choirs, every Sunday ushers, Sisters of the Skillet (kitchen crew), and the group that counts the offering every Sunday—all can become "family" to one another over years of sharing. Congregations often claim the language of intimacy in describing the church, sometimes in promoting their assets: We are a church family.

But "family" is not the same as *ekklēsia*.[46] The intimate community is difficult for an outsider to enter, and difficult for a leader to change. It finds its identity in past experiences and nourishes its strength in familiar repetition. The very intimacy which shares feelings and shapes values makes entry and change difficult. *Ekklēsia* implies not only intimacy but also something more structured, accessible, and future oriented. From the beginning the New Testament included elements of institutional organization to complement the warmth of the intimate community, to provide a backbone for the continuity of the church.

Institutional organization provides rational order for leadership and membership alike. With an understood and agreed structure the group can face the future, make decisions, and manage its affairs based on recognized tradition and anticipated changes. Church boards tend to be more organizational than intimate, particularly if they have a turnover in membership drawn from a cross section of the groups within the congregation. (At least they go through the motions of the democratic process even if their decisions reflect more intimate commitments.) Task-oriented groups tend to follow more structural procedures, and new church groups often find that formal organization is helpful, at least until more familiarity allows the group to become "a family."

In its sources, *ekklēsia* reflects both the more intimate covenant of Jewish heritage and the more structured process of Greek community councils. Although some groups gravitate toward one emphasis or the other for natural and understandable reasons, both elements must be present in a healthy group. Despite the inclination of some to romanticize the stories of intimacy with Jesus, we find both elements embedded in the biblical sources from the earliest memory of the church in both Paul and the Gospels. In program development, we hope some of the tension between these elements may be reduced with the recognition that the church did not "decline" from some cozy intimacy with the Lord but that both caring and structure are recorded as essential to the church from the beginning.

The Social Dynamics of Church Size and Location

Using the distinction between intimate community and organizational society, church leaders can better understand and work with congregations in very different social settings. Bruce Reed, for example, speaks of "communal" and "associational" churches and applies these concepts to the influence of social location on particular congregations.[47] He notes that communal churches tend to be smaller, more local, grounded in rural communities which share its values and its history. Associational churches are capable of larger memberships and tend to flourish in urban communities of diverse and transitional populations where values differ substantially among the population and between the church and its community.

On this basis, for example, procedures appropriate to the development of leadership of typically rural congregations, for extended family churches, will be distinguished from those for more organizational congregations. This distinction provides the basis of a variety of literature on the small church[48] which emphasizes caring and communal aspects—even the busybody character of its intimacy—as compared with larger, more organized congregations, often in the suburbs. Suburban congregations with their mobile management-oriented membership tend to be seen as the acme of religious organizational structure, while many city churches appear as a curious combination of enduring organization and cultural intimacy.[49] In every situation the generic denominational program materials for worship, stewardship, evangelism, community concerns, and the like must be "translated" into the climate of the congregation, based on the particular mix of intimacy and institutional character of that congregation.

The Social Dynamics of "Community" Congregations

Congregations with a strong base in an ethnic, nationality-based, or blue-collar community often develop a substantial institution based more on extended family and traditional religion than on the clarity of organizational functions. In defining ethnic consciousness, Michael Novak writes, "Ethnic memory is not a set of events remembered, but rather a set of instincts, feelings, intimacies, expectations, patterns of emotion and behavior; a sense of reality; a set of stories for individuals— for the people as a whole—to live out."[50] In contrast with the Protestant church, which Novak finds too organizational and individualistic, the "Catholic difference . . . weights against the myth of personal success both by its sense of communal interdependency and by its wholistic sense of society. In its view, society is not a machine composed of individual atoms, but an organism giving life to families, and through them, to persons."[51] Within this communal consciousness, as we noted in the New Testament community, language takes on its own meaning: "Words like 'conscience,' 'family,' 'loyalty,' 'work,' 'meaning,' 'suffering,' 'sacrifice,' 'ideals,' and even 'law' have a different ring in Catholic than they do in Protestant ears."[52]

Reflection on the bonding power of blue-collar churches follows similar lines. According to Tex Sample, congregations of working-class families are communal, with three characteristics: they are (1) "more like a family than an organization," (2) "not primarily goal oriented but rather are gathering oriented," and (3) "focused not so much on program as on events."[53] Unlike the small and rural congregations, these ethnic, nationality-based, and blue-collar churches can achieve substantial size and impressive organizational proportions, but they retain their extended family roots, relationships, and leadership styles. In a way not envisioned by Reed, they mix communal and associational elements by developing substantial size and organizational complexity but by retaining a more intimate style of participation, leadership, and church activities.

Personal Needs and Leadership Styles

The distinction between relational caring and organizational tasks has also been used to identify the personal needs and various motivations of volunteers in congregational and community activities.[54] In a widely used approach to roles of group leadership, Robert Bales[55] claims that social groups should have a "task leader" and a "social leader" who make essential but different contributions to the life and work of social groups, including churches. Consultants to business and industry have used this distinction to show the orientation of managers to people or to production. The Blake-Mouton grid, for example, has become a familiar way for group leaders to score concern for people and concern for production in their management style.[56]

Lyle Schaller has suggested that this distinction provides a "basic principle" of church management: "Most leaders are predominantly task-oriented or predominantly people-oriented . . . some by 70–30 margin, others may be 60–40 or 80–20."[57] Schaller understands the necessity for both functions to carry the life of individual groups and the congregation as a whole. He suggests that a congregation with a more "pastoral type" (social leader) might want to identify the person(s) who is (are) the task leader(s) in the social dynamics of congregational management, such as a church officer, secretary, or spouse. Each needs the other, and the group needs both.

Mutual Dependency of Intimate and Institutional Styles

The tension between intimate community and organizational society is a common experience in the work of pastors and church leaders. The two distinctive emphases we have noted in the biblical text often result in counterpoint within a particular congregation. Sometimes they provide the basis for "misunderstandings" between relational groups which have gathered for prayer, Bible study, and mutual support, and more management-oriented councils and committees organized for decision, administration, and action. Sometimes differences are presented in a confrontational manner; for example, the church officer who quotes the pastoral epistles to command the respect due those in authority, or the quiet, caring member who wants no church organization but longs rather for "the spontaneous warmth of Christian love to which we should return."

Like the epistles of Paul and the New Testament as a whole, the healthy church must weave these themes together. Thus its worship includes both confessional clarity and the softness of music, its sermons make theological points and contain memorable stories, its stewardship is constructed on a rational budget and explained by beloved leaders. The tension between these two poles can be complementary and creative for the life of the congregation.

In the first section of this chapter we suggested that faith language and symbolic universe were symbiotic: each needs and supports the other. In this second section we noted the social backbone provided by intimacy and organization. These two pairs of concepts are foundational for the development of a Christian community, then or now. We began with these basic tensions since they are relatively simple, absolutely essential, and easily identifiable in the biblical record and in the common life of the church. They may be so commonplace that they have been taken for granted, overlooked, or ignored in far too many situations. They are New Testament tensions which remain essential for healthy churches.

However, these concepts are so foundational that they apply to all communities, Christian and secular. We may adapt them for Christian purposes but there is nothing uniquely Christian in them as borrowed from the social sciences. In the chapters that follow we explore those processes and beliefs that make the church more distinctively Christian.

TWO

THE ENERGY OF
COUNTERCULTURE
CHRISTIANITY

The New Testament is characterized by remarkably high energy. From
the Gospels through Revelation the reader can feel the pulse of
commitment and conflict which has stimulated the church through the
centuries. This energy far exceeds what would be required for the
institutional maintenance of the Christian community we discussed in
chapter 1. From the New Testament we gather that the early Christians
saw themselves, in the hands of God, as unique and special in the
history of the world. They were in active tension with the culture of
their time, especially resistant to other religious groups and competing
faith commitments. This tension between church and society is so
significant that we can trace the growth and strength of the church by
its opposition to the surrounding culture.

The early Christian communities defined themselves as the lively
alternative to the existing religious institutions throughout the empire.
The language and vision that provided the inner strength of the
congregation were energized by the communities' rejection of the
surrounding world and their feelings of being rejected by it in return.
The Christ whom they served called them to be counter to the culture
of the world from which they came. From this distinctiveness arose
the energy to challenge and change the world.

This tension between the gospel and the world remains in our time,
reflected in the words, actions, and life style of every congregation.
Tension between church and culture, then and now, directly affects
the people who join, the energy a congregation has to work with, and
the expectations of its leaders. In this chapter we consider the early
church as a countercultural movement in the earliest responses that we
note in the churches to which Paul wrote, in the variety of attitudes

which developed in New Testament churches toward the *ptōchoi*, "the poor," and in the characteristic expectations and behavior of church leaders. Although the term "counterculture" is freighted in American society with overtones from the 1960s, we recognize its broader implications as a force throughout Christian history.

COUNTERCULTURE MOVEMENTS

When the earliest Christians gathered in communities based on a common vocabulary of faith and vision for God's activity in history, they found unity in a common belief that God had rejected the other alternatives and had chosen them for a special message of hope to the world.

But they also found unity through what they rejected. The Jesus movement turned its back on much of the religious, social, and economic establishment of its time. To understand these attitudes we need to remember that during the first century, until the war of A.D. 70, Palestine was a land of unrest. It was a minor subprovince on the edge of the Roman Empire where the Romans generally did not send their most talented officials (Pilate hardly stood high in Roman affairs), a place where the native Jews, who had a high consciousness of their own superiority, were constantly rubbed the wrong way by a large gentile population that was both fascinated by them and yet held them in contempt. Taxes were heavy and often punitive, and people of all classes lived in fear of economic disaster. It is instructive to note how many of Jesus' sayings and parables deal with such tensions: for example, "Make friends quickly with your accuser" (Matt. 5:25–26); "You cannot serve God and mammon" (Luke 16:13–14); the two versions of the parable of the Unjust Steward (Matt. 18:23–35 and Luke 16:1–9). Cultural tensions were also high as the Jews felt themselves pulled between concern for the preservation of their ancient traditions and pressures to modernize their ways of thinking and their life style in the direction of Hellenistic and Roman culture. Thus social pressures on their perceptions of reality were extreme and highly unsettling. People's foundations were being shaken violently. Such insecurities permeated all levels of society, just as today the millionaire in a high-rise, the executive in the suburbs, the farmer on family land, and the "bag lady" in a shelter can all experience a deep uneasiness about the security of the culture we live in.

In such situations of widely felt insecurity, people who join groups typically exhibit one of two reactions:[1] withdrawal or resistance. Gerd Theissen has spoken of these as "evasive" and "aggressive" behaviors.[2]

Evasive or passive rebels demonstrate their rejection of the situation by withdrawing from society and creating their own world. They consciously give up on society as it is, narrow the limits of their world to their own group, and seek to create manageable social space in which they can build an ideal society. Characteristically, such groups are highly disciplined. As examples, one is reminded of the Essenes in the Judean desert at Qumran, of early Christian monasticism, and of various nineteenth-century American utopian experiments.

Aggressive or active rebels can stand the situation no longer and are willing to stake their lives on the possibility of building a better society by force. Often they are less disciplined than passive rebels. The prime example in New Testament times of this reaction was the Zealots, whose opposition to the Romans and their supporters led to two ill-fated revolutionary wars in A.D. 70 and 135.

Both passive and active rebels are characteristically rootless in the sense that they have given up on their social worlds. The one withdraws physically from the world and shuns it emotionally, denying normal roots of family and friends; the other remains physically in the world but declares itself to be the world's enemy.

There is much in the gospel story and in the teachings attributed to Jesus that reflects this physical and cultural rootlessness. Jesus is said to declare: "The Son of man has nowhere to lay his head" (Matt. 8:20), and when his disciples are sent out, as we have seen in the previous chapter, they are expected to follow their master in a similar life style (Matt. 10:5–25; Luke 10:1–12). When Jesus commissions his disciples, there is every reason to believe that they will preach a gospel that is greeted with public disapproval (Matt. 10:5–42; Mark 6:8–11; Luke 9:3–5; 10:4–12). In Matthew's form of Jesus' instructions, which certainly also reflects the experiences of later wandering Christian preachers, the disciples are fearlessly to expect persecution. They are to be "wise as serpents and harmless as doves," but this is because the world into which they go is a world of wolves (Matt. 10:16). It seems clear, then, that Jesus and his followers are definitely to be seen as among the restless who stood in tension with their society and sought a better world.

But in comparison with the two options suggested by Theissen, the Jesus movement adopted a third way. They were consciously different from both the Essenes, who withdrew physically from society, and the Zealots, who sought to destroy it by violence. Their response to social insecurity can be seen in a three-point program. They gave up possessions and depended on others for support (Matt. 19:27; Mark 1:16–17; Luke 8:3); they sought to permeate their society by wandering, especially from village to village; and they proclaimed a new order of society, "the kingdom of God/Heaven," which, at least as it was understood after Easter, was coming to them where they were by God's powerful act, not by withdrawal or by revolution (note Luke 17:21: "The kingdom of God is in your midst").

THE SOCIAL DYNAMICS OF A SECT

In a number of ways the early church resembled what some sociologists have called a "sect."[3] Although there are significant differences between a classic or contemporary sect and the early church, some points of comparison are instructive. Sect is a common designation for religious groups which find their identity in their efforts to reject and reform the religions from which they are drawn. Sects are usually in tension with the established "church" and culture in which they live.

Ernst Troeltsch has succinctly contrasted sect and church:

Sects are comparatively small groups; they aspire after personal inward perfection, and they aim at a direct personal fellowship between the members of each group. . . . Their attitude towards the world, the State, and Society may be indifferent, tolerant, or hostile, since they have no desire to control and incorporate these forms of social life; on the contrary, they tend to avoid them; their aim is usually either to tolerate their presence alongside of their own body, or even to replace these social institutions by their own society. The Church [on the other hand] is that type of organization which is overwhelmingly conservative, which to a certain extent accepts the secular order, and dominates the masses; in principle, therefore, it is universal, i.e., it desires to cover the whole life of humanity.[4]

In effect, the sect is a counterculture group that defines its identity by offering an alternative to the established religion. It is a gathering of voluntary believers who willfully reject religions of higher status in which belonging seems inherited and faith assumed. Believers are energized by the clarity of their opposition. Thus, H. Richard Niebuhr emphasizes the energy of choosing to belong: "Members are born into a church while they must join a sect."[5]

But a typical dynamic of change has often been observed: a group that begins as a counterculture "sect" becomes an acceptable "church" within a generation or two. This social, economic, and religious transition seems an almost natural consequence of the values and behavior of sect movements, such as their emphasis on personal discipline, vocational commitment, and communal support. Liston Pope, in a study of the sect groups of Gaston County, North Carolina,

summarized many ways in which such groups move from sect to church:
- from propertyless to property owners
- from economic poverty to economic wealth
- from cultural periphery to cultural center
- from experiential religion to social institution
- from ridicule toward other churches to cooperation
- from suspicion toward rival sects to disdain for all sects
- from moral community excluding the unworthy to embracing members who are socially compatible
- from unspecified, untrained, part-time clergy to full-time professional ministry
- from a psychology of persecution to a psychology of success
- from an emphasis on conversion to an emphasis on religious education
- from stress on the next world to an interest in a future in this world
- from congregational participation to delegation of responsibilities
- from fervor in worship to restraint and passive listening
- from a large number of services and activities to fewer and more scheduled ones
- from spontaneous "leadings of the spirit" to an order of worship
- from lively folk hymns to more stately music of a liturgical tradition
- from adherence to strict biblical standards, such as tithing or nonresistance, to acceptance of general cultural norms for religious practices[6]

From this brief discussion, we note two characteristics of sectarian movements. First, they release great energy in believers who find their identity by holding values different from those of the groups they oppose. Second, they are seen to move from positions of social marginality and alienation through discipline and organization toward positions of social acceptance and "success."

TENSION BETWEEN COUNTERCULTURE COMMITMENTS AND SOCIAL ACCEPTANCE

As a counterculture movement, the church has benefited from sectarian energy and struggled against "success." This distinction is pivotal in our understanding of the development of the Christian community. It has been frequently argued that the church began as a sectarian movement of the poor who found their strength in believing but who lost their purity as they became prosperous. We will take a somewhat different position. We observe that inclination to compromise with the culture is reflected in the earliest documents of the New Testament church, the writings of Paul. We also observe that reaffirmation of counterculture commitments can be found in the final documents of the New Testament. There is no clear movement from early purity to later decadence, but a constant tension which continues in our time.

As a framework for understanding this struggle, we examine first the tension between church and culture reflected in the writings of Paul. Here we note three characteristic ways in which the early church moved from a position of marginality toward more socially acceptable behavior: (1) the settled life of Christian communities, (2) urban, social, and economic adjustments in urban societies, and (3) the struggles of authority in the family and the community. These early accommodations to cultural pressure seem too clear for reasonable doubt. At the same time we note characteristic ways by which the church resisted assimilation: (1) the personal morality of believers, (2) the unique qualities of spiritual gifts, and (3) the persistence of old ideals from the Jesus movement and the earliest community in Jerusalem. Each of these gave rise to controversy but continued as cherished ideals.

The remainder of this book discusses other responses to pressures toward cultural assimilation. Later in this chapter we set the issue in a larger context by discussing several ways in which "the poor" function to recall the church to the focus of its counterculture identity. In subsequent chapters we show the importance of cognitive dissonance, conflict, and ritual in providing a barrier against erosion and a resource for renewal of the Christian vision. Here we note only that the struggle against compromise began with the birth of the church. If there ever was a time of pristine purity (a Garden of Eden for the Christian church), it was prior even to the earliest documents we have received. The tension between church and culture existed from the beginning of recorded memory.

From Rootlessness to Settled Life

Using the churches of Paul as a lens through which to view early Christianity, we note a striking shift in the first century from a socially rootless and sometimes wandering group or groups of believers in villages to settled communities in more urban environments. As we have already seen, this development was not initiated by Paul but came about in the very early years of the church and may well be traced to the Jerusalem community immediately after Jesus' death. But it is with

Paul that we are most directly in touch with it, and in his churches we find our most readily available examples. In the previous chapter we noted that settled Christians who stayed put were counted among Jesus' followers from the beginning, but these were not dominant in the ethos of the Jesus movement. Now, however, settled Christianity appears to have become normative. This shift was doubtless an evangelistic strategy. After Easter, itinerant missionaries went where concentrations of prospective converts were found; as the most likely converts were Jews, who outside Palestine tended to congregate in urban settings, the large cities offered the most promising areas for the proclamation of the gospel.

The general direction of this movement is recognizable: from spontaneous to organized, from smaller to larger, from rural to urban, from independent to mutually supportive. Wandering missionaries such as Peter, the other apostles, Jesus' brothers, and their wives (1 Cor. 9:5) lived at the expense of those to whom they preached. As soon, however, as this extension of the Jesus movement ventured into major urban centers where sizable numbers of converts were made who could themselves neither take to the road nor completely fade back into synagogue life as Jesus-believing Jews, it was inevitable that the majority among Christian adherents quickly shifted to those who were leading sedentary, income-producing lives. The characteristic Christian was no longer the wandering follower of Jesus in Palestine, but an urbanite, either Jew or Gentile, who continued life in the world of work and other everyday activity. In this shift of locale they gave up some symbols of their rootlessness but did not lose their identity as Christians.

Urban Social and Economic Pressures

The shift to the city is evident in the early Christian attitude toward the economic world. Those who earn their livelihood in the world cannot completely repudiate it. Thus Paul, concerned with the acceptance of the church in the larger world, felt the need to declare to the Corinthians, "I wrote to you in my letter not to associate with immoral men; not at all meaning the immoral of this world, or the greedy and robbers, or idolators, since then you would need to go out of the world. . . . For what have I to do with judging outsiders? . . . God judges those outside" (1 Cor. 5:9–10, 12–13). Similarly the antithetical stance toward established institutions that characterized the Jesus movement was now giving way to a conscious concern for acceptance in the eyes of the world. What had proved a powerfully attractive quality to the oppressed people of Palestine was no longer an ingredient in successful evangelism. In this vein Paul admonishes his readers, "Give no offense to Jews or to Greeks or to the church of God, just as I try to please all men in everything I do, not seeking my own advantage, but that of many, that they may be saved" (1 Cor. 10:32–33). Climaxing his discussion of speaking in tongues, he declares, "All things should be done decently and in order" (1 Cor. 14:40). In a strong admonition to the Christians at Thessalonica, he tells them they should "aspire to live quietly, to mind your own affairs, and to work with your hands" and "to be dependent on nobody" in order to command public respect (1 Thess. 4:11–12).

Paul's insistence on earning his own living is doubtless also to be seen in this perspective. Though entitled as an apostle to support from the community, he refused this because he was concerned to adapt himself to the situation of those to whom he preached; he wanted the gospel to be "free of charge" and so had made himself a "slave to all, that I might win the more.[7] To the Jews I became as a Jew, in order to win Jews; . . . to those outside the law I became as one outside the law . . . that I might win those outside the law" (1 Cor. 9:18–21). In their transition to an urban environment early Christians cast down economic roots and surrendered much of their independence from social values.

The Struggle for Authority in Family and Community

In Paul's battle to bring Gentiles and Jews together in the church he declared, "There is neither Jew nor Greek, there is neither slave nor free, there is neither male nor female; for you are all one in Christ Jesus" (Gal. 3:28). Such an ideal appears frequently among sectarian groups. At times, however, in response to cultural pressures Paul accommodated himself to local norms.

In discussing sexual relationships, he declared that "the husband should give to the wife her conjugal rights, and likewise the wife to her husband. For the wife does not rule over her own body, but the husband does; likewise the husband does not rule over his own body, but the wife does" (1 Cor. 7:3–4). This position finds analogies in ancient Jewish law (*Mishna Ketuboth* 5.6), where it does not imply any general equality between husbands and wives. Similarly Paul could make marked distinctions between men and women in worship (1 Cor. 11:3–16; and perhaps in 14:33–36 [which may not be from Paul]), a context in which one would have expected his declaration in Gal. 3:28, if anywhere, to have been effective. What seems to be operative here, however, is the priority of conformity for the sake of evangelistic effectiveness.

Similarly Paul's declaration in regard to slavery in Gal. 3:28 did not carry through on the social level; he showed no indication that Christians should necessarily emancipate their slaves and admonished: "Every one should remain in the state in which he was called. Were you a slave when called? Never mind. . . . For he who was called in the Lord as a slave is a freedman of the Lord. Likewise he who was free when called is a slave of Christ" (1 Cor. 7:20–22). The ideal that "there is neither slave nor free" thus appears for Paul to have been a theological concept to which he could actually turn in support of the social status quo.[8]

In the writings that come to us from the Pauline circle, such attitudes are even more clearly stated. In Eph. 5:21, speaking to married couples, children and slaves, the writer declares as his ideal, "Be subject to one another out of reverence for Christ." What this actually means for him, however, is "Wives, be subject to your husbands, as to the Lord. For the husband is the head of the wife" (Eph. 5:22–23). In return husbands are told, "Love your wives, as Christ loved the church and gave himself up for her" (Eph. 5:25). The ideal, which might appear to be one of equality, is understood rather as one of reciprocal beneficence. The attitude is similar in the case of slaves, though even more sharply differentiated: "Slaves, be obedient to those who are your earthly masters, with fear and trembling, in singleness of heart, as to Christ . . . rendering service with a good will as to the Lord and not to men. . . . Masters, do the same to them, and forbear threatening, knowing that he who is both their Master and yours is in heaven, and that there is no partiality with him" (Eph. 6:5–9). Similar "household codes" are found in Col. 3:18—4:1; 1 Pet. 2:13—3:7. In these passages we see how radical ideals characteristic of a rural counterculture movement were modified to meet the realities of the urban social system.

The trend to reestablish family and other authority reaches its height in the pastoral epistles. In these church documents high priority is placed on projecting a strong, positive public image before the pagan world: Christians are to pray for kings and governors, "that we may lead a quiet and peaceable life, godly and respectful in every way" (1 Tim. 2:2); church leaders ("bishops" and "deacons") are to be men of impeccable character, "well thought of by outsiders" (1 Tim. 3:7). Christians in general are "to be submissive to rulers and authorities, to be obedient, to be ready for any honest work, to speak evil of no one, to avoid quarreling, to be gentle, and to show perfect courtesy toward all men" (Tit. 3:1–2). In the matter of women and slaves, all evidence of the nuanced idealism we noted with Paul and in Ephesians has disappeared. Women are to "learn in silence with all submissiveness.

I permit no woman to teach or to have authority over men; she is to keep silent." This is a position characteristic of rabbinic Judaism (e.g., *Mishna Kiddushin* 4.13), and it is here bolstered with an argument in a typically rabbinic key: "Adam was not deceived, but the woman was deceived and became a transgressor." A woman's salvation will be "through bearing children, if she continues in faith and love and holiness, with modesty" (1 Tim. 1:11–15).

Similarly the instruction to slaves is entirely one-sided: "Let all who are under the yoke of slavery regard their masters as worthy of all honor, so that the name of God and the teaching may not be defamed. Those who have believing masters must not be disrespectful on the ground that they are brethren; rather they must serve all the better since those who benefit by their service are believers and beloved" (1 Tim. 6:1–2). There is no reciprocal instruction for masters as to their conduct toward their slaves. Although the tension apparently remained in the dynamics of the early church (as we discuss in chap. 4), in the pastoral epistles we are left with only one perspective. Here the typically counterculture commitment to abolish distinctions of social status, gender, and nationality is gone.

For contemporary readers who wish the church to be a solid bulwark of counterculture commitments, these examples of compromise and capitulation are disturbing—they occur early in the history of the church and they challenge many values precious to the twentieth century, such as abhorrence of slavery and advocacy of equality between marriage partners. But Christians in a Pauline church would not have seen it that way. Such believers maintained counterculture commitments in more personal and spiritual ways.

COUNTERCULTURE RECLAIMED

Although the early church believed that it lived in the final days before the second coming of Christ and was driven by evangelistic zeal to bring the message to as many as possible before the end of time, they did not completely give up their counterculture commitment for the sake of evangelistic success. In significant ways Paul and his congregations continued to maintain counterculture attitudes. Here we note patterns of maintaining such a stance that have been resources of the church under pressure through the centuries.

Personal Morality

On a moral plane, which had implications for practical life, Christians and the world were to stand distinctly apart; Paul, or perhaps another early Christian, could write, "Do not be mismated with unbelievers. For what partnership have righteousness and iniquity? Or what fellowship has light with darkness?" (2 Cor. 6:14).[9] As a practical outcome of this stance, Christians were, for instance, not to go to court against fellow Christians: "When one of you has a grievance against a brother, does he dare to go to law before the unrighteous instead of the saints?" (1 Cor. 6:1).

This sense of standing apart from the world, and indeed in many instances over against it, is pervasive throughout the thought of Paul. We have noted the power of language—vocabulary freighted with in-group meanings, phrases that have special significance for the attitudes and life of the community, and liturgical formulations of particular power. Such special vocabulary also functions at times to set the community off from the world around it. Wayne Meeks has written of this as "the language of separation."[10] Thus even when Paul abdicates passing judgment on "immoral men," he can still refer to them as "outsiders" because they are not among those who are "inside" the church (1 Cor. 5:12–13; cf. 1 Thess. 4:11–12).

This stance of apartness, even while maintaining on-going day-to-day relations with the world, of being in the world but not of the world, is raised to the level of scathing execration in the "catalogues of vices" which Paul details with gusto. Thus in Rom. 1:29–31 and again in Gal. 5:19–21 he heaps up lists of evil deeds and attitudes that characterize those who "suppress the truth" and do "the works of the flesh." In Gal. 5:24, he climaxes his catalogue with the assurance, "Those who belong to Christ Jesus have crucified the flesh with its passions and desires." Such stylized lists of vices as Paul presents were common in the writings of Hellenistic moralists and are found in Philo of Alexandria as well (Sacrifices 32), where they are intended to awaken the soul to recognize good from evil. The nearest parallel to Paul's use of them, however, is found in the Dead Sea Scrolls (Manual of Discipline 4), where they are "the ways of the spirit of falsehood" whose followers stand in contrast to "the sons of truth in this world."[11] Here the catalogue of vices is used to set the sect of Qumran off from the world around it; in the same way Paul employs such catalogues not merely as moral instruction but particularly as a means of establishing a sense of separation from and antipathy toward the ways of the world. As at Qumran, so here, the literary device of a resounding litany of vices strengthens the sectarian stance of the community. The more positive effect of such catalogues, of course, was to emphasize the essential importance of personal rectitude for membership in the community, which is also a characteristic earmark of counterculture commitments.[12]

Spiritual Gifts

Another element in the experience of the early Christian community that contributed to distinctiveness was its understanding of the action of the Spirit. Significantly, the Greek word that Paul used for a "gift" of the Spirit is *charisma*, literally, a "gracement." This emphasizes the thought that what is received is indeed a gracious gift: the recipient is the object of special favor not vouchsafed to the world at large. Thus, in a general sense, Paul could say, "the gift (*charisma*) of God is eternal life" (Rom. 6:23), and for him and his congregations, at least at Corinth, the possession of special gifts to be apostles, prophets, teachers, workers of miracles, and so on (1 Cor. 12:28; cf. 8–10) was tangible evidence of this. In discussing these gifts, Paul's overriding concern was that they not be divisive of the community; the community is like the human body with all members interacting for the common good: "If one member suffers, all suffer together; if one member is honored, all rejoice together" (1 Cor. 12:26). Paul was clear that the purpose of these gifts is the well-being (shalom!) of the community: "Since you are eager for the manifestations of the Spirit, strive to excel in building up the church" (1 Cor. 14:12).

To appreciate the significance of Paul's concept of the gifts of the Spirit, it is important to recognize that he understood them eschatologically. Christians have the "first fruits of the Spirit" (Rom. 8:23); that is, the gift of the Spirit is a down payment, a guarantee, looking toward that day when "what is mortal may be swallowed up by life" (2 Cor. 5:4–5; cf. 1:22). Such an understanding of the gift of the Spirit meant not only that Christians saw themselves as recipients of a special gift of divine grace now but also and more that this gift set them apart, marked them (note 2 Cor. 1:22: "He has put his seal upon us") as destined for "a house not made with hands, eternal in the heavens" (2 Cor. 5:1). In this way they sensed themselves by divine grace to be set apart sharply from the world around them.

Persistence of Old Ideals

We have seen a variety of ways in which early Christians moved toward more socially acceptable behavior and ways by which, at the same time, they resisted assimilation. The tension is evident early in Christian history in the Pauline churches. From other areas we can sense a persistence of the original counterculture ideals, as the Gospel writers reminded the community late in the first century. Thus Jesus is quoted as declaring, "Do not think that I have come to bring peace on earth; I have not come to bring peace, but a sword. For I have come to set a man against his father, and a daughter against her mother, and a daughter-in-law against her mother-in-law; and a man's foes will be those of his own household. He who loves father or mother more than me is not worthy of me; and he who does not take his cross and follow me is not worthy of me" (Matt. 10:34–38).[13]

Jesus is also portrayed as having breached established relations between the sexes as they were observed in respectable Jewish society. Thus in a society where a woman "should seek a life of seclusion" and "not show herself off like a vagrant in the streets before the eyes of other men, except when she has to go to the Temple" (Philo, *Special Laws* 3.171; Loeb Classical Library; cf. *Mishna Aboth* 1.5; *b. Berakoth* 43b), the Gospels report that as Jesus "went through cities and villages, preaching and bringing the good news of the kingdom of God," his entourage included women, of whom one was Joanna, the wife of Herod's steward, and "many others" who were well enough to do to provide financially for Jesus (Luke 8:1–3). These were not women of the ʿammêi hā-āreṣ, the lower classes, whom the Pharisees deprecated as "knowing not the law" and thus not abiding by established social conventions. Similarly, on his final arrival in Jerusalem, according to what is certainly a tradition related to that in Luke, Jesus is reported to have been accompanied by "many . . . women who came up with him to Jerusalem from Galilee" (Mark 15:40–41). In a quite separate tradition, even Jesus' disciples, when they found him speaking openly with the Samaritan woman, are depicted as being shocked "that he was talking with a woman" (John 4:27).

The impact of these counterculture values would have been severe. A movement that sought to abolish levels in society, to create a new family out of disparate social classes, made itself immediately suspect of being subversive of public stability. The notion of dominant and subordinate classes as being essential to the structure of both the state and the family and the conviction that each was necessary to the other were deeply rooted in Greek and Roman philosophy and political theory. Disruption of such relationships within the family, therefore, was seen as a threat also to the constitution of the state.[14]

The traditions handed down regarding the earliest urban community, that in Jerusalem after Easter, also evoke the old ideals. Christians could envision a time when "all who believed were together and had all things in common; and they sold their possessions and goods and distributed them to all, as any had need" (Acts 2:44–45). This accords with another report which seems to indicate that the Jesus movement, or at least Jesus and his disciples, lived with a common purse (John 12:6; 13:29), which in view of their general mode of life, is entirely credible. To what extent the picture given us of the "communism" of the Jerusalem community is idealized we cannot say, but in view of the existence of other, contemporary groups who held their goods in common, such as the Qumran community and the Therapeutae near Alexandria, it is reasonable to think that the earliest Christians could have attempted such a way of life. Although there is no further evidence in the New Testament of other such experiments, similar attempts at a common life are frequent among later sectarian groups (many of them, indeed, in conscious imitation of the Jerusalem Christians). The fact that Christians preserved a tradition that their earliest settled community had lived in this way indicates that the counterculture ideal persisted for many decades.

Here are at least two major streams of countercultural Christian expression. In the Pauline church, we see many characteristics often associated with contemporary conservative and evangelical churches. They are similar in their urgency to evangelize more members, in their emphasis on "the last days," in their concern for personal morality, and in their expectation of the intervention of the Holy Spirit. We acknowledge the biblical foundations for such congregations, which see themselves living at the end of time and allow evangelistic zeal to set their social priorities.

What we miss in Paul is a discussion of poverty or a clear effort to change the status of "the poor." The absence of concern for the *ptōchoi* is even more startling when we recall how the sociological literature of "sect" argued that the poor provided the core of the counterculture movement of the early church. The other stream of countercultural Christianity, seen in the persistence of old ideals carried by the Gospels, suggests a later struggle in the early church to recover a concern for "the poor" which had become obscured in the evangelical zeal of the first and perhaps second generation of Christians. To understand these tensions, we offer four definitions of *ptōchos* used by early Christians in developing communities.

THE ENERGY FROM "THE POOR"

In the context of countercultural energy in the early church, concern for "the poor" took on particular potency. The counterculture and the poor are not necessarily identical groups of people. In early Christianity there was a powerful though not entirely consistent interaction between them that played a significant role in the attitudes of Christians, the formation of community life, and the reenergizing of the faith in the first century, and every century since.

During the period when social scientists associated counterculture movements generally with "lower classes,"[15] it was also common to portray early Christianity as a religion made up in largest part of the poor and powerless. Thus in 1911, writing of Paul, Adolf Deissmann declared,

> It appears to me to be certain, that Paul of Tarsus, although his native city was a seat of Greek higher education, was not one of the literary upper classes, but came from the unliterary lower classes and remained one of them. . . . As a missionary chiefly working amongst the unliterary masses of the great cities, Paul did not patronizingly descend into a world strange to him: he remained in his own social world.[16]

In the same rather romantic vein, H. Richard Niebuhr idealized the studies of Troeltsch with a broad generalization about religion in the lowest economic segment of the population. According to Niebuhr,

> In the religion of the poor . . . one finds, more than anywhere else, appreciation of the religious worth of solidarity and equality, of sympathy and mutual aid, of rigorous honesty in matters of debt, and the religious evaluation of simplicity in dress and manner, of wisdom hidden to the wise and prudent but revealed to babes, of poverty of spirit, of humility and meekness.[17]

In more recent years, both the understanding of the seedbed of sectarianism as being the poor, characteristic of Troeltsch and Niebuhr, and of the socioeconomic texture of early Christianity as being similar, popularized by Deissmann and others, have shown themselves to be too narrow. Poverty and lack of education are but two elements of a much broader spectrum of frustrating circumstances that give rise to groups that identify themselves over against "the world," the dominant order of things. Neither can our modern concept of socioeconomic class be transferred directly to the situation of the ancient world. As Meeks has pointed out, it is rather the category of *status* that is "the most generally useful one for forming a picture of stratification in the Greco-Roman cities."[18] Status is a complex phenomenon made up of a variety of factors which in any one individual's existence may be of varying levels of strength. A person with economic power may be fearful of political reprisal, a celebrity may feel outclassed for lack of education, while a respected academic may suffer a sense of making no meaningful impact on the "real" world. All such persons share with the poor the problem of low status crystallization; the disjunctions in the dynamic elements of their lives can lead them to form or to join communities that, as we have seen, set themselves off from the world in order to remake that world or to create their own hoped-for utopia.

Unrest both in Palestine among the Jews and more broadly across the Roman Empire fits this wider understanding of counterculture dynamic.[19]

The expanded biblical concept of "the poor" (the *ptōchoi*), described in the previous chapter, reflects a similar category of people. We have seen how already in the Old Testament "the poor" similarly had come to have a wider sense, embracing not only those who were deprived economically, but also those who lived under a variety of pressures. Early Christians inherited this broadened sense of the term, along with the tradition of Israel as "the poor." As persons standing over against the world, whatever their economic status, they could more easily sense themselves as being among "the poor." Such persons, even though they may be led, and even at times composed largely of persons of means and education, have often been concerned for economic issues.

It is against this background that we should evaluate the counterculture nature of early Christianity. Recent analysis of its communities has shown that rather than their having been made up almost exclusively of the poor and the powerless, they represented a cross section of Hellenistic-Roman society. The New Testament reports the presence in these communities of government officials, functionaries of the civil service (the "household of Caesar," Phil. 4:22), persons of wealth sufficient to allow them to serve as patrons of congregations, landowners, army officers, and business people. There were also large numbers of common people, most of whom were probably artisans and tradesmen, and there were slaves. What is missing is evidence of the nobility and the very rich on the one hand, and of the abjectly poor on the other.[20]

In light of this analysis, it is clear that economic deprivation per se did not give rise to the sectarian stance of early Christianity. Rather, counterculture movement is grounded in a more general ambiguity of status arising from a variety of disjunctions in the lives of people from many social and economic levels. Sharing a sense of frustration, they found common ground in Christianity's position over against this world and its offer of community now and of a better world coming.

In the New Testament, the term "the poor" refers at times to the economically destitute, at times is spiritualized, and yet again in other contexts projects a more holistic view. Attitudes toward the poor in these various senses vary considerably. This doubtless reflects equally varying attitudes among Christian leaders and in the communities from which these writings sprung. We shall trace these attitudes with particular attention to (1) the traditions of the Jesus movement and its appeal to the poor, (2) Paul's attitude in light of eschatological and evangelistic priorities, (3) Luke's concern for the poor, and (4) James's rejection of the rewards of "success." We shall also note the mixed reactions that emerge in the second century.

The Jesus Movement: Appeal to the Poor

The traditions of the Jesus movement in regard to the poor, filtered as they are through the later experiences of various Christian communities, are not easily evaluated with precision. However, the evidence is convincing that Jesus and his disciples maintained a counterculture stance. The statement we have noted in Matt. 10:34–38 is doubtless an accurate appraisal of the social results of their preaching: "Do not think that I have come to bring peace on earth; I have not come to bring peace, but a sword." In view of the social and political tensions with which Palestine was fraught at this time[21] it is reasonable to think that the report "the great throng heard him gladly" (Mark 12:37) genuinely reflects the appeal Jesus' message had for common people. Many of these were economically oppressed and an even larger number could be included in the broader definition of the poor. As we have seen, Jesus' message in the face of such tensions was neither one of withdrawal from society nor of incitement to violence toward the establishment; it was rather the proclamation of a kingdom in which the established relationships of the world people knew were inverted, where the "first will be last, and the last first" (Mark 10:31).[22]

Paul: Eschatological and Evangelistic Priorities

Turning to the epistles of Paul, it is striking how little he was concerned for the economically depressed or for the poor in the broader sense, as well. Nor did Paul indulge in denunciation of the rich. Two reasons for this appear probable. First, "eschatological pressure" was keen for him. In view of the imminent consummation of history, social issues seem at times almost to come to a standstill: "Everyone"— circumcised, uncircumcised, slaves, the married, and the unmarried— "should remain in the state in which he was called" (1 Cor. 7:20), because "the appointed time has grown very short" (1 Cor. 7:29). Second, there was evangelistic pressure to become acceptable. Earning money and financial stability were now essential in the urban environment of the Pauline congregations, and Paul had himself forgone living on charity and was modeling an economically independent way of life (1 Cor. 9:3–18; 2 Cor. 12:13). While there were "not many" among them who were "powerful" (1 Cor. 1:26), Paul could still count among his friends and fellow Christians "Erastus, the city treasurer" (Rom. 16:23). In sharp contrast to those congregations from which the Gospels

emerged, where oral traditions of Jesus-sayings were extensively preserved, the Pauline communities appear to have been in possession of
little of this material, if Paul's epistles are characteristic of their
understanding of the gospel (cf. Gal. 1:11–12).[23]

Nevertheless Paul was committed to the "poor among the saints in
Jerusalem," and used their condition to bind congregations into an
awareness of the larger church in Jesus Christ (see chap. 5). Although
he did not dwell on the problems of the poor, in 1 Corinthians he
denounced the rich for their discrimination against the poor in their
agape meals (although his concern was with the divisions in the
community that this produced rather than with the fact of their
poverty). Despite the diversity of status represented in congregational
life, Paul crystallized their unity in their independence from cultural
rewards: "Not many of you were wise according to worldly standards,
not many were powerful, not many were of noble birth" (1 Cor. 1:26).
He lauded the Macedonian congregations for their liberality toward
the Jerusalem Christians in spite of their own "extreme poverty" (2
Cor. 8:2). As in the case of slavery (1 Cor. 7:20), Paul cannot be
ranked among those early Christians who intentionally raised their
voices to change the status of the poor.[24]

Luke: Caring for the Poor

Three of the Gospels say little about the poor. This is not surprising
in a culture in which although people gave alms there was little positive
appreciation of poverty.[25] Mark scarcely goes further than to tip his
hat to the giving of one's wealth to the poor in a passage that has
rather to do with the problems of the rich (Mark 10:21), while John
ignores their situation entirely. Matthew in one instance portrays Jesus
as claiming the words of Isa. 61:1 for himself: "The poor have the
good news preached to them" (Matt. 11:5).[26]

What is more surprising than the general lack of concern for the
poor in Mark, Matthew, and John is Luke's highly intentional focus
on them.[27] At the beginning of his Gospel, in the Magnificat, Mary
praises God because "He has filled the hungry with good things, and
the rich he has sent empty away" (Luke 1:53). In Luke's portrayal of
John the Baptist, the latter admonishes the multitudes, "He who has
two coats, let him share with him who has none; and he who has food,
let him do likewise" (Luke 3:10–11). Luke thus sets the tone for a
continuing emphasis on the needs of the poor which he lays out
programmatically at the beginning of Jesus' career. There he depicts
him as reading Isa. 61:1–2 in his home synagogue: "The Spirit of the
Lord is upon me, because he has anointed me to preach good news to

the poor . . ." (Luke 4:18). Jesus then claims this to be fulfilled in his own ministry.

There is also a second reason for concern that goes beyond the physical well-being of those who are poor. In the first Beatitude, whereas Matthew has "Blessed are the poor in spirit,"[28] thus spiritualizing the notion of poverty, Luke states flatly, "Blessed are you poor" (Luke 6:20). That he intends this literally is evident both from the fact that none of his other beatitudes is spiritualized ("you that hunger," "you that weep," "you when men hate you," Luke 6:21–22), and that the following woes, which stand in parallel with his beatitudes, likewise are clearly directed at literal classes ("you who are rich," "you that are full," "you that laugh," "you, when all men speak well of you," Luke 6:24–26). While Luke shows no concern here for the alleviation of poverty, what is important for our study is that his eschatological message ("Rejoice in that day . . . your reward is great in heaven," Luke 6:23) is directed to those who literally are poor, hungry, sorrowful, and persecuted, the "poor" in the broad sense we have seen in the Old Testament. As Hengel points out, Luke's beatitude is the first instance of "direct praise of the poor."[29]

In Luke 14 two passages deal with the poor. When invited to dinner at the home of a "ruler who belonged to the Pharisees" (v. 1), Jesus admonished him, "But when you give a feast, invite the poor, the maimed, the lame, the blind" (v. 13). This is followed immediately by the parable of the Great Banquet, to which the invited guests refuse to come. As substitute guests the master then orders his servant to invite the same classes, "the poor and maimed and blind and lame" (v. 21). These sayings have a double implication for Luke. On the one hand they stress concern for the plight of the poor, while on the other they point to the eschatological banquet (v. 15) to say that the kingdom of God is for the powerless, the marginal, and the outcast.[30] The same point is made in the story of the Rich Man and Lazarus (Luke 16:19–31).

Luke's more holistic concern for the poor and underprivileged may be related to his special understanding of the place of the Christian movement within history. The authors of Matthew and Mark, each in his own way, while recognizing the validity of the gentile mission, write with a sense that the climactic point is reached in the death and resurrection of Jesus. Subsequent events until the Parousia are interlude. "Eschatological pressure," an urgent sense of the nearness of the Parousia, is high. It is to this imminent turning point in history that the poor and oppressed can look for redress and reward.

While, as we have seen, Luke shares this anticipation, he also has another concern: for him the life and experience of the ongoing

Christian communities since Easter constitute not only a time of waiting for the Second Advent. This period is also theologically significant in the divine scheme of history. This is reflected in the fact that the narrative he presents in Acts is declared to be in accord with God's foreordained program (Acts 1:6–8). This explains, then, Luke's double concern for the poor that we have noted: the gospel is not only to lift their eyes to promised relief in the future kingdom but also to inspire a concern for their material well-being now. Writing for Christians in the late first century, Luke thus draws on the traditions of Jesus' teachings and deeds to emphasize this dual concern.

James: Rejecting the Rewards of Success

The other side of the early Christian appeal to the poor lay in a frequent denunciation of wealth. Such a rejection of worldly honors and rewards was essential to maintain the ideology and the energy of the counterculture. It was implicit in Jesus' and his disciples' own renunciation of private material goods (cf. Peter's declaration, "Lo, we have left everything and followed you," Mark 10:28; Matt. 19:27; Luke 18:28; cf. Luke 14:33). This attitude found vivid expression in numerous sayings preserved by the Christian communities: the camel and the needle's eye (Matt. 19:23–24; Mark 10:23–25; Luke 18:25), the difficulty of the rich entering the kingdom (Mark 10:21–22; Matt. 19:21–22; Luke 18:22–23), the woe upon the rich (Luke 6:24–25), and the declaration, "You cannot serve both God and mammon" (Luke 16:13).

In contrast to the absence of primary attention to wealth in Paul stand the ringing denunciations of the Epistle of James. Writing probably some thirty to forty years after Paul, but obviously conscious of his teaching (cf. James 2:21–24 with Rom. 4:1–5), the author of this epistle is more directly concerned for "good works" than is any other writer in the New Testament. Accordingly the plight of the poor at the hands of the rich is particularly important for him. Adopting the literary form of the diatribe, a popular give-and-take style of address to an audience, he directs a series of striking rhetorical questions to his readers: "Listen, my beloved brethren. Has not God chosen those who are poor in the world to be rich in faith and heirs of the kingdom which he has promised to those who love him? But you have dishonored the poor man. Is it not the rich who oppress you, is it not they who drag you into court? . . . If a brother or sister is ill-clad and in lack of daily food, and one of you says to them, 'Go in peace, be warmed and filled,' without giving them the things needed for the body, what does it profit?" (James 2:5–6, 15–16).

But James's sharpest fire is reserved for a direct assault on the rich:

"Come now, you rich, weep and howl for the miseries that are coming upon you. . . . Behold, the wages of the laborers who mowed your fields which you kept back by fraud, cry out; and the cries of the harvesters have reached the ears of the Lord of hosts. You have lived on the earth in luxury and in pleasure; you have fattened your hearts in a day of slaughter" (James 5:1, 4–5). That this broadside is calculated to be a comfort to poor Christians is clear from the following verses, where they are told to "Be patient, therefore, brethren, until the coming of the Lord. . . . Do not grumble, brethren, against one another, that you may not be judged; behold, the Judge is standing at the doors" (James 5:7, 9). Here we see, in contrast to Paul, much the same attitude as that of the Synoptic tradition, and particularly that of Luke. James states it more stridently, and combines denunciation of the rich with eschatological consolation of the poor, while also showing concern for their present well-being.

The Second Century: A Mixed Picture

Moving into the second century we find in *The Shepherd of Hermas*, a Christian work written at Rome, yet another attitude toward rich and poor. Hermas stands in the traditions of Luke and James in his concern for the poor. It is apparent, however, that the number of well-to-do persons in the Roman church had increased to the point that the rich could no longer simply be the object of denunciation. Rather than decrying riches, Hermas calls upon the rich to act responsibly in the use of their wealth, and to show charity to the poor.[31]

An even more conservative attitude is reflected in the *Didache*. Elaborating on the saying found in Matthew and Luke, "Give to all who ask of you and don't ask for it back" (cf. Matt. 5:42; Luke 6:30), the author comments, "But it has also been said concerning this matter: Let your alms sweat in your hands until you know to what end [or, to whom] you are giving."[32]

These attitudes toward the poor are part of a more general, mixed picture of attitudes toward culture and counterculture reflected in Christian documents of the second century. Thus, while wandering apostles still existed in the Christian communities a century after Jesus, they often were viewed with suspicion and their activities were subjected to regulations—exactly opposite in nature to their own charismatically directed proclivities! Thus the *Didache*, our earliest handbook of church order, offers this instruction:

Every apostle who comes to you should be received as the Lord. But he should not remain more than one day, and if there is some necessity a second as well; but if he should remain for three, he is a false prophet.

And when the apostle departs, he should receive nothing but bread until he finds his next lodging. But if he requests money, he is a false prophet. . . . If he wants to settle among you and knows a trade, use your own judgement to determine how he should live with you as a Christian without being idle. But if he does not wish to cooperate, he is a Christ-peddler. Beware of such![33]

At the same time, a keen sense of their apartness from the world continued to characterize the lives of many Christians. The anonymous apology for Christianity known as *The Epistle to Diognetus*, probably from the first half of the second century, is eloquent in this regard:

Christians are not distinguished from the rest of mankind by either country, speech or customs; the fact is, they nowhere settle in cities of their own; they use no peculiar language; they cultivate no eccentric mode of life. . . . Yet while they dwell in both Greek and non-Greek cities, as each one's lot was cast, and conform to the customs of the country in dress, food, and mode of life in general, the whole tenor of their way of living stamps it as worthy of admiration and admittedly extraordinary. They reside in their respective countries, but only as aliens. They take part in everything as citizens but put up with everything as foreigners. . . . They find themselves "in the flesh," but do not live "according to the flesh." They spend their days on earth, but hold citizenship in heaven.[34]

These tensions continued to be characteristic of Christianity in greater and lesser degrees throughout the third century as well, much depending on the extent to which Christian communities experienced persecution, continued to be in the minority, or grew to enjoy positions of public influence in their particular localities. Although in many ways Christianity became a "church" in the late first and second centuries, elements of the countercultural commitments remained even after its establishment as the official religion of the Roman Empire in the early fourth century. The church not only became assimilated as an institution, but in time provided the backbone for the continuity of Western culture.

"THE POOR" AS A SOURCE OF
COUNTERCULTURAL ENERGY

Our brief study of the concept of the poor, *ptōchoi*, deprives us of simple stereotypes or singular theological perspectives on which to construct the contemporary church. The poor are treated differently in various phases of early church development. We are denied, for example, any simple progression from an alienated sect to a socially accepted church. It is not possible to claim that early Christians were largely from people in poverty, or even that they called themselves the poor. Characteristics of a sect appear in the Jesus movement, but elements of church are also woven into the earliest Gospel records of that movement. In the writings of Paul compromise has already blunted some basic values for the sake of others, for example, equality for the sake of evangelism. Later images of the church, in James and Revelation, seem closer to counterculture commitments. We see not a simple movement from sect to church[35] but a continuing tension between the ideals of the Jesus movement and the hard realities of the world, with the ideals continuously being compromised and constantly rediscovered.

This variety of viewpoints frustrates the idea of a single New Testament theology of poverty or a single sociological pattern of church development. The tensions of congregational development are not only between the church and the world but within the various viewpoints which the church espouses. Although this diversity frustrates those who advocate a single approach, it is equally liberating to those who have experienced the variety of views toward poverty held in the contemporary church. The way Christians approach the *ptōchoi*, the poor, is more diverse and contextual than any single ideology espouses.

The New Testament does not validate whatever the believer might choose to believe, but several biblically based perspectives can be identified. Rather than endorsing any one of these, our biblical study of the poor helps us honor several of the approaches which also appear in the contemporary religious situation. Particularly notable are (1) the waves of restless reform groups that the gospel inspires in every new generation of the church. We consider (2) the continuing tension between "evangelical" religion which senses the urgency of personal salvation and for which the question of poverty often is secondary, and "mainline" religion which sees itself in history and seeks a more holistic, long-term ministry to the poor; and (3) the importance of the church identifying with the poor, which is basic to its counterculture character, as seen most recently in the development of liberation theology. For all of these approaches there is solid biblical foundation and mutual tension within the contemporary church.

Restless Reform Groups

The energy of the church resides not in the glacial momentum of its institutional structure but in the waves of reform movements which arouse the imagination of the public and cut across the structures of organized religion. Historically these groups have seen it their task to cleanse the churches of North America through renewal of concern for the poor as inspired by the example of the gospel. Some of these, like the Methodists, felt themselves called to bring the gospel to the alienated working class, as a renewal movement within the Anglican tradition. Others, like the Christian Scientists, began with more independent roots but also hoped to offer new direction and commitment in what they perceived to be a declining religious environment. Some, like the Jesus people (once called the Jesus freaks), pattern their group discipline on their reading of the New Testament. The Jesus people provoke a range of direct comparisons with the first-century Jesus movement, from their initial restlessness, financial dependency, and sexual "scandal" to their contemporary economic, familial, and community disciplines. Each of these reform groups has drawn from those who were restless in the ranks of established religion, and each has followed a different course—the Methodists to become a church, the Christian Scientists to become an established sect, and the Jesus people to remain a (self-declared) "Christian community in an alien world."

In addition to the many groups that have become institutionalized, the Gospels have inspired "movements" which have refocused on the plight of the poor. By remaining relatively loose in structure, they have attracted the commitment of kindred spirits from a wide range of existing religious institutions. The Young Men's and Women's Christian Associations (YMCA/YWCA), for example, shared a history of evangelical zeal in membership recruiting and in serving the needs of the poor while participants could remain active in home churches. In the 1970s and 1980s these movements have expanded numerically, combining a far greater number of issues with much more limited focus in each group. Thus the concept of the poor has come to mean ever more specific populations which feel they have been alienated or oppressed. We have moved from a general concern for civil rights to concerns for the specific rights of blacks, Native Americans, Hispanics, elderly, women, and homosexuals. The general concern for peace has become specific in the campaigns for sanctuary, antinuclear freeze, and nuclear-free zones. Some movements stress social concerns, such as overnight shelters and health programs; others are more traditionally religious, such as community Bible study fellowships and charismatic worship groups—all have grown in membership and diversity. In many cases church members will change denominational affiliation but retain their "membership" in particular campaigns.

More than radical sects or denominational bodies, these movements which sweep through national religious consciousness revitalize faith commitments even as they challenge the institutional church. "The role of the reform movements in religious revitalization is perhaps the most straight forward," observed Robert Wuthnow; "Many such movements have as their explicit aim some form of religious renewal. . . . Most result neither in new religions nor in distinct denominations, but such movements have repeatedly shaped the direction in which religious efforts are focused."[36]

Evangelical Urgency and Mainline Historical Consciousness

The sharpest tension in the contemporary church is exposed in our brief study of differing attitudes toward the *ptōchoi*, the poor. Evangelistic religion, in the tradition of the early Pauline communities' zeal to witness to Jesus Christ in the last days, emphasizes personal morality and spiritual gifts. It often is not unconcerned for the poor, but places a higher priority on the preparation of the individual for the kingdom which is to come; similarly, efforts for the poor characteristically focus on direct aid to individuals. "Mainline" religion, drawing on a more extended sense of history reminiscent of that of Luke-Acts, takes a "responsible" role toward the ongoing life of the community. Included in that public responsibility is a holistic concern for those who are poor which is expressed in programs aimed not only at individuals but also at changing society as a whole.

In these differing attitudes toward the poor we see the split between fundamentalist and evangelical conservatives on the one hand, and liberal mainline Christians on the other. It is a difference between evangelistic emphasis on the world to come and mainline emphasis on responsibility in this world as we find it, between evangelistic accent on personal ethics and private faith and mainline expectations which include the social ethics of a "public church." The term "public religion," which Martin Marty attributes to Thomas Jefferson and Benjamin Franklin[37] at the founding of the republic, contrasts the major features of mainline Christian commitment to public concerns with the more private and individualistic expressions of conservative groups.

Just as we noted biblical foundations in Pauline material for evangelistic zeal under "eschatological pressure," so we also find support in the writings of Luke for the longer historical perspective of mainline churches. In the case of Luke, this perspective, along possibly with the traditions of a caring physician (which he may have been), seems to have led him to more awareness of the church's responsibility for the poor in its midst.

In contemporary churches this difference between historical consciousness in this world and an urgent preparation for the next has been identified as the most significant feature to distinguish congregational mission. According to David A. Roozen, William McKinney, and Jackson C. Carroll, who conducted an extensive study of congregations in Hartford, Connecticut:

> The mission orientations divide along this-worldly versus otherworldly lines. As the distinction suggests, the former takes with considerable seriousness this present world as an important arena for religiously motivated service and action. . . . In contrast, the otherworldly orientations tend, either explicitly or implicitly, to devalue life in the world and stress salvation for a world to come.[38]

Roozen, McKinney, and Carroll provide ten case studies organized around similarities of congregational mission, based on those which were more active in the community or more membership-centered within the congregation. In rich detailing of contemporary congregations, the study shows the continuing presence of Pauline urgency to "bring souls to Christ," and the Lucan effort to be a "responsible congregation in the life of the community." Their report also documents the mutual misunderstanding that often exists between these two biblical perspectives.

Ironically, churches that appeal to people who feel alienated in this world and promise a better life in the world to come seem to be more successful as institutions in this world here and now. Sociologist Dean Hoge has shown a remarkable correlation in the growth of churches that project an image of separation from the cares of the world, and the decline of churches that embrace and seek to guide the culture.[39] He says that such growth is most pronounced where the population feels "alienated from the world."

We see similar appeals to those who feel alienated in secular movements that build on a sense of "deprivation" and provide energy to the cutting edge of change. Gary Schwartz, for example, has identified several areas of "relative deprivation"[40] which do not reflect objective measures of being deprived, but are based on the feelings of the persons involved. Relative deprivation can occur even when a person is physically comfortable: one may have wealth, but feel deprived when compared relatively with others in one's social world. Relative deprivation may be experienced in numerous areas other than wealth.[41] Thus in a variety of deprivations people can feel that they are alienated and marginalized, that they are "the poor."

Social Dynamics of Church Development

The poor are important to the church, because God cares for them. But they are also important sources of strength. Programs that provide a relationship to the poor have, in many congregations, generated membership energy which cannot be matched by any activity directed at their own internal self-interests. Such programs range from soup kitchens and food pantries to personal counseling and national peace advocacy. Invariably the church initiates the program to help others, and the members conclude that "we get so much more from it than the people we are trying to help."[42] In such settings, the congregation reclaims its identity with the poor, a reunion in which all have some needs, and all have something to share. No congregation is so poor or so thoroughly endowed that it cannot gain by giving. Recognition of the poor, among us and in us, can bring out the best in the church.

In a more radical way, "the poor" offer a measure of protection against the coopting of the church by cultural rewards of affluence, power, and success. In the biblical tradition of rejecting "the world," especially in James and Revelation, the counterculture commitments of the church are affirmed by the denial of secular values and the affirmation of Christian relationships. Thus rejection of the world and identification with the poor saves the church from compromise and assimilation.

Recently liberation theology has highlighted the pivotal role of the poor in the maintenance of the Christian faith. Liberation theology reverses the paradigm from sect to church, from alienated sinner to acceptable Christian. Rather than the bottom rising to higher levels, liberationists see privileged Christians reclaiming their poverty. Based on Dietrich Bonhoeffer's admonition "to see the great events of world history from below, from the perspective of the outcast, the suspects, the maltreated, the powerless, the oppressed, the reviled," Robert McAfee Brown defines liberation theology as "preeminently a way of looking at life 'from below,' from the perspective of the poor, the dispossessed, the marginalized."[43]

This reversal of the flow provides a different interpretation of Pauline theology: Paul does not ignore the plight of the poor, but points to God as the one who joins in their suffering (2 Cor. 8:9). But this reversal also creates a dilemma, since liberationists know that poverty is not romantic. Rather liberation theology views association with poverty as a means of sifting and testing the commitment of church members. "The vocabulary of poverty is the idea of a faithful 'remnant,' " says José Miguez Bonino. "Christian poverty, the believer's humility before God, incarnates itself in the solidarity with the poor and oppressed."[44] Miguez Bonino proceeds to quote Gutiérrez approvingly:

> Poverty must be assumed for what it is—as an evil, in order to protest against it and to fight for its abolition. . . . Christian poverty as an expression of love, is solidarity with the poor and it is a protest against poverty.

Thus the counterculture assumes different expressions in the church. These can be identified by several attitudes toward the poor, each of which has biblical foundations in the early church and currency in our time. Each emphasizes different values, and each has limitations. (a) The counterculture characteristic of the Jesus movement gathers the restless and seeks to reform the church and society to bring it back to basic values. (b) The counterculture of the evangelistic church emphasizes personal morality and the participation of the Holy Spirit. (c) The countercultural style of the "mainline" churches feels a responsibility for the whole society, and seeks holistic ministry to the poor of the community and throughout the world. (d) Counterculture in liberation theology rejects worldly honors and success by rejoining the poor and experiencing life from their perspective, not to romanticize poverty but to destroy it. Each of these perspectives claims center stage on occasion, and sometimes denies the validity of the others. In our view, each has a valid but limited grasp of truth. One emphasis may be more appropriate in a particular setting, but together they form a more complete presentation of biblical theology and contemporary witness.

In contemporary congregations, the countercultural faith assumes different expressions when faced with particular oppressive situations. In the despair of the inner city, counterculture is hope. In the barren anonymity of the business district, counterculture may be a community of the lively arts. In the survival struggle of the working class, counterculture may be disciplined achievement. In the competitive individualism of business success, counterculture may be a cooperative community. In the consumer society, counterculture is sacrificial sharing. In the destructive forces of addictive alcohol, drugs, and family dissolution, counterculture is a group of caring people. In the face of oppressive powers, counterculture is the voice of courageous truth. When confronted by aggressive nations, counterculture is a commitment to a just peace. In the materialism of all human achievement or disaster, counterculture recalls spirituality that makes possible our relationship with a transcendent God. In all, counterculture seeks *eirēnē*, right relations among God's people.[45]

LEADERSHIP: AN APPEAL FOR BALANCE

Much of what has been said regarding the energy generated by the counterculture element in Christianity comes to focus in its leadership. Our understanding of leadership combines the major themes discussed in chapters 1 and 2 and rests on both biblical sources and contemporary application of basic concepts. In chapter 1 we noted two significant elements in the social dynamics of group process, the intimate community and the organizational society. Max Weber offered two similar "types of solidarity" in the development of social groups.[46] One was based on the way affectionate ties become traditional feelings and the other on rational judgments which become normative rules. For each of these Weber identified the expectations of the group that would be satisfied by each "legitimated" leadership style.

The validity of their claims to legitimacy may be based on:
1. Rational grounds—resting on a belief in the "legality" of patterns of normative rules and the right of those elevated to authority under such rules to issue commands (legal authority).
2. Traditional grounds—resting on an established belief in the sanctity of immemorial traditions and the legitimacy of the status of those exercising authority under them (traditional authority).[47]

These two styles of leadership are basic to institutional growth and stability, as noted in chapter 1. The rational style is essential for effective organizational leadership. Such people keep appointments, run the meetings, stick to the agenda, plan the program, press for results, and, if appointed, preach a proper sermon of "three points, a poem, and a prayer." Organizational leaders take justifiable pride in their qualifications and performance. They are "professionals," even if they volunteer. Without them the church organization would be disorganized and frustrating.

Traditional leaders depend more on relationships than on official status. They keep in touch with people, even if they are running off schedule. They allow meetings to wander if the conversation is a way of keeping in touch. They plan for the next generation but not necessarily for tomorrow. They solve problems not by the analysis of issues but by finding people who care. If appointed, their preaching may not be clear or even theologically consistent but it is marked by human interest stories about people who sound familiar. Traditional leaders may not run the institution very well but they make the membership feel good about belonging.

Both rational and traditional leaders are essential for the social dynamics of congregational development, as we suggested in the first chapter. Their symbiotic interdependence maintains the church alive and strong as long as there is no need to challenge the culture or step off in a dramatic departure from the past.

But if the church is to sustain its countercultural heritage, another leadership style is equally essential. Although the church after Constantine became the backbone and carrier of culture, the church also supplied many of the fresh initiatives of cultural critique and massive social change. This dynamic of change prompted Ernst Troeltsch to

develop the concept of sect, which introduced our discussion of the
countercultural elements in Christian faith. To interpret the leadership
style that makes possible a countercultural movement, Troeltsch used
a third style of leadership suggested by Weber. From the Greek, Weber
employed a New Testament word to describe the characteristic quality
of a leader who is especially "gifted," or "graced by God:" *charisma:*

> Charismatic grounds—resting on devotion to the specific and exceptional
> sanctity, heroism and exemplary character of an individual person, and
> the normative patterns or order revealed or ordained by him (charismatic
> authority).[48]

The charismatic individual is seen to have gifts of body and spirit,
of vision and strength, which are specific, extraordinary, and even
sometimes supernatural. Such persons are not appointed or dismissed.
They make no claim to a career ladder, salaried position, or credentials
of institutional preparation. They are not "controlled" by agencies of
advancement or accountability. Thus Weber writes, in the unconsciously sexist language of his time, reminding the church of one root
word for leadership:

> Charisma knows only inner determination and inner restraint. The holder
> of charisma seizes the task that is adequate for him and demands obedience
> and a following by virtue of his mission. His success determines whether
> he finds them. His charismatic claim breaks down if his mission is not
> recognized by those to whom he feels he has been sent. If they recognize
> him, he is their master—so long as he knows how to maintain recognition
> through "proving" himself. But he does not derive his "right" from their
> will, in the manner of an election. Rather, the reverse holds: it is the duty
> of those to whom he addresses his mission to recognize him as their
> charismatically qualified leader.[49]

Rational and traditional leadership are not unimportant, but each
serves different needs and behaves in different ways. Weber says that
"charismatic domination is the very opposite of bureaucratic domination" and is in "sharp contrast" to any traditional or patriarchal
structure. As we have seen in the Jesus movement, the charismatic
leader often "deliberately shuns the possession of money and pecuniary
income per se" but rather is supported by "gifts, donations or other
voluntary contributions."[50] Thus the charismatic leader has a direct
appeal to those who follow, but a kind of independence in spirit from
the mundane demands of surrounding society. Such charisma is not
limited to leadership, but is shared by all who accept the challenge:
"In order to do justice to their mission, the holders of charisma, the
master as well as his disciples and followers, must stand outside the
ties of this world, outside the routine occupation as well as outside the
routine obligations of family life."[51]

Charismatic leaders are seen to arise by those who follow them when the established traditional and organizational institutions no longer reflect the needs or commitments of their constituencies. As we have noted regarding the rise of counterculture movements, the crisis or distress that calls forth a response to charismatic leaders may be physical, medical, psychological, social, political, philosophical, economic, ethnic, ethical, spiritual, or—more likely, some combination of these needs. These sectlike movements need charismatic leaders to focus concerns and mobilize their energy, whatever the cause. In this sense, "Ronald Reagan is the Che Guevara of capitalism,"[52] offering charismatic leadership to a movement that needed focus. Such leaders at times may see themselves beyond the law:

> In meaning and content the mission may be addressed to a [very specific] group. . . . Its "objective" law emanates concertedly from the highly personal experience of heavenly grace and from the god-like strength of the hero. Charismatic domination means a rejection of all ties to any external order in favor of the exclusive glorification of the genuine mentality of the prophet and hero. Hence, its attitude is revolutionary and transvalues everything; it makes a sovereign break with all traditional or rational norms: "It is written, but I say unto you."[53]

The strength of charismatic leadership lies in the high level of commitment it produces. The difficulty lies in its instability. In challenging the status quo, the movement and its leaders become changed as well. Although this may appear to be a loss of vitality, it also signifies that the changes the movement has urged are becoming more acceptable generally. Weber calls this the routinization of charisma, and sees it as inevitable. "It is the fate of charisma, whenever it comes into the permanent institutions of a community, to give way to powers of tradition or of rational socialization."[54] Although we have not found that charismatic authority inevitably "gives way" as Weber proposed, we find that charismatic leadership was active in the New Testament church, and the hope for charismatic leadership lives on in the contemporary church. We believe that all three leadership styles—rational-organizational, traditional-relational, and charismatic—are essential for a balanced understanding of professional and lay church leaders.

NEW TESTAMENT LEADERSHIP

The New Testament remembers the heroes of the early church in a way that reflects each of the three types of legitimate authority—legal, traditional, and charismatic. Because, however, these types as described by Troeltsch are ideal types, and Christianity in the first two centuries was an organism in constant process of social development, we cannot expect to find entirely discrete examples of each of these types. But the "types" are valuable in identifying traits in various individuals in the early communities which signal the developments that were taking place.

Jesus. The historical Jesus, the man of Nazareth, stands as our prime example of a charismatic leader.[55] Without formal qualifications or traditional status, he gathered a following and energized a movement through the power of his person, his teachings, and his acts. "The great throng heard him gladly" (Mark 12:37).

The early Christians understood this charismatic authority to have been passed by Jesus to his disciples. Thus in the commission to the seventy, Luke reports a saying that must have reflected a common conviction of early preachers of the gospel: "He who hears you hears me" (Luke 10:16). A similar understanding is stated in Peter's explanation of the power by which he had healed the lame man: "Be it known to you all . . . that by the name of Jesus Christ of Nazareth . . . this man is standing before you well"(Acts 4:10). Authority does not rest primarily in the persons of the disciples but is delegated by the charismatic leader and is thus on the way to becoming traditional. After Peter's speech to the rulers, Luke reports that the latter recognized that the disciples "had been with Jesus" (Acts 4:13).

This transmission of authority was closely connected with the experience of the Spirit. "You shall receive power when the Holy Spirit has come upon you, and you shall be my witnesses in Jerusalem and in all Judea and Samaria and to the end of the earth"(Acts 1:8). A particular manifestation of this is found in the wandering preachers and the prophets, itinerant and settled, who continued into the second century to be a characteristic of Christianity. Philip's four virgin daughters and Agabus (Acts 21:9–10) are examples of such persons who clearly were notable and spoke with authority; they are even depicted as admonishing Paul.[56]

The Twelve Apostles. While Jesus' transmission of authority to his disciples was understood broadly, at least in Luke's view (cf. "The Seventy," Luke 10:1), it is in this concept of "apostle" that we move a step nearer a traditional type of leadership figure. The story of the choosing of Matthias to fill the place of Judas reveals a sense of the uniqueness of the Twelve as contrasted with other followers of Jesus. When he was chosen, Matthias was then "enrolled with the eleven apostles" to be in a special way "a witness to his resurrection" (Acts 1:15–26). The official, almost legal tone of these proceedings also reflects attitudes in the church a half-century after the events.

Paul. Paul's struggle to be accepted as an "apostle" gives evidence, however, that these attitudes were indeed present at an earlier period. This is clear from his argument with those who would deny him apostleship. Having "seen Jesus our Lord" (1 Cor. 9:1; cf. Acts 1:21–22) and having the proof of a fruitful ministry were also key prerequisites to recognition as an apostle (see also 2 Cor. 12:11–13). Paul thus laid claim to apostleship on traditional grounds. At the same time, there was much in the force of his own personality that would characterize him as a charismatic leader. Perhaps for this reason he was at constant pains to conceal himself behind the figure of Christ (note especially how both these characteristics emerge in 2 Cor. 11:21—12:13, where he "boasts" but confesses that "I am speaking as a fool"; cf. 1 Cor. 2:1–5). This tension within Paul between his own charismatic genius and his devotion to Christ may also be reflected in the fact that it is the crucified and risen Christ, rather than the teacher and miracle worker of Nazareth, to whom he constantly appeals.

James, the Brother of Jesus. Another mixed form of leadership, tending toward the traditional, is found with James "the Lord's brother." The New Testament tells us little of James other than that he was a witness to the resurrection (1 Cor. 15:7) and that he was one of the "pillars" of the Jerusalem congregation (Gal. 2:8) to whom, along with Peter, Paul first introduced himself after his conversion (Gal. 1:18). His leadership role can be traced in this way to within less than ten years after the death of Jesus. Luke portrays him as having been spokesman, and probably leader, of the congregation some twenty years afterward (Acts 21:18–25). A much later tradition, though likely a basically authentic one, describes James as having been intensely pious and because of his piety having exercised wide influence not only on the Christian community, but on the Jewish public as well.[57] In James's exercise of authority we can see then a combination of factors: personal charisma supported by a family relationship with Jesus which seems to have placed him in a specially intimate relationship with the Twelve (cf. Acts 1:14).

Peter. The case of Peter is somewhat different. Possessed of a dynamic personality, he was from the outset a central figure in the Jesus movement. In the early traditions of the Jerusalem community (Acts

1—5; 15), he is portrayed as the functional leader, though without specific portfolio beyond the apostleship he shared with the other eleven. That this tradition has substance, however, is probable from Paul's account that on his first visit to Jerusalem as a Christian, he went up "to visit Cephas and remained with him fifteen days" (Gal. 1:18). The degree to which Peter's leadership may have rested on a specific authorization of Jesus is impossible to say. Some years after Peter's death Matthew records a Jesus-saying that, if not authentic, at least enhanced his image in the memory of the church: "You are Peter, and on this rock (*petra*) I will build my church" (Matt. 16:18). What Peter's role was in the founding of the congregation at Rome is equally unclear, but that he was involved with that church and that he died there is virtually certain.[58] Analyzing what we can know and can reasonably conjecture regarding Peter's position, we can see that he too stands on the boundary between charismatic authority and that based on traditional grounds of recognized apostleship. Whether or not at the end of his life he occupied a more "rationally" founded position as "bishop" at Rome, as traditionally conceived, is beyond the limits of our sources to determine.

Church Officers. The beginnings of such leadership on rational or legal grounds can first be detected clearly in the presence of officers in at least some of Paul's congregations. Thus there were "bishops" and "deacons" at Philippi (Phil. 1:1) and a woman, Phoebe, who was a "deacon" at Cenchraea, near Corinth (Rom. 16:1). Luke understands that there were "elders" in the congregation at Ephesus who "bishoped" (Greek, *episkopeō*) the community there (Acts 20:17, 28). We cannot say to what degree the holders of these positions were officials in an institutional sense. In view of the existence of counterparts to some degree in the synagogues, however, it is reasonable to conclude that we do have here the beginnings of authority vested on rational grounds. In chapter 1 we traced the way in which such offices continued to develop in the second century.

The Christ: Charismatic, Traditional, and Rational. In their understanding of Christ as seen through the light of Easter, the early Christians perceived a figure of authority that combined the elements we have been discussing. The *charismatic* qualities of Jesus were given full play: "No man ever spoke like this man!" (John 7:46); and the stories of his miracles were told in such a way as to point to his divinity (e.g., Matt. 14:22-23; Mark 4:36-41; John 11:25-27).

The *traditional* grounds for his authority were also enhanced through the vision of his ministry, and his death and resurrection as a fulfillment of God's intention foretold in the Old Testament. Paul understood that "when the time had fully come, God sent forth his son" (Gal. 4:4), and that "of first importance" to the gospel message was that Christ died "in accordance with the scriptures, that he was buried, that he was raised on the third day in accordance with the scriptures" (1 Cor. 15:3–4). The Gospels each elaborate this sense in telling the story of Jesus' passion by drawing heavily on Old Testament themes. Luke is especially vivid; the Risen Lord tells his disciples in regard to his death: "These are my words that I spoke to you while I was still with you, that everything written about me in the law of Moses and the prophets and the psalms must be fulfilled" (Luke 24:44). John, from his unique perspective, ties Christ not only into the Old Testament but also into the whole cosmic scheme: "In the beginning was the Word. . . . He was in the world, and the world was made through him, yet the world knew him not" (John 1:1, 10–11; cf. 1 Pet. 1:20).

The *rational* or legal grounds of Christ's authority are developed especially in the Epistle to the Hebrews, where he is "designated by God a high priest after the order of Melchizedek" (Heb. 5:10). This image is then elaborated in terms of the rituals of the Israelite sanctuary (Hebrews 8—9), and Christ's authority for the believer is strikingly portrayed: "We have such a high priest, one who is seated at the right hand of the throne of the Majesty in heaven, a minister in the sanctuary and the true tent which is set up not by man but by the Lord. For every high priest is appointed to offer gifts and sacrifices; hence it is necessary for this priest also to have something to offer. . . . He entered once for all into the Holy Place, taking not the blood of goats and calves but his own blood, thus securing an eternal redemption" (Heb. 8:1–3; 9:12).

In these ways, then, as authority in the church developed, early Christians were able to subsume its various manifestations in their understandings of Christ and to draw from those understandings a christological basis for the sociological developments taking place among them.

LEADERSHIP IN CONTEMPORARY CHURCHES

Charismatic, traditional, and rational styles of leadership, as introduced by Weber, are all essential to the continuing life of the local church. Thus James D. Anderson and Ezra Earl Jones write,

An underlying assumption of our model is that church leadership is required to fulfill three basic tasks. . . . (1) Associational [traditional]

leadership: to provide effective guidance for the gathering church, helping the membership clarify directions and associate together with a free commitment to the mission of the church. (2) Organizational [rational] management: to provide efficient organizational management. The brick-and-mortar, bureaucratic aspects of church life demand careful, efficient administration and execution. (3) Spiritual [charismatic] direction: to provide authentic spiritual direction—congruent, authoritative teaching, preaching, counsel, and witness in order to help people know themselves and the world through the eyes of faith.[59]

In the social dynamics of congregational life, these three functions of leadership are shared among the membership. The roles are usually allocated unofficially but everyone "knows" who contributes each of the styles to make the pattern complete. Usually people accept a particular role, although sometimes one person may have more than a single function.[60] The "organizers" (rational leaders) are the easiest to locate. They are the recognized managers and leaders of activities and organized groups. The associational (traditional) leaders provide the social glue to hold the church together: the entertainers, communicators, and gossips; the community "mothers," storytellers, and even the grumblers. The organizational leaders will keep the activities alive, and the social leaders will be in touch with the people. The spiritual (charismatic) leadership of the church is often exempted from normal activities and vested with special powers. They are the "saints," the consolers, confidants, and care-givers who have come to symbolize what it means to belong in that particular congregation. Taken together these people share the function of leadership in the local church, although many would not appear on an organizational chart.

There are people in the congregation who will expect each of these functions from the pastor, and the pastor will feel the pressure to provide all three. For some members, the pastor is the manager and director of the congregational organization. She may be expected to be proficient in management skills, from the supervision of staff to the details of machine operations—except, of course, for financing, where most congregations do not expect (have learned not to expect?) that pastors have any natural gifts. For some members the pastor should be more proficient in social skills—a visitor and counselor, a storyteller and telephoner, a group processer and personal friend. These roles are essential to the strength and growth of a healthy congregation, and pastors should be as prepared as possible in each.

But of the three leadership roles, the charismatic style seems most hoped for, in quality if not quantity.[61] Urban Holmes has called the pastor "theotokas," the bearer of the holy.[62] Holmes argues that the primary strength of the pastor is not the associational or organizational,

but is found in the charismatic "gifts" of the leader who is strong
when others are weak. Pastoral leadership is needed most when members
of the church experience times of loss and transition. The pastor should
be strongest when others are in greatest need, to stand with them in
"their wilderness" and walk with them through "the abyss." Holmes
suggests that such leadership is not learned with advanced degrees,
but acquired as a gift from God in the midst of "the poor," a people
who know they are in need.

Robert Greenleaf as a consultant in industry developed and popularized the concept of servant leader. In applying this concept to the
church (from which it came in the first place), Greenleaf suggests[63]
that the strongest leader is one who imagines and articulates alternatives
for the community. Such a person embodies the sense of hope and
willingness to risk, as the charismatic leader, and inspires others by
life style as much as language. The community believes in the leader
because they believe through her or him. The charismatic leader does
not need to be dramatic or flamboyant, only strong when others are in
need, especially in the transitional seasons in the lives of individuals
and the church.

Role confusion and pastoral burnout can be caused by trying to
fulfill too many expectations of others—church members, family, local
community, denominational leaders, and even residual images from
seminary days. The social analysis of biblical and contemporary
leadership functions should help to sort out those expectations and to
remind us of our strengths and weaknesses. As protection against
burnout it is helpful for the pastor to recognize personal limitations
and the need for others to share in the leadership of the church. The
biblical record provides a welcome relief. None of the New Testament
leaders were remembered as capable in all three areas. Only the figure
of Christ—in memory—provides a prototype to legitimate all three in
a single person.

The church must be like other human groups, both an intimate
community and an organizational society, and the leadership must help
it happen. But the church is also expected to be more: a resource for
human living over against life's mundane and destructive elements. In
charisma—that gift of leadership which comes from beyond—the church
has become a counterculture time and again, for the salvation of
individuals and reclaiming of society.

The charisma from God can be recognized by its fruits. In the New
Testament communities we have seen charisma in the counterculture
of the church at work in the world: in the Jesus movement, the
gathering of restless people, and the restoration of lost values; in the

Pauline communities, the emphasis on the Holy Spirit and individual morality; in Luke's historical church, a more holistic ministry with the poor; in the later concerns of James and Revelation, rejection of worldly success and reclaiming a place with the poor. Each of these is an expression of the counterculture church. Taken together they are evidence of the continuing energy of God's charisma at work in the world.

THREE

FAITH CRISIS AND CHRISTIAN WITNESS

From any rational perspective, the New Testament church never should have happened. The church began with two crises of faith, either of which alone could have destroyed the embryonic gathering of believers. But inspired by its counterculture foundations and its charismatic leaders, the early Jesus movement and later the young church were able to transform initial challenges to their faith into even stronger commitments to ministry and mission.

The first crisis arose in Jerusalem within the Jesus movement, and revolved around an understanding of "kingdom." But following the crisis of the crucifixion, evangelism abruptly exploded. The second crisis was anchored in the growing disappointment over a delay in the expected return of Jesus. In each instance an apparent setback became the trigger to mobilize an even greater zeal. Disappointment did not lead to disillusion.

The sources are clear that Jesus proclaimed the imminence of "the kingdom." It was about to break in on the existing order of things, its coming would be largely unexpected except as people accepted his announcement, and its coming would be God's act. Thus it would be distinctly messianic. It is understandable that Jesus' Jewish hearers, including his disciples, interpreted his words in terms of *their* expectations of an earthly, political Messiah, a conclusion repeatedly reflected in the Gospels (e.g., Mark 8:31–33; Luke 24:18–21; John 6:14–15).

As we try to understand the significance of eschatology for the development of early Christianity, we take as our point of departure the fact that at Jesus' death, his disciples found themselves faced with acute disappointment. The one whom they had expected would usher in the messianic "kingdom of God" had instead been executed as a

76

criminal. When the crisis came he had not even delivered himself, as was doubtless aptly pointed out by their enemies (cf. Mark 15:30–31). Here we see a double threat to the community's perception of its own reality: internally their understanding of themselves was threatened by the disappearance of the one who embodied their expectations; externally they no longer could claim credibility from the public.

Just beyond this experience of the utter devastation of their hopes lay the outburst of energy and commitment, of evangelistic zeal that carried the gospel "to every nation" (Matt. 28:19). This conversion of a faith crisis into a committed witness is the organizational miracle of the New Testament.

The second phase can be seen in the church of the late first century, also threatened by confusion and uncertainty, this time concerning the eschaton and the second coming: Would the second coming occur within their lifetime? Why had Christ not yet returned? Was their hope in vain?

Initially this does not appear to have been a pressing question. As late as the fifties, when Paul wrote to the Christian community at Thessalonica, he and they shared the expectation that the return of Christ, the Parousia, would occur in the near future. This is clear from the fact that when one of the believers there died, Paul assured the survivors that when Christ returned, the dead would, in fact, rise first before "we," the living, are "caught up together with them in the clouds to meet the Lord in the air" (1 Thess. 4:16–17). Paul classed his readers and himself among those who would live to see the Parousia. Some years later his anticipation is shown to have been heightened by a sense of urgency, when, writing to the Corinthians, he could declare, "The appointed time has grown very short" (1 Cor. 7:29).

Moving on into the latter decades of the first century, however, we can sense a growing concern over the fact that Christ had not returned. This is reflected in the way questions from Jesus' disciples are nuanced by writers at this time. Thus Mark's form of Jesus' apocalyptic discourse, written about A.D. 70, is introduced by a question regarding the destruction of the temple; but in Matthew's form of the same question, written after the temple was gone, the disciples ask instead, "What will be the sign of your coming and of the close of the age?" (Matt. 24:3). Similarly Luke shows the disciples asking Jesus again, just before his ascension, "Lord, will you at this time restore the kingdom to Israel?" (Acts 1:6). These were not only questions that might have been asked by the disciples of Jesus; they also reflect increasingly pressing questions for the Christians among whom the Gospels and Acts were written some half-century later.

Written sometime in the late first or early second century, the *First Epistle of Clement* to the Corinthians reflects a growing sense of doubt among some regarding the coming of the Parousia. Quoting what was probably a Jewish writing (which it refers to as scripture), it declares,

> Far be that Scripture from us which says, "Wretched are the double-minded, those who harbor doubts in their souls and say, 'We have heard these things even in our fathers' time, and yet here we are, already grown old, and none of these things has happened to us' "[1]

The sharpest formulation of the issue, however, arises in what is doubtless the latest book of the New Testament, 2 Peter, written probably during the first half of the second century. The author addresses himself "to those who have obtained a faith of equal standing with ours . . . First of all you must understand this, that scoffers will come in the last days with scoffing, following their own passions, . . . saying, 'Where is the promise of his coming? For ever since the fathers fell asleep, all things have continued as they were from the beginning of creation' " (2 Pet. 1:1; 3:3-4). Here we are dealing not simply with growing doubt but with outright rejection of those who still after a century expect the Parousia.

Either of these profound disappointments, one virtually instantaneous at the cross, the other a matter of growing uneasiness and doubt across many decades, could have destroyed the church in infancy. In both cases, the church grew stronger and larger. We have noted that almost immediately after the death of Jesus, the believing community launched a program of intense missionary activity. And, decades later, when increasingly insistent questions arose regarding the Parousia, we see evidence of additional evangelical commitment. How can we account for such positive reactions when Christians were confronted with these crises in faith?

COGNITIVE DISSONANCE AND THE CRISES OF FAITH

Based on broad social research in the elements involved in making decisions, Leon Festinger has developed a theory to describe the behavior of people who experience a "crisis" between their expectations or beliefs and the objective data from a historical event. Festinger calls this disconfirmation and the behavior that follows "cognitive dissonance." He has developed extensive data about reactions in the experience of cognitive dissonance and applied his research to a wide variety of social issues such as eating habits, world peace, racial prejudice, teacher grading practices, fairness in sports, commercial advertising, and social lives of homosexual men.[2] Cognitive dissonance is not necessarily an unusual or exotic experience, but rather is associated with those shocking moments when we realize that the way we have organized our world is no longer functional or confirmed by the sources of reality we have come to trust. It is experienced in the collapse of our "symbolic universe" and the subsequent urgency to put our world together again.

Cognitive dissonance may happen when a marriage dissolves and the partners realize—through sudden discovery or through erosion and apathy—that their relationship is dysfunctional. Once they believed, but now they have no more faith in each other: the magic is gone. Cognitive dissonance happens when a dream is lost, when a faith is broken, when a "world" dissolves. Festinger has studied the variety of responses that occur in these crises of faith.

Cognitive dissonance as used by Festinger suggests a causal relationship between the disconfirmation of belief and the energy to proselytize new believers. Festinger, with others, found these principles operative in religious behavior through an extensive study of a "Lake City" group which believed they could date the end of the world. In analyzing the behavior of group members, he identified five conditions that must be present to produce an increase in evangelistic zeal.[3] These include (1) commitment to a belief (2) which is important and (3) subject to disconfirmation; (4) following an unequivocal experience of disconfirmation, (5) those for whom the community remains intact respond with an evangelistic effort to win converts to some form of the belief that has been disconfirmed. The Festinger study showed these conditions in operation: when the date on which the group under study anticipated to be the end passed without noticeable alteration in the cosmos, the group did not dissolve but rather expanded its efforts to recruit new members. Following their crisis of faith, they evangelized. Festinger observes that under some conditions "it may be less painful to tolerate the dissonance than to discard the belief."[4]

In discussing the implications of cognitive dissonance for interpreting the New Testament, John Gager[5] notes the importance of Festinger's study for understanding faith crises in the early church.[6] In establishing essential similarities, Gager proposes modifications in the theory of cognitive dissonance that emphasize the importance of group development at the time of the event, the public response to the event, and significant social support during the transitional time:

   1. Proselytism as a means of reducing cognitive dissonance will appear primarily in new groups, like early Christianity, whose existence has been occasioned by or associated with a belief that is subsequently disconfirmed.

2. Public ridicule at the time of disconfirmation may play an important role in turning such a group toward missionary activity.

3. The limit beyond which belief will not withstand disconfirmation is a function of the degree to which identification with the group supplants the original belief as a basic motivation for adherence to the group.[7]

In addition, Gager further reminds us that new explanations or rationalizations accompany the proselytizing of new members. The faith crises of the early church can be understood in terms of such cognitive dissonance. We can witness, even at this distance, how the emphasis on preaching and spreading the gospel was accompanied by the development of explanations which interpreted and modified the initial shock of disconfirmation. Even through the several layers of New Testament memory, we see this pattern twice: first at the shock of the crucifixion, and second in a more gradual adjustment to the nonoccurrence of the Parousia.

RESPONSES TO THE CRUCIFIXION

Paul: Preach Christ!

Paul provides our earliest insight, writing some quarter-century after the event of the crucifixion. He had become a Christian soon after Jesus' death and was in close touch with those who had experienced it (Gal. 1:18; Rom. 16:7). In Paul we hear the most forthright statement of faith in the face of the crucifixion: Jesus *is* the Messiah, the Christ. In this way he took that which appeared to be denied by Jesus' death and made it the central assertion of his proclamation: "For the foolishness of God is wiser than men, and the weakness of God is stronger than men" (1 Cor. 1:25). This startling challenge to dissonance was possible for Paul through a rationale that is both brilliant and understandable in light of Festinger's model.

Paul argued:

a. Jesus' death was a part of God's mysterious plan. It was the doing of demons (1 Cor. 2:7–10), but God worked it out to his glory and humanity's salvation. Paul's relative disinterest in Jesus' life and teaching (he says nothing about the kingdom of heaven) gives emphasis to this focus on his death. It is precisely this event, which would seem to be the weakest point of all, that Paul makes dynamically significant (1 Cor. 2:2; 1:23–25; Gal. 1:4).

b. That Jesus' death has such a positive dynamic is proved by his resurrection; thus the normally unbelievable is called up to bolster the "weak" point. Paul asserts it as utterly believable (1 Cor. 15:1–4), and substantiates it by eyewitnesses (1 Cor. 15:5–8).

Jesus' resurrection and exaltation are God's action in direct recognition of his humiliation and death (Phil. 2:5–11, a pre-Pauline Christian hymn).

c. Jesus' resurrection is the guarantee of ours (1 Cor. 15:12–19; Rom. 8:11; 2 Cor. 4:14; Phil. 3:10–11).

Having thus turned the death of Jesus inside out, and integrated it into a mysterious divine plan, Paul (and the earliest Christians generally) could then adapt the familiar Jewish apocalyptic scenario of their time to their Christian expectations. The risen Christ is the "first fruits" of the resurrection of the dead (1 Cor. 15:20, 24), which will take place in full apocalyptic glory (1 Thess. 4:14–18). This will, however, be preceded by a period of trouble ("the birth-pangs of the Messiah," in Jewish parlance; cf. 2 Thess. 2:1–12). After the resurrection, there comes "the end," the goal toward which all is moving, when Christ will "deliver the kingdom to God the Father" (1 Cor. 15:24–28).

Here we see a striking example of the reaction of the early Christian community to the cognitive dissonance brought on them by Jesus' death. Paul was convinced that this reorientation came to him by divine revelation (Gal. 1:11–12) though much of it was also shared by the Christian community more generally. Thus Meeks describes how Paul brought in a "radically new vision" but oriented it to the older expectations:

> In these two ways, using revelations and eschatological language to legitimate a radically new vision of the divine-human order and incorporating into that vision and that legitimation the old scriptures and traditions, the Pauline movement resembles the modern millenarian model.[8]

For Paul, the direct result of this resolution of cognitive dissonance was his missionary activity. After listing the eyewitnesses to the resurrected Lord, he says:

> Last of all, as to one untimely born, he appeared also to me. For I am the least of the apostles, unfit to be called an apostle, because I persecuted the church of God. But by the grace of God I am what I am, and his grace toward me was not in vain. On the contrary, I worked harder than any of them, though it was not I, but the grace of God which is with me. Whether it was I or they, so we preach and so you believed (1 Cor. 15:8–11).

Mark: The Dynamic of the Messianic Secret

A different approach to Jesus' death is offered by the Gospel of Mark. Like Paul, this Gospel reflects a keen concern for the cognitive dissonance experienced by the Christian community. Also like Paul,

Mark asserts that Jesus was the Messiah (Mark 8:29–30). This confession was at the base of Christianity and about it there was no question to be raised; it was only to be explained, and an explanation, a rationale, was essential to the resolution of the cognitive dissonance occasioned by the undeniable fact that this Messiah had died. Though he wrote some forty years after the event, it is obvious from Mark's Gospel that the issue was still a live one. How does Mark explain it?

Mark's rationale is couched in what is known as "the Messianic secret." This is a major theme in his Gospel and involves the gradual unfolding of a consciousness of Jesus' messiahship and divinity. At the outset, Mark shows Jesus' identity to be known only to the supernatural world of the heavenly voice, the angels, Satan, and his demons (Mark 1:11, 12–13, 24–25, 34). It is to be kept a secret from human beings and to be revealed only gradually as God wills. This theme then becomes a pattern in Mark, where Jesus repeatedly commands silence on the part of those he heals (Mark 1:43–44; 3:11–12; 7:36).

At the same time, Mark offers a series of miracles that have symbolic significance to the insightful reader, so that while Jesus' public remains in the dark, Mark's public is allowed to see who he is (Mark 2:10; 4:41; 6:51–52; 8:14–21). For Mark the turning point in the revelation of the secret is reached at Caesarea Philippi, where Jesus asks his disciples, "Who do men say that I am?" (Mark 8:27). After receiving various answers he then asks, "But who do you say that I am?" whereupon Peter makes the crucial declaration, "You are the Christ," the Messiah (Mark 8:29).

The secret now is out, among the disciples. But they still fail to understand its implication. Mark declares, "He began to teach them that the Son of man must suffer many things, and be rejected by the elders and the chief priests and the scribes, and be killed, and after three days rise again" (Mark 8:31). The disciples, imbued as they are with the common idea of the Messiah as a conquering king, refuse to accept a concept so antithetical to their expectations. Thus while Jesus' messiahship is no longer a secret, the real cause of cognitive dissonance, his death, is now the focal issue, and from this point to the end of his Gospel Mark is at pains to clarify that issue for his readers. As Jesus and his disciples proceed on to Jerusalem and his passion, he keeps on trying to explain to them the reality of his death, "saying to them, 'The Son of man will be delivered into the hands of men, and they will kill him; and when he is killed, after three days he will rise'" (Mark 9:31), to which Mark comments again, "But they did not understand the saying, and they were afraid to ask him" (Mark 9:32).

For Mark the story climaxes when the death and resurrection of

Jesus actually occur as he had been predicting (Mark 15, 16). Mark has thus built up the drama of the messianic secret in such a way that Jesus' death, instead of disproving his messiahship, becomes a proof of it. Jesus had kept his messiahship a secret, so the world at large did not recognize him. His disciples had finally caught on but could not grasp the idea that he was going to die. But the reader, who has the full view from the beginning, can see that Jesus turned out to be exactly the kind of messiah he said he would be: one who would suffer and die! Things were right after all. The problem lay not in Jesus' dying but in the disciples' lack of understanding of what was really going on, in *their* miscalculation.[9]

How then does Mark's resolution of the problem of Jesus' death lead on to evangelistic activity? How does he understand Jesus' death and resurrection to be the basis for a mission to the world? It may be that we cannot give a full answer to this question because the ending of Mark's gospel is probably lost. But we do have a hint of Mark's concern for the mission to the world in the text as it stands. Mark reports that just before his betrayal Jesus told his disciples, "You will all fall away; for it is written, 'I will strike the shepherd, and the sheep will be scattered.' But after I am raised up, I will go before you to Galilee" (Mark 14:27–28). Here we see portrayed in miniature the cognitive dissonance experienced by the community at Jesus' death. When the shepherd is stricken, the sheep are scattered. But immediate reassurance follows: they will meet him again in Galilee. How do these two concepts relate to each other? Why Galilee?

Merely to return to Galilee, or even a postresurrection appearance there after the glory of Easter, would seem anticlimactic. We are led to feel that something more significant must be intended. This is suggested by the full form of the name "Galilee" in Hebrew, *g^elîl haggôyim,* "the circuit, or territory, of the Gentiles" (Isa. 9:1 [Heb. 8:23]; cf. Matt. 4:15). Jesus had "walked ahead" of his disciples on the way to his passion at Jerusalem (Mark 10:32), now he will again "go before" them (the Greek verb is the same in each case, *proagō*) as they carry the gospel to the gentile world, and in this way they will "see" him, will have full vision of who he is. In the early Christian community the messianic secret thus finally issues in the evangelization of the world.

Matthew: The Gospel Commission

Matthew does not appear to be as interested as Mark in the notion of secrecy regarding Jesus' messiahship. While he does include instances of Jesus' commanding silence in regard to his miracles (e.g., Matt.

8:4; 12:16), he repeatedly lacks such instructions where Mark has them (cf. Matt. 8:16–17 with Mark 1:32–34; cf. Matt. 15:29–31 with Mark 7:31–37). More importantly, he does not build this theme of the secret into a dramatically structured rationale as does Mark.

Matthew is, however, clearly concerned with the relation between disillusionment over Jesus' death and mission to the world. We have seen how Mark connects these through Jesus' prediction that the disciples will desert him and the assurance that he will meet them again in Galilee. Matthew gives the passage in almost identical words (Matt. 26:31–32), but he makes it clear that it has special meaning for him by the way in which he treats the theme after the resurrection. There he makes explicit what is implicit in Mark: when the disciples arrive in Galilee and meet Jesus on a mountain, a characteristic setting for divine revelation, his message is the great commission: "Go therefore and make disciples of all nations" (Matt. 28:18–20). The relation of this passage to Jesus' prediction of their defection (Matt. 26:31–32) suggests that Matthew sees the commission not only as a universalization of the original commission in Matt. 4:18–19 but also as a reinstatement of all the disciples after their desertion of him. For Matthew and his time these words are thus a reassurance to all believers who may have been led to doubt. Like the disciples, their doubt is reversed and directed into a new commission to evangelize the world.

Luke: Discovering the Meaning of History

Luke, in contrast to Matthew, vividly reflects the dissonance felt by the disciples on the death of Jesus, and in so doing doubtless speaks to such concerns in his own time. However, rather than developing a theme such as that of the "secret" running throughout Jesus' ministry, as in Mark, he emphasizes the instruction of the Risen Lord as offering the solution. In the words of the disciples to Jesus on the road to Emmaus, Luke offers our most striking example of the cognitive dissonance brought about by Jesus' death: " . . . how our chief priests and rulers delivered him up to be condemned to death, and crucified him. But we had hoped that he was the one to redeem Israel" (Luke 24:21). Jesus' reply is that this was all in the plan of God and had been foretold in the Scriptures: "Beginning with Moses and all the prophets, he interpreted to them in all the scriptures the things concerning himself" (Luke 24:27; cf. Luke 24:45–49). But the disciples fail to comprehend until they sit with Jesus at table when he takes bread, blesses it, breaks it, and gives it to them; then their eyes are opened and they recognize him (Luke 24:30–31). Finally they are able to respond, "Did not our hearts burn within us while he talked to us on the road, while he opened to us the scriptures?" (Luke 24:32). When they arrive back in Jerusalem and tell their story to the apostles, Luke says, "Then they told what had happened on the road, and how he was known to them in the breaking of the bread" (Luke 24:35).

That Luke intends this story to reflect the ongoing experience of the Christian community is suggested by his repeated reference to this revelatory experience with the Lord as having occurred "on the road" (Greek, *en tē hodō*), which can also be translated "in the way." Later, in the Acts, "the way" is a familiar term of Luke's for the Christian movement (Acts 9:2; 19:9, 23; 22:4; 24:14, 22). That he sees the word as having metaphorical value in his narratives is suggested by his use of it in the story of Paul's conversion, where Ananias declares to him, "Brother Saul, the Lord Jesus who appeared to you on the road ['in the way'] by which you came, has sent me" (Acts 9:17); and Barnabas later introduces him to the apostles at Jerusalem, declaring to them "how on the road ['in the way'] he had seen the Lord, who spoke to him" (Acts 9:27). Similarly the slave girl at Philippi declares of Paul and Silas, "These men are servants of the Most High God, who proclaim to you the way of salvation" (Acts 16:17). All these examples suggest that for Luke it is "in the way," within the community of belief, that the resolution of dissonance takes place; true insight into the meaning of Jesus' death is revealed there. And it is particularly in the central act of the community, the breaking of bread, that the fullest understanding of the divine plan realized in Jesus will come.

Of all the Gospel writers, Luke is the most explicit on the relation between cognitive dissonance and evangelistic zeal. As Jesus appears to his disciples on the night following his resurrection, Luke says, "Then he opened their minds to understand the scriptures, and said to them, 'Thus it is written, that the Christ should suffer and on the third day rise from the dead, and that repentance and forgiveness of sins should be preached in his name to all nations, beginning from Jerusalem. You are witnesses of these things. And behold, I send the promise of my Father upon you; but stay in the city, until you are clothed with power from on high' " (Luke 24:45–49). Here, in contrast to the tradition in Matthew and Mark, Luke places the great commission in Jerusalem rather than in Galilee and specifically says they are to remain in Jerusalem (cf. Luke 24:6–7 with Mark 16:7) because he wishes to use a different geographic symbolism. Rather than Galilee representing the world, for him Jerusalem is the base from which the world is to be evangelized. He goes on to make this clear throughout the Book of Acts.

Further, the dynamic tie between the resolution of dissonance and the proclamation of the gospel for Luke is the gift of the Holy Spirit. According to Acts 1:2, Jesus' final words to the disciples in Luke 24:45–49 were given "through the Holy Spirit." At Pentecost the same Spirit descends on the disciples and energizes them for their work of preaching to the world. The rest of Luke's narrative in the Acts is the story of how this took place.

John: Dissonance Resolved

In the Gospel of John, probably written about the end of the century, we can sense that the tension over Jesus' death has been resolved in the Johannine community to the point that it no longer needs addressing as such. From the very beginning Jesus can be declared publicly to be "the Lamb of God who takes away the sin of the world" (John 1:29), "the Son of God," and "the king of Israel" (John 1:49). It is no longer necessary to build a rationale as to why the Messiah died; that appears to be understood. John can simply assert, "He came to his own home, and his own people received him not. But to all who received him, who believed in his name, he gave power to become children of God" (John 1:11–12). The original cognitive dissonance has now been resolved in the success of the movement: the gospel has now gone far and wide and this is itself proof of its validity.

THE POSTPONED PAROUSIA AND NEW ENERGY

The second occasion of major cognitive dissonance in early Christianity, that brought about by the nonoccurrence of the Parousia, also receives much attention in the New Testament. While Paul responded to concerns of Christians at Thessalonica (1 Thess. 4:13–18) and Corinth (1 Corinthians 15) in regard to the death and resurrection of believers, he and they still stood strongly within the generation that expected to be alive "until the coming of the Lord." As far as we can tell from our sources, it was with the destruction of the temple in A.D. 70 that a turning point was reached in Christian thinking about the Parousia.

By then, forty years had passed since Jesus' death. The careers of Peter and Paul and doubtless of the other apostles were in the past. Thousands of mature Christians had been born since Jesus died, and not a few had been Christians all their lives. Cognitive dissonance in the communities was taking a new form. The question now was not only, Why did the expected Messiah die? but also, Why have all these years passed with business as usual, if he really was the Messiah? In our time we can add the further question, In the face of the reality of

Jesus' not having returned, how did they account for this in such a way that their faithfulness not only was not diminished, but actually encouraged?

Mark: Countdown to the End

The Gospel of Mark can be called "the Gospel of A.D. 70": it was written either just before the destruction of the temple or shortly afterward. In either case there shine through it at a number of points evidences of the Christian community's concern for the return of Christ in light of the events of that year.

It is clear from Mark that Christians were concerned over the fact that Jesus had not come back. We can sense this from the way in which he puts together two sayings that combine a command to witness with a startling reassurance regarding return: "If any man would come after me, let him deny himself and take up his cross and follow me. For whoever would save his life will lose it; and whoever loses his life for my sake and the gospel's will save it. . . . Truly, I say to you, there are some standing here who will not taste death before they see the kingdom of God come with power" (Mark 8:34–35; 9:1). Such statements functioned to strengthen faith. As long as an apostle still lived, his presence remained a reassurance that hope of the Parousia was not in vain and provided a motivation for continuing to proclaim the gospel.

In the context of such doubts and reassurances we can read the apocalyptic discourse of Mark 13, where the events of A.D. 70 are especially in view.[10] Here the introductory question of the disciples, which is also that of Christians in Mark's time, is phrased in such a way as to combine the Parousia with the destruction of the temple.[11] In response to Jesus' declaration that the temple will be destroyed, the disciples ask, "Tell us, when will this be, and what will be the sign when these things are all to be accomplished?" (Mark 13:4). As used here, the verb "accomplished" is "an almost technical expression for the events of the end-time."[12]

Certainly Christians living at this period could easily have seen in the disasters of the Jewish-Roman War with its destruction of the temple the evidence of their long-anticipated expectation. Mark's report of Jesus' discourse, then, disabused them of this idea. Note how he develops his argument: "And Jesus began to say to them, . . . when you hear of wars and rumors of wars, do not be alarmed; this must take place, but the end is not yet. . . . This is but the beginnings of sufferings. . . . They will deliver you up to councils, and you will be beaten in synagogues; and you will stand before governors and kings for my sake, to bear testimony before them" (Mark 13:5–9). Here we see again the close connection between a realization that the "end is not yet" and continued zeal for preaching the gospel. The fact that the cataclysmic events occurring about them are not harbingers of the Parousia, rather than dampening their ardor for evangelism heightens it and gives them courage to face increasing persecution. Mark then breaks into his sequence of thought, or possibly his source, to add a saying calculated to give courage to the doubting and to stimulate ongoing evangelism: "And the gospel must first be preached to all nations" (Mark 13:10). Rather than following the conventional wisdom which might consider the postponement of the Parousia a reason for relaxing evangelistic effort, this saying stands such thinking on its head by making evangelism the reason for the postponement!

Mark moves on to describe further the tribulations of the war: "But when you see the desolating sacrilege set up where it ought not to be (let the reader understand), then let those who are in Judea flee to the mountains . . . " (Mark 13:14). He then makes clear again that these disasters are not the final ones: "But in those days, after that tribulation, the sun will be darkened, and the moon will not give its light. . . . And then they will see the Son of man coming in clouds with great power and glory" (Mark 13:24, 26).

In spite, however, of Mark's concern that Christians not interpret the events of A.D. 70 as the final ones, neither are they to consider the postponement to be for the long term. "Truly I say to you, this generation will not pass away before all these things take place. Heaven and earth will pass away, but my words will not pass away" (Mark 13:30–31). The fact that no one knows the day or the hour of Jesus' return is itself to be a cause for alertness and continued labor: "It is like a man going on a journey, when he leaves home and puts his servants in charge, each with his work, and commands the doorkeeper to be on the watch" (Mark 13:34).

We can see clearly how Mark countered the miscalculations of Christians in regard to the events of A.D. 70 and provided a rationale for the cognitive dissonance that they either had experienced or were about to encounter when those events did not issue in the Parousia. While denying their immediate expectations, his explanation provided instead renewed impetus for evangelism.

Matthew: The Urgency of Faithfulness

Matthew must have written a decade or more after Mark. The disasters of the Jewish-Roman War were now in the past, and anticipations of the Parousia raised by those events were no longer burning issues. But as time passed, the problem of the postponement of the Parousia inevitably became more urgent. Matthew had essentially the same saying as Mark regarding those "standing here who will not taste death before they see the Son of man coming in his kingdom" (Matt. 16:28; Mark 9:1), and he doubtless understood it in much the same way as did Mark. But he had another saying that is unique to his Gospel: when Jesus sends out the Twelve to preach and heal, he tells them, "When they persecute you in one town, flee to the next; for truly, I say to you, you will not have gone through all the towns of Israel, before the Son of man comes" (Matt. 10:23). Whatever intention this saying may have conveyed at an earlier stage in Christian history, in Matthew's community, concerned as it was with relations between Christians and Jews, it can be seen as reflecting the issue of the Parousia; it offered a rationale for those Christians who found themselves in tension between their ardent desire for the return of Christ and the evident fact that Jews in large part had not accepted the gospel. Must they wait for the conversion of the Jews? For Matthew and the Christians of his circle, at least, a saying such as this could offer reassurance that the Parousia was not contingent on the completion of the mission to the Jews ("through all the towns of Israel").[13] Here again, the question of the Parousia is coupled with the issue of mission, but in a new way.[14]

In Jesus' apocalyptic address (Matthew 24), in contrast to Mark, Matthew focuses the weight of the disciples' initial question on the time that the Parousia would occur: "Tell us, when will this be, and what will be the sign of your coming and of the close of the age?" (Matt. 24:3). Matthew shares with Mark the warnings that the tribulations connected with the Jewish-Roman War are not to be seen as the final events (Matt. 24:6, 8). But the striking difference between Mark and Matthew is the latter's keener sense of the imminence of the Parousia. After describing the events of the past war (Matt. 24:4–28), Matthew says, "Immediately after the tribulation of those days the sun will be darkened, and the moon will not give its light . . . then will appear the sign of the Son of man in heaven . . . and they will see the Son of man coming on the clouds of heaven with power and great glory" (Matt. 24:29–30). Whereas for Mark these final events occur simply "after that tribulation" (Mark 13:24), in Matthew's scenario they are immediate.

In the context of the years following the destruction of the temple, words such as these reflect the growing urgency of the question regarding the end. To a point at least, the longer it was delayed the nearer it must be. This insight makes possible an understanding of the difference between Mark's and Matthew's forms of the saying regarding the preaching of the gospel. Mark's "The gospel must first be preached to all nations" (Mark 13:10) is in line with his warning that "the end is not yet" (Mark 13:7). But Matthew's "This gospel of the kingdom will be preached throughout the whole world, and then the end will come" (Matt. 24:14) is, in the context of the previous verse ("but he who endures to the end will be saved"), a promise of the certainty of the Parousia. The gospel will be preached and the end will come. The word "world" (Greek, *oikoumenē*) can be understood to refer to the Roman Empire in general, without insisting that every nook and cranny must have been evangelized. Such an achievement, if not already seen as having been realized by Matthew's time, must have seemed realizable in the near future. Matthew was certainly not expecting a long-delayed event. He follows Jesus' apocalyptic discourse with a series of parables and other admonitions that emphasize the importance of watchfulness and faithfulness to duty in light of the impending end (Matt. 24:37— 25:46). For Matthew, then, the fact that the Parousia had not occurred was only a reason for greater earnestness in ministry and proclamation.

Luke: All in God's Plan

As we have already seen in regard to his understanding of the death of Jesus, so in the question of the Parousia Luke had a different approach from that of Mark and Matthew. In response to this problem he wrote a whole volume, the Acts, to show that everything that had happened since the crucifixion fulfilled the divine plan based in Scripture and outlined by the Risen Lord in Luke 24:46–49.

From this point of view we can better appreciate the differences that set Luke off from the traditions shared by Mark and Matthew. For the Jesus-saying regarding those who will not die before the end, Luke has simply, "There are some standing here who will not taste of death before they see the kingdom of God" (Luke 9:27). Luke thus lacks the distinctly apocalyptic nuances of Mark ("the kingdom of God come with power," Mark 9:1) and Matthew ("the Son of man coming in his kingdom," Matt. 16:28). This is in harmony with his different understanding of "the kingdom." For him its nature is ethical. This is clear from Luke 8:9–15 in which Jesus tells the disciples, "To you it has been given to know the secrets of the kingdom of God" and follows immediately with the explanation of the parable of the sower, ending with praise for those who "bring forth fruit with patience." Similarly when asked by the Pharisees when the kingdom will come, he answers, "Behold, the kingdom of God is in the midst of you" (Luke 17:20–21); it is already here. Such a concept of the kingdom fits Luke's extended view of the history of salvation and his understanding of the Parousia in light of that.[15]

Luke's treatment of the apocalyptic discourse (Luke 21) shows evidence of a similar point of view. Like Mark and Matthew, he begins Jesus' recital with the same forecast of false messiahs but adds that such persons will say, "The time is at hand!" to which Jesus warns, "Do not go after them" (Luke 21:8). Whereas Mark and Matthew imply that wars, disasters, and persecution all lead up to the destruction of the temple, Luke separates his section on persecution from the other woes by making it anterior to them: "But before all this they will lay their hands on you and persecute you. . . . This will be a time for you to bear testimony" (Luke 21:12–13). This difference is an important one for it warns Christians against interpreting persecution as a sign of the imminent end and it creates theological space for the Book of Acts. There Luke will describe the development of a worldwide church beset by persecution, but with no indication that either development is related to an imminent Parousia. In harmony with this, Luke has no parallel to either Mark's or Matthew's sayings regarding the preaching of the gospel to the world being a prerequisite to the end (Mark 13:10; Matt. 24:14).

Even more clearly than Mark or Matthew, Luke fixes his focus on the fall of Jerusalem (Luke 21:20) and builds it into his scheme of sacred history: "And Jerusalem will be trodden down by the Gentiles, until the times are fulfilled" (Luke 21:24). Only after this statement does he turn to a description of the portents leading directly to the Parousia (Luke 21:25–28). In this way again he has lengthened his vision of the future by postponing the Parousia until "the times [of the Gentiles] are fulfilled." At the same time, Luke does not think of a delay of great length, for he can still join Mark and Matthew in the saying, "This generation will not pass away till all has taken place" (Luke 21:32).

Comparing Mark's, Matthew's, and Luke's approaches to the problem of the nonoccurrence of the return of Christ, we see that while they all expected it within "this generation," each had a different concern and emphasis. Mark, writing in the hurly-burly occasioned by the Jewish-Roman War, was concerned that Christians not interpret that as a sign of the imminent end; but it would be soon and they were therefore to be ever more watchful and zealous. Matthew, at a somewhat later period, doubtless in the face of mounting anxiety regarding the Parousia, was particularly insistent that it was not far off; for this reason Christians were to be alert and to spread the gospel. Luke, confronted by similar questions, offered a distinctly different rationale:

the passage of time since Jesus' death and resurrection was an essential part of God's plan, so that the Gentiles might hear the gospel. Persecutions occasioned by preaching the gospel were not a sign of the end, but were also a part of the divine plan. Different as these approaches were, each offered an explanation of the dissonance caused by the postponement of the Parousia that led not to disillusionment but to increased zeal in preaching the gospel.

John: Focus on the Presence

By the end of the first century two generations had passed since Jesus' death. Explanations advanced by the writers of the seventies and eighties for his not having returned were increasingly difficult to sustain. The last of the apostles probably was dead, the apocalyptic vision of Mark 13 had not worked out, and even the rationale offered by Luke showed little evidence of climactic fulfillment. It was no longer possible to take literally the saying, "This generation will not pass away before all things take place" (Mark 13:30).

New understandings were imperative. Three documents, the Gospel of John, the *First Epistle of Clement,* and the Second Epistle of Peter, all precisely undatable but doubtless written between the last years of the first century and the middle of the second, deal with this problem from quite different perspectives. They show us how divergent Christian thinking on this common problem had become.

The solution offered by the author of the Gospel of John is to say that the return of Christ has happened after all but not according to the anticipated apocalyptic scenario. What had been expected to occur in the future had already happened and was happening in the Holy Spirit: "Truly, truly, I say to you, the hour is coming, and now is, when the dead will hear the voice of the Son of God, and those who hear will live" (John 5:25). He does not deny apocalyptic expectations in the future ("The hour is coming when all who are in the tombs will hear his voice and come forth," John 5:28–29), but he places emphasis on fulfillment in the present, so that the future expectation becomes less immediately important.

John has no parallel to the apocalyptic discourses in Mark, Matthew, and Luke, but he does discuss the return of Christ: "In my Father's house are many rooms; if it were not so, would I have told you that I go to prepare a place for you? And when I go and prepare a place for you, I will come again and will take you to myself, that where I am you may be also" (John 14:2–3). At first sight this would appear to be a reiteration of the future expectations familiar to us from Paul and the Synoptic Gospels. But as one reads on through the chapter it

becomes clear that something different is in view. This coming again
is an experience that is now available to the believer and is made
possible through the Spirit (John 14:16–29).

In accord with John's sense of immediacy, compared especially with
Luke, he places the gift of the Spirit on the day of the Resurrection
rather than later at Pentecost. But he shares with Luke the understanding that the Spirit is given to prepare the church for its mission. The
Risen Lord says to his disciples, "Peace be with you. As the Father
has sent me, even so I send you," to which the writer adds, "And
when he had said this, he breathed on them, and said to them, 'Receive
the Holy Spirit. If you forgive the sins of any, they are forgiven; if
you retain the sins of any, they are retained' " (John 20:21–23).

The solution of the Gospel of John, then, is not to deny the
expectation of a future, climactic consummation, but to deemphasize
it by stressing the present significance of the promises cherished by
the church. This reinterpretation in no way slackens the importance
of mission; rather, by making the Holy Spirit the mediator of these
eschatological realities in the present, it strengthens the basis for
ministry. John shares with Luke an emphasis on the role of the Spirit
in ministry but goes beyond Luke in tying the Spirit directly to the
realization of the Parousia.

The Second Century: Preparing for the Long Haul

The *First Epistle of Clement* takes a distinctly different approach to
the problem of the Parousia. Its author finds himself confronted by
scoffers who point out, "Here we are, already grown old, and none of
these things has happened to us" (*1 Clement* 23:3). He meets this
complaint head-on. Rather than offering a new explanation, in the
manner of John, he asserts the old expectation and argues for it: "Truly
his purpose will be quickly and suddenly accomplished, just as the
Scripture confirms when it says, 'He will come quickly and not delay,
and the Lord will come suddenly to his temple . . . ' " (*1 Clement*
23:5). He then shifts focus to the resurrection and marshals arguments
for the reasonableness of such a hope: the cycle of nature and the
phoenix. Of the latter he asks, "Are we to think it then a great and
wondrous thing if the Creator of all things causes to be raised from
the dead those who have served him . . . , when even in the case of a
bird he shows us the greatness of his promise?" (*1 Clement* 26:1).
Clement's final argument is the faithfulness of God: "He it is who
commanded us not to lie: how much the more will he not lie himself!
. . . Let our faith in him then be rekindled in us, and bear in mind
that all things are near him. . . . When he wills and as he wills he

shall accomplish all things, and not one of the things he has decreed can fail" (*1 Clement* 27:2, 3, 5).[16]

It is important to note that while Clement, in contrast to John, has kept the future hope firmly in center stage, he no longer deals with the question of the nearness of the Parousia, as earlier writers had done. It can be expected to happen suddenly, but there is no sense of imminence, nor is there any apocalyptic scenario. The key issue now is the resurrection, and of this Christians can be certain. Probably because of this shift in focus, he goes on to emphasize the importance of holy living rather than of evangelistic effort.

Sometime probably during the first half of the second century, the letter we know as 2 Peter was written. The author of this epistle was confronted by questions similar to those faced by Clement: "First of all you must understand this, that scoffers will come in the last days with scoffing, following their own passions and saying, 'Where is the promise of his coming? For ever since the fathers fell asleep, all things have continued as they were from the beginning of creation' " (2 Pet. 3:3–4). Unlike Clement, however, this author does not avoid the question of time. Rather, he resorts to a theological explanation based upon Scripture: "Do not ignore this one fact, beloved, that with the Lord one day is as a thousand years, and a thousand years as one day" (2 Pet. 3:8, following Ps. 90:4). (That such an argument was a telling one, at least among Jewish readers, is evident from the fact that the same passage in the Psalms was used by rabbis to interpret the days of creation in Genesis 1.) Here the author goes on to explain that the fact Christ has not returned is not due to slowness "as some count slowness," but because he "is forbearing toward you, not wishing that any should perish, but that all should reach repentance" (2 Pet. 3:9).

In this explanation, we can see how once again the issue of the nonoccurrence of the Parousia is turned inside out. Recalling Mark 13:10, the delay is not really a delay but is intentional on the part of God so that the purpose of the gospel may be realized.

When the concepts of cognitive dissonance are applied to the New Testament, the patterns of energy and commitment anchored in the event of the crucifixion and the nonevent of the Parousia become clear. (*a*) Conviction and commitment were profound. (*b*) Disconfirmation was unequivocal at the cross in as far as Jesus' temporal messiahship was concerned, and gradually became unequivocal for many, at least in regard to an imminent return. (*c*) But social support was massive within the community of belief, and (*d*) persecution only enhanced the importance of proclamation. (*e*) The result was an unparalleled evangelical zeal, (*f*) accompanied in time by theological interpretations of these events which (g) also absorbed additional events into the history of salvation. The behavior anticipated by cognitive dissonance theory is in striking coincidence with scholarly consensus regarding the dating of the New Testament documents, which tends to confirm the usefulness of this theory.

At the same time, in dealing with a paradigm such as that offered by cognitive dissonance theory, it is important to avoid falling victim to reductionism. Insights from the social sciences do not necessarily explain the whole of what may have happened. The cognitive dissonance paradigm describes a socio-psychological process and thus may "track" aspects of the development of faith. In itself it says nothing as to the truth or falsity of the explanations or rationalizations that emerge from dissonance. Christians today can appreciate the dissonance experienced by early believers and can sense the variety of ways in which they explained their disappointments. What is of abiding significance, however, is that to which all these explanations pointed them—the presence of Christ as Lord and Savior.

IMPLICATIONS FOR CONTEMPORARY MINISTRY

Cognitive dissonance is the experience of seeing the world differently with such a dramatic impact that the believer wants to share this newly discovered world with others to confirm its "social reality." As used by Festinger and others, cognitive dissonance includes the entire sequence of behavior from disconfirmation through evangelical zeal and eventual interpretation of the event. As such it is a description of that threshold experience which contributes to strong convictions and active commitment to any cause or movement. In its broadest application, it presents the dramatic form of transition from outsider to insider through which a believer passes in order to be fully a member of a movement or campaign.

For congregations cognitive dissonance has several areas of programmatic implication: (1) programs of evangelism, (2) pastoral leadership, (3) the function of doubt, and (4) the function of need. We shall also consider how cognitive dissonance operates positively outside the context of crisis.

Programs of Evangelism

Overwhelming evidence shows a direct relationship in the New Testament church between crisis and evangelism, accompanied by theological interpretation of events. By contrast in our contemporary society most members of mainline churches appear comfortable with the easy relationship between the church and the world as it is. There appears no sharp distinction between the symbolic universe of the nation and the church; there is no crisis of faith which creates a mental or spiritual wilderness of cognitive dissonance required for entry into the contemporary church.

As a result, many churches have turned to other means for growth. Most often they rely on friendship evangelism in its many forms, such as community growth, family friendship, shared social concerns—all extensions of the "homogeneous unit principle" advocated by the Church Growth Institute.[17] Unfortunately, some congregations are simply in the wrong location to achieve much numerical success, since what happens in the surrounding community usually determines the growth possibilities within the congregation.[18] Further, churches do not achieve growth simply because they are friendly, especially if there are no prospective members in the area; and they do not grow simply because they have a committee on evangelism. In fact there is no statistical evidence that evangelism committees significantly aid membership growth.[19] Some type of cognitive dissonance seems essential for long term evangelism.

But for many people in established churches, cognitive dissonance is a disturbing concept which is associated with marginal groups and unpleasant experiences. They remember being challenged with "Brother-are-you-saved?" language which seems limited and legalistic to the outsider. Such cognitive dissonance is characteristic of Christian sects, cults, and pseudoreligious political movements. Radical forms of cognitive dissonance, with sometimes violent results, can be seen in certain church-related movements, such as some antinuclear and right-to-life activities, whose members are so frightened by the world they see that they take extreme measures to call it to the attention of others.

Despite these risks, we cannot ignore the community coherence and evangelical energy that cognitive dissonance made possible in the life of the early church. The threshold of doubt and assurance of faith provided a barrier within which the believers knew who they were, and who they were not. In the enthusiasm of their new identity, they drew others to themselves. Further, in the community of the resurrected Jesus, they left behind the social hierarchy of the secular society (wealth, education, gender, nationality, etc.). Cognitive dissonance made community pluralism possible because a more powerful experience gave them unity. In this dramatic new reality, they could share their worldly wealth since they assumed that others who joined would see the world as they did. Even, or especially, the boundary of death was overcome. In the cognitive dissonance of the early Christians, paradox was experience: Jesus who was dead had become the Christ, the fulfillment of the past (Luke 24:44–46), and the source for the future (Luke 24:47).

Like the earliest Christian movement, the contemporary church must be united in more than language or interpretation: the symbolic universe makes sense when sealed by faith, by a community experience of cognitive dissonance. As we noted in our discussion of counterculture commitments (chap. 2), this is not a once-in-a-lifetime experience, but a continuing tension in the lives of members and the church. Cognitive dissonance takes many forms: the conquest of death in Jesus Christ, the acceptance of self in a loving God, the unity of Christians which crosses social barriers, the denial of worldly honors and success for the sake of a more lasting community, the sharing of worldly possessions in a more compelling commitment. Crossing these thresholds of faith provides the challenge that has unified the church and energized evangelism throughout history.

Without such cognitive dissonance, the basis of church membership becomes social and the urge to invite others becomes institutional.

Pastoral Leadership

Cognitive dissonance is appropriately associated with charismatic leadership expected in the pastoral office. It is not surprising that such movements find their warrant in the conversion, ministry, and letters of the apostle Paul for as we have seen his charismatic leadership remains a prototype for the early church. His conversion confirmed their faith, his writing interpreted it in God's plan.

Paul utilizes the sharply dissonant experience of Jesus' death and resurrection as the cornerstone of Christian experience. Like the faith challenge of all subsequent centuries, Paul turns the cross from a symbol of death and destruction to a promise of resurrection and life eternal. Through cognitive dissonance we see with faith-eyes what is foolish to the surrounding world. That faith is the strongest force of continuing evangelical activity.

In the experience of cognitive dissonance, the leader is expected to remain strong when others are weak. Based in confidence that the pastor has a sustaining relationship with the transcendent God, members of the congregation assume that the pastor is a trusted guide through the crises of their lives. Pastoral leadership is strongest at the points of weakness in the lives of others. The official functions of the pastor are anchored to the symbolic turning points in life's journey—birth and death, marriage and community, vocation and retreat. The work of the pastoral leader, says Urban Holmes, "is by necessity to share deeply the antistructural dimensions of people's lives, to face the erotic realities both in their demonic and angelic form, and to discern what makes whole and what destroys."[20] In the wilderness of their lives, people look to the religious leader for strength and guidance. In the pastoral ministry, every other relationship is a consequence of this primary function.

One seminary student, while serving as an intern in a small church, describes her encounter with cognitive dissonance the first time she stood at the head of an open grave:

> A member of the congregation died and I was to have his funeral. I met with the family in their home and heard their cries of disbelief. "Why Bill?" "He had so much to live for." "How am I going to get on without him?" I joined silently in their cries, "Why me, God?"
>
> There I was at the time of the service, scared stiff, never having done a funeral before, feeling alone. We were all treading through foggy, unfamiliar ground. I felt as if my senses had left me, blind and groping for the right words and actions. And yet it was me, shaking, blind, nearly unable to speak in the face of such pain and confusion, it was me to whom they turned for support, for good news in this darkness. I was the one among the believers gathered who was expected to stand in that place between their pain and the hope that is our faith. I felt the tension even in what I was wearing, the pull between the black robe and the cotton dress beneath. But in that gathering I felt the support of believers not only in that congregation but of all those who had gone before. There in our midst was Christ, speaking through all of us, through even me, words of assurance—proclaiming the hope and joyous news of the gospel to all who had assembled. In that service we were all given the ability to go on assured anew of God's grace. We were able to feel the pain and yet continue because of our faith and the renewing presence of the Spirit working in our lives.[21]

Ordained clergy are not the only guides through such wildernesses since many church members are pillars of strength to each other and, as the student felt, to the clergy. Cognitive dissonance makes the most profound demands on all who give pastoral care and provides the most unique satisfactions. Like the disciples before us, the gospel begins at the grave.

The Function of Doubt

Cognitive dissonance invites believers to explore the mysteries of their lives. Doubt is not the enemy of faith but the entry into it. The most convinced believers have journeyed through the abyss of losing loved ones and the feeling of being lost themselves. The concept of cognitive dissonance denies any easy solutions or obvious answers. We must travel through dissonance before we find faith, or it finds us. Festinger's elements of cognitive dissonance experience are what we need on the journey: personal and social crisis and a supporting community which cares but cannot deny our pain, and the Christian confession of a transcendent God whose home is beyond us but whose love is available.

Alcoholics Anonymous has built a movement on the dynamics of cognitive dissonance. For members to enter the group they must give up any denial of problems with alcohol and any confidence in themselves to solve their problem alone. Only when they see the world differently, accept a new symbolic universe, can they become members of the transforming community. In the beginning of each gathering the members must confess that they have a problem and that they cannot solve it alone. Cognitive dissonance admits a sense of mystery and mutual dependency. Only by doubting the past can we begin anew.

The Function of Need

Cognitive dissonance suggests that people in crises and transition are particularly ready to hear the gospel if it is offered as a guide through the wilderness and offered by a community who is seen as caring. Thus people who are faced with traumatic change and reorganization of their lives may appreciate the direct and personal attention of the Christian community. Thomas Holmes and Richard Rahe have listed the most demanding events of crisis and readjustment, beginning with death of a spouse, divorce, separation, jail, personal injury or illness, change or loss of employment (including retirement), pregnancy, change in financial status, and many others.[22] The community that is alert to such crises may be especially helpful.

In a less dramatic but more accessible way, an awareness of cognitive dissonance directs our attention to those broad groups within the community who may be especially responsive to hearing the gospel as they struggle with their situations. Among the reasons people join churches, Edward Rauff[23] has reported, are the following:

(a) a search for community, which is "crucial in times of crisis"; (b) a feeling of emptiness, which may happen "even if things seem to be going well"; (c) the end of rebellion, when people want to "return to their values"; (d) a response to fear and guilt, with a need for "reassurance and celebration"; (e) God's Kairos, often the "result of a sacred act such as the funeral or wedding of a close friend."

COMMITMENT WITHOUT CRISIS

Although cognitive dissonance as outlined by Festinger is helpful in interpreting the community building and evangelical zeal of the early church, it is clearly not the only avenue to Christian commitment. We will not offer a survey of alternatives, but we wish to suggest two concepts of the social sciences that build on the same themes in different directions. Following the distinctions set up by Weber and Tönnies, one of these builds on the traditional continuity of the Christian community, and the other emphasizes more rationally disciplined dimensions of Christian experience.

Liminality as Cognitive Dissonance

In the continuity of the traditional community, cognitive dissonance may be carried through a process Victor Turner has called "liminality." Liminality describes the transition within the community from limited or lower levels of understanding to higher and more inclusive awareness. Turner[24] observes an "oscillation" between the intimate relationships of *communitas* and the transforming experiences of liminality. The experience of liminality, called "anti-structure" to emphasize its contrast to the organized community, has many similarities to the experience of cognitive dissonance upon entering a counterculture community:

> Equality, anonymity, absence of property (. . . for property rights are linked with structural distinction both vertical and horizontal), reduction of all to the same status level, . . . sexual continence (or its antithesis, sexual community, both continence and sexual community liquidate marriage and the family, which legitimate structural status), minimization of sex distinction, . . . unselfishness, total obedience to prophet or leader, sacred instruction, maximization of religious . . . attitudes and behavior, suspension of kinship rights and obligations, simplicity of speech and manners, sacred folly, acceptance of pain and suffering (even to the point of undergoing martyrdom), and so forth.[25]

Turner assumes that communities need both structural continuity and transitional liminality. Such ritual occasions are the means both by which individuals are brought into the community and those who already belong are able to intensify their commitments. But liminality should be a memorable experience (as, for instance, baptism by immersion) apart from the mundane routines of daily living. This oscillation[26] between structure and liminality, according to Turner, transforms the individual, renews the community, and inhibits the natural forces of institutional atrophy.

The genius of the early church is a challenge to contemporary congregations. Where in the life of our churches do we find powerful celebrations of liminality to match the early Christian baptismal experience which Wayne Meeks graphically reconstructs as it might have been practiced in the first-century Roman world?[27] Noting that early Christian baptism was more sophisticated than the more primitive rites of passage studied by Turner, Meeks finds remarkable similarity in the language of death—naked descent into the place of washing/

burial, and rising-reclothing/new virtues—entrance into a community of new life on the other side. Baptism for the early church provided a ritual that affirmed cognitive dissonance reenacted to celebrate the entry of new members and the renewal of the community.

Events of liminality may be seen as cognitive dissonance in slow motion, measured by the presence of the attributes noted by Turner, "equality, anonymity, absence of property, . . . unselfishness; . . . obedience, . . . simplicity," and others.[28] Baptism and the Lord's Supper are natural candidates for such shared liminal experiences. Greeting new members and welcoming the communicants' class may be times when shared liminality can rekindle commitment throughout the congregation. Weddings and funerals can be celebrations of individual and communal liminality if they are not too well encased in socially determined behavior.

More creatively, some congregations have risked the intentional use of life crises as a basis for congregational affirmation—illness and unemployment, leaving home and loneliness, divorce and death of a loved one. In these circumstances we may experience the shock of cognitive dissonance—when the world no longer makes sense. The power of cognitive dissonance in general, and the event of liminality in particular, can effect the conversion of loneliness and doubt into community and faith. Worship events have been built around times of crisis, transition, and opportunity. Some churches schedule seasonal times of liminal-like escape and renewal: the church has weekend retreats for spiritual renewal and marriage or personal enrichment, and networks of people who care, listen, and sometimes simply share "space" in silence. In this kind of liminality, cognitive dissonance can be encouraged to run in slow motion, but it should not be denied or avoided.

Rational, Disciplined Cognitive Dissonance

Insights gathered in a "moment of illumination" have remarkable parallels to cognitive dissonance without being associated with an obvious crisis or communal threat. James Loder's description of a "transforming moment," for example, sounds like a kind of cognitive dissonance in a personal experience. Loder reaffirms the social basis of a faith which is experienced individually: "We compose 'worlds' and reflectively set the 'out there'; they in turn feed back and 'compose' us. . . . "[29] The transforming moments of special consciousness are, he says,

> . . . a mixture of continuity and discontinuity. . . . Continuity may be conceived as a linear gestalt . . . held together by an inherent or immanent principle . . . [but] the very heart and center of this sequence depends

upon a mediating discontinuity . . . a gift that takes awareness by surprise. . . . Discontinuity effected by an imaginative construction is the key and center of the knowing event; indeed, it is just this discontinuity that makes transformation possible.[30]

Discontinuity is to the mind what liminality is to the social world, a description of a costly (dissonant) experience through which the believer must pass before believing becomes intellectually persuasive and emotionally compelling.

Loder provides a summary of the "key steps in transformational logic" which are remarkably parallel with the expectations of cognitive dissonance cited from Festinger at the beginning of this chapter. Loder lists: (1) conflict, (2) interlude for scanning, (3) constructive act of imagination, (4) release and openness, and (5) interpretation.[31] Although he explores its implications in science, esthetics, therapy, and religion, he might have been listing the experiences we have traced in the New Testament. Faith is compelling when it grows out of "conflict," is nourished by "scanning" and "imagination," and is shared in the "release" of energy and the "interpretation" of experience. In moments of illumination the crisis may not be acute. In fact, individuals may not realize that they are experiencing cognitive dissonance—until, abruptly, "That's it!" and the world makes sense in a different way.

To nourish such moments of illumination the church has traditions of disciplined study, spiritual exercise, and communal sharing. Such activities are significant disciplines for maintaining the strength of the church. Loder's transforming moment is a helpful example of various ways in which cognitive dissonance can be experienced without the impending trauma of life-threatening events.

In short, what cognitive dissonance dramatizes, liminality rehearses, and the transforming moment illuminates quietly in fine detail.

SUMMARY

In this discussion we have used cognitive dissonance as a tool for appreciating the crisis of the early church and the resulting Christian witness. We have seen the correlation between cognitive dissonance and evangelical zeal: proselytizing is strongest when (a) disconfirmation is clearest, (b) the group is youngest, (c) the outside world is most hostile, and (d) the identity of the believer is invested in a commitment to the cause.

Cognitive dissonance contributes to the energy of congregations and to an understanding of pastoral leaders. It can be rediscovered and shared in the exercises of liminality and individual moments of illumination. However, as we have seen in the aging process of the institutionalized church, when the urgency of cognitive dissonance declines, the energy of the church shifts from evangelical effort in the outside world to more comfortable living within the Christian community.

Without the faith commitment of cognitive dissonance, evangelical enthusiasm declines. No other social process or organizational push can so well ignite the passion that characterized the early church.

FOUR

USING CONFLICT
CONSTRUCTIVELY

Conflict is one area of comparison in which the New Testament church differs significantly from contemporary congregations. While some issues of conflict are common to both, others are unique to one or the other. But in their constructive use of conflict, the early church offers a challenging model for church leaders today. How, for example, did diversity in race, culture, and society contribute to the strength of Christian communities then, while providing today an almost insurmountable problem to most congregations?

Symbols of power and status, including differences between women and men, were muted in the earliest phases of the Christian movement. Why did these differences become divisive issues at an early point and remain areas of conflict in contemporary congregations?

Personal squabbles and group rivalries typical of every human community are evident in the early church. How did they handle their petty jealousies and power plays differently from many churches in our time?

Although parallels between the early Christians and contemporary churches must be approached with care, one thing is clear: the friction of conflict created heat and energy then as it does now. If by conflict we mean the struggle between competing individuals, ideologies, or forces, then the vigor and danger of conflict seems similar across the centuries. In the New Testament as now, conflict is reported as an experience of high energy.

Such conflict was not the opposite of peace, but its prerequisite. Biblical peace is not based on the dominance of one group and the oppression of others. Rather, as we have learned in chapter 1, the kingdom of God, characterized by *eirēnē* (shalom), results from right relationships with God and among people in the human community.

The struggle to develop and maintain *eirēnē*, to build those right relationships, is the basis for biblical conflict. Therefore, some enemies are natural and essential to maintain the integrity of the church.

POSITIVE FUNCTIONS OF SOCIAL CONFLICT

To examine the uses of conflict in the New Testament church, we have adapted three axioms from the work of Lewis Coser.[1] These will also be helpful in guiding our comparisons of conflict in Christian communities. Each of these axioms is based on a pair of concepts in necessary tension.

1. Conflict may contribute to growth. Conflict provides the opportunity for individuals and groups to define their boundaries, discipline their members, and exercise the social consciousness of belonging. New Testament writers clearly understood that conflict made a positive contribution to the strength and growth of the early church (e.g., Acts 15:6–29; 2 Cor. 7:8–13; Phil. 1:12–14; 1 Pet. 3:13–16).

Conflict may, of course, also be destructive of individuals and relationships, and lead to the decline of the church; this has contributed to its bad reputation. The early Christians, however, involved themselves in conflict not because they were malicious. But with the convictions we have suggested in previous chapters, conflict is an inevitable consequence. Conflict is a theological necessity and can be socially constructive.

In this chapter we explore several implications of the tension between conflicts that build and strengthen the Christian church, and other conflicts that may be dishonest, lack integrity, and be destructive of individuals and community.

2. Intimacy and ideology can intensify conflict. Coser identifies these separately, but they may be in tension and they always interact with one another in church dynamics.

Intimacy. In situations of conflict, the closer the relationship the more intense the hostility.[2] Such hostility is often experienced, for instance, in divorce. In reviewing the growth of the early church, John Gager extends a similar concept to some phases of church growth and compares it to the identity crisis of a young child: "The search for identity is often reached through a process of rebellion against one's immediate parents."[3] The early church "chose its enemies" from those groups which offered the most lively alternative for potential members. Therefore evidence of intimacy-hostility can help to determine the social location of the church. The "chosen enemies" of the church are one factor in defining its growing edge at different periods of history.

Ideology. Ideology sets the conflict in a larger context, linking particular events to a pattern of activities which takes on greater significance. Thus Coser observes, "Conflicts in which the participants feel that they are merely the representatives of collectivities and groups fighting not for self but openly for the ideals of the group they represent are likely to be more radical and merciless than those that are fought for personal reasons. Elimination of the personal element tends to make conflict sharper. . . . "[4] Thus ideology carried in dogmatic statements is often more forcefully expressed than the faith which is carried by narratives or taught by parables.

Clearly, the symbolic universe of the church is an expression of its commitments carried in language (chap. 1), demonstrated in its countercultural stance (chap. 2), and experienced by new members in cognitive dissonance of entry and renewal (chap 3). The church is grounded in ideology. But that theology is remembered in many ways: in creed and story, in preaching and music, in doctrine and action, in intimate community and institutionalized structure.

These two elements of personality and principle are the sources and carriers of conflicts. Through individual advocates and their issues, conflicts become identified and social movements are mobilized. We will note how these two dimensions interact in the New Testament and in contemporary churches in sometimes healthy and sometimes destructive ways.

3. Conflict unifies by defining boundaries and demanding adherence. Thus two arenas of conflict are defined by (a) the recognition of boundaries and (b) the demand for loyalty. The first is between the group and the rest of the world, between "them" and "us." The other conflict arena is within the group and among the members. Coser points out that since classical times "a distinction between conflicts over basic matters of principle and conflicts over matters presupposing adherence to the same basic principle"[5] has been common in political theory. In the early church both forms of conflict—between the church and "others," and within the church—produced stronger community. External and internal conflict are different in style, risk, and contribution to the growth and strength of the church. The inability to distinguish between these two has led many congregations to seek to avoid conflict altogether.

In our discussion of the New Testament and the contemporary church, we distinguish between these two arenas: external conflict between the church and the world, and internal conflict within the church. In both the early and contemporary church we note a few areas of conflict that seem symbolic of each period. For both external and internal conflict we will explore the interaction of personality and ideology. Although we emphasize the constructive use of conflict, we will note that destructive dimensions are also present.

CONSTRUCTIVE USE OF EXTERNAL CONFLICT

When we examine the role of conflict in the New Testament, much of what we have previously discussed can be refocused in new ways. In chapter 1 we suggested the complex interplay of diversity and unity that characterized the world of early Christianity. Diversity and unity were also significant in the maintenance of community in an almost opposite way: the Christian struggle for unity within the diversity of the Roman world precipitated conflicts which in many instances gave strength to the nascent church.

As we have seen, in the biblical scholarship of an earlier day it was the general consensus that the early Christians, with a few notable exceptions, came from the lower socioeconomic classes. But today we know that such a picture was oversimplified. The membership of the early Christian communities reflected much of the mélange that constituted Greco-Roman society. It is difficult to locate the earliest Palestinian Christians in terms of their socioeconomic origins, which were probably thoroughly mixed (cf. Luke 8:3). The significant factor is that the Jesus movement tended to bring together people of widely different socioeconomic strata. Concern for the poor reflected in the gospel traditions (cf. chap. 2) suggests that these pronouncements were intended both for the poor and for those who were not. Similarly a parable like that of the rich farmer is hardly directed only to the poverty-stricken! The traditions in the early chapters of Acts reflect a community of Christians from a mixed socioeconomic background who had laid these distinctions aside (Acts 2:44–45). The picture here is one of general well-being, not because there were no poor but because the Christian community included an economic mix. Their struggle (as noted in chap. 2) was not economic mobility, but unity (community) in the midst of diversity.

Changing the Focus: From Pharisees to Sadducees

The transition from Jesus movement to early church is characterized by a shift in the antagonists they identified. For the most part, in the Gospels Jesus' opponents are the scribes and Pharisees. By contrast, in the early chapters of Acts these groups largely disappear and the Sadducees take the stage as the persecutors of the community.

In recognizing this opposition, the early church attacked both the ideology and the political position of their enemies. From a theological point of view, the scribes and Pharisees were preeminently the guardians of the law. One of the earliest rabbinic dicta we possess declares that "the men of the Great Synagogue" (the successors of Ezra) said, "Be deliberate in judgement, raise up many disciples, and make a fence around the Law" (*Mishna Aboth* 1.1). In accord with this injunction, the Pharisees sought to protect the integrity of the law by elaborating hundreds of subsidiary regulations touching every aspect of life, in order to make the law genuinely livable. The scribes, most of whom were Pharisees, were the professional expounders and teachers of the law. As leader of a counterculture movement, Jesus inevitably came into conflict with them. Thus in the Gospels, the scribes and Pharisees are the enemy to be acknowledged. After Easter, when the doctrine of the resurrection became the centerpiece of the apostles' preaching, the Sadducees became the antagonists: while the hope of resurrection was dear to the Pharisees, it was rejected by the Sadducees, which made them the natural opponents of the new Christian proclamation.

Theology, however, does not tell us the whole story. There were sociological grounds for these shifts as well. The Pharisees were rooted in the synagogues spread across Palestine. The synagogues were not only houses of worship; they were community centers where instruction was given, court was held and punishment meted out (cf. Matt. 10:17), ritual ablutions were performed, and at times travelers were given accommodation. They were found in towns and villages throughout the land. With such places as their power bases, the Pharisees were constantly in touch with life at its roots and exercised wide influence over common, daily life. From this standpoint it is understandable that as long as the Jesus movement remained chiefly in the towns and villages, it was the Pharisees and their attendant scribes with whom Jesus' adherents were thrown into conflict. They would have had relatively less contact with the Sadducees, who held the high priesthood and related to the elite and whose power base lay in the one temple in Jerusalem.

But when the apostles settled in Jerusalem the poles of tension shifted. Jesus' action in the temple just before his death and the accusations brought against him at his trial reflect tension with the temple establishment.[6] The tradition is strong in the early chapters of Acts that the Christian believers made the temple the chief setting of their worship and proclamation (Acts 2:46; 3:1; 5:12, 20–21, 42), and this brought them into direct collision with the Sadducees. Thus it was not only what the apostles preached but where they preached it that determined who their antagonists were. The shift from the rural, small-town setting of Jesus to the urban context of the apostolic community was a basic factor in determining their chief opponents.

After the Jews' defeat in A.D. 70, the situation changed again. With the loss of the temple the Sadducees' base of power understandably declined and they virtually disappear from history. Although there had also been wide destruction of synagogues during the war, the Pharisees, whose influence was more diffused throughout the nation, survived to assume ideological and religious leadership in the succeeding decades. Their appeal to legal traditions served to rally a broken nation that had lost its point of focus on the temple. We can understand how, in this post-temple era, the memory of Jesus' conflicts with the Pharisees should be of continuing importance to the church, and that in recording these traditions, the Gospel writers would reflect the issues of their own times as well as those of Jesus. Virtually all of the points of conflict with the Pharisees have to do with matters of the law: washing hands before meals, keeping the Sabbath correctly, fasting, and paying tithe and taxes. With the increased emphasis on the observance of the traditional body of law after the disaster of A.D. 70, in many places these issues doubtless became the source of even sharper conflict with Christians than previously. The result of such tension is aptly described by Matthew in terms of Jesus' instruction to his disciples: "Beware of men; for they will deliver you up to councils, and flog you in their synagogues" (Matt. 10:17).

Tension With the Romans

Within Palestine, Christian attitudes toward the Romans shifted during the years leading up to the Jewish revolt of A.D. 68–70. As conflict between the Jews and their Roman rulers heightened, the strength of radical, anti-Roman elements among the Jews increased. This intensification also influenced the Christian community, as is apparent from the story of Paul's encounter with James, the Lord's brother, on his final return to Jerusalem (Acts 21:17–25). Set sometime in the late fifties, the account has James, then leader of the Christian community, saying to Paul, "You see, brother, how many thousands there are among the Jews of those who have believed; they are all zealous for the law" (Greek, *zēlotai tou nomou*, "zealots of the law"). While this does not necessarily mean that thousands of Christians were adherents of a Zealot political party that advocated violence against the Romans as the way by which the messianic kingdom was to be brought in, it does suggest that the growing public sentiment for a stand against the Romans on the basis of traditional Judaism did not leave the Christian community untouched. This trend was probably also in the background of Paul's controversy with Peter at Antioch (Gal. 2:11–14).

While our evidence in regard to Jewish-Christian attitudes toward the Romans at this time is meager, we can nevertheless sense intricate interweaving of theological, political, and social tensions with which Christians in Palestine had become involved by the mid-first century.

Revelation: The Church Against the World

Written near the end of the first century, the Book of Revelation offers a dynamic portrayal of conflict between the church and the world. Our best evidence, both from tradition and historical probability, dates it during the reign of Domitian (A.D. 81–96).[7] The author, whose name was John, places himself on the island of Patmos in the Aegean Sea, which, taken with the seven letters to the churches of Asia with which the book begins, relates it to western central Asia Minor. Adela Yarbro Collins has described at length a variety of tensions that characterized social and economic life in western Asia Minor during the latter part of the first century: resistance to Rome, particularly because of economic conditions, and socioeconomic unrest which could at times erupt into mob violence were coupled for Christians with their own increasingly ambiguous status vis-à-vis the Roman government.[8] While the long-held notion that Christians were the object of a bitter persecution by Domitian has recently been shown to be groundless,[9] the situation of Christians as reflected in Revelation clearly was one of unrest in the world around them and of increasing insecurity within their congregations. While there was apparently no general persecution, Christians did face sporadic martyrdom and other forms of violence (e.g., Rev. 2:10, 13; 6:9–10).

John is clear about the enemies of the faithful, identifying Rome, celebrating martyrs, and renewing the church's resistance to wealth. The keenness with which he senses these pressures is revealed in the vividness of his language and absolute quality of his condemnation.

Rome. John denounces Rome, especially for its economic transgressions. Prophesying the destruction of Rome, he declares, "Fallen, fallen is Babylon the great! It has become a dwelling place of demons, . . . and the merchants of the earth have grown rich with the wealth of her wantonness" (Rev. 18:2–3; cf. 18:19).

John names individuals and particular congregations. Himself a Christian prophet (Rev. 1:3), he fulminates against prophets and teachers in several of the churches, whom he identifies as Nicolaitans, Balaam, and Jezebel. These persons teach their brethren to "eat food sacrificed to idols and practice immorality" (Rev. 2:14; cf. 2:6, 20). As Collins has pointed out in light of Old Testament imagery where "immorality" (Greek, *porneia*) denotes acceptance of idolatrous practices, we have here more than a dispute over specific sins; rather, these accusations reflect the much broader issue of Christian attitudes toward a surrounding culture.[10]

The prophets denounced here sought to solve the difficult problem of how Christians could relate to a pagan culture which they could not avoid in daily life. Their solution doubtless appeared to them to be realistic accommodation.[11] To refuse to eat food offered to idols made business relationships and, especially, participation in socioeconomic societies difficult; those who partook of such food could appeal to Paul's instruction on the matter (1 Corinthians 8), which had been written from one of their own churches. Those who may have worked out some accommodation in regard to idolatry ("immorality") as it related to emperor worship (which was being promoted in the East under Domitian) could defend themselves with the argument, also from Paul, that " 'an idol has no real existence,' and that 'there is no God but one' " (1 Cor. 8:4).

Similarly, Revelation stands in striking contrast to Paul (Rom. 13:1) and the author of 1 Peter (1 Pet. 2:13, 17) in regard to relationships with the Roman state. While they call for loyalty, in Revelation Rome is "Babylon the great, mother of harlots and of earth's abominations" (Rev. 17:5). Rome is the enemy.

Martyrs. In his description of the One Hundred Forty-four Thousand (Rev. 14:1–5), John presents a special group of saints who "follow the Lamb wherever he goes" and "have been ransomed as the firstfruits of humanity for God and the Lamb" (Rev. 14:4, NEB). Collins has argued reasonably that following the Lamb "wherever he goes" (i.e., even to death) and their being "firstfruits" indicates that they are martyrs. These persons are also described as celibate ("who have not defiled themselves with women," [Rev. 14:4]). It appears, then, that for John martyrdom and virginity, which a century later were prominent marks of special sanctity, were already considered characteristics of a select group of super-Christians.[12] At this point John is in line with certain strains in the Jesus traditions (Mark 8:35; Matt. 19:12) and is followed by other Christian writers in the second century.

The Poor. A third area of tension for John is reflected in his radical stance toward wealth. The letter to the church at Laodicea is filled with imagery that reflects, on the one hand, the fact that the Laodiceans were among the wealthiest people in the province of Asia, and on the other, that the Christians there because of this had become complaisant over their situation: "Because you are lukewarm, and neither cold nor hot, I will spew you out of my mouth. For you say, I am rich . . . not knowing that you are wretched, pitiable, poor, blind, and naked" (Rev. 3:16–17). Such a rebuke could only come from one who saw wealth as an insidious cause of spiritual debility. As we have already seen, much of John's polemic against Rome is also directed toward her riches, which he interprets as her means of leading the world astray: "For thy merchants were the great men of the earth, and all nations were deceived by thy sorcery" (Rev. 18:23).[13] As Rome is a political enemy, Wealth is the spiritual enemy.

In a variety of ways, then, the Book of Revelation can be seen to promote a social, political, and economic radicalism reminiscent of the counterculture stance of the Jesus movement. Revelation is the revival of the revolution, the conscience of the early Christian church, resisting accommodation to the evils of the world. It insists on disciplined commitment against both the natural inclination toward institutionalization and a concern for respectability that we have noted elsewhere among Christians of the first century.

IMPLICATIONS OF EXTERNAL CONFLICT

Group cohesion through identification of a common enemy is the most obvious and accessible positive result of conflict, and the early church put it to good use. In simplest terms, the first-century Christians saw themselves as a culture counter to the "world." As we discussed earlier, Christian hostility to the world expressed itself differently in the Jesus movement, the evangelistic emphasis of Paul, the more historical consciousness of Luke, and the social concerns of James and Revelation.

"Christian conflict" seems a contradiction of terms when we view the faith from the comfort and nurture of contemporary Sunday worship. But Christians involved in the civil rights movement with the Rev. Dr. Martin Luther King, Jr., experienced the constructive power of a militant faith. As the church seeks *eirēnē*, a more Christian world, such conflict is inevitable and essential. Thus external conflict (1) energizes Christian community, (2) clarifies positive identity, (3) defines negative alternatives, and (4) produces creative leadership and committed membership. For each of these areas we note examples of tensions and we remember the guidance of Dr. King.

Energizes Community

The counterculture vision of a unified community that transcends racial, cultural, and national differences may have sounded ideal, but it was energized by the recognition of threats to its existence. The Christian vision became a social reality when the enemies were recognized. Thus Coser says, "Conflict with out-groups increases internal cohesion. . . . A state of conflict pulls the members so tightly together and subjects them to such uniform impulse that they either must get completely along with, or completely repel, one another."[14] In the ancient and contemporary church we see this principle applied in several ways.

Christian conflict with the "world" generated the basis for a new community in the midst of Roman diversity. The Christian alternative provided both the vision and the energy that made community possible. In the excitement of this ideal, differences from the old world became irrelevant. Race and nationality, gender and social standing faded. In response to the initial question of this chapter, differences were dissolved in resisting the enemy.

The rejection of the old world and victory of the new reality are "proven" in the diversity of people who belong. Multicultural communities were not accidental in the early church: they were the essence of opposition to the established order. The inclusive character of the Christian community demonstrates its most profound conquest over the old world by rejecting the separations and symbols of status by which the old world lives. People who would otherwise be fractured and divided find common ground in "the body of Christ," the "new creation."

In this conflict with the world, both ways of generating intensity are united in Jesus the Christ: ideological commitment is focused in the symbol of Christ, and the power of intimacy is linked to the person of Jesus. Believers are united in "the body of Christ." The intensity of commitment can be measured by the barriers crossed to become followers of "the way" (Acts 18:25, passim).

In our century, those churches that absorb racial and ethnic change tend to claim a theology in which Christ transcends cultural differences in worship and parish programs.[15] Congregations that do not survive these cultural changes often huddle with old members to perpetuate the past. Even some congregations that romanticize the culture of the new residents (by, for instance, introducing gospel music to attract blacks to a white congregation) have overcompensated and failed to survive the transition. Rather, those congregations that seem most able to bridge the cultural barriers are able, like the early church, to find a common ground for their unity in Jesus Christ. They are more apt to be clear than fuzzy about the basic tenets of their beliefs and therefore more likely to be conservative than liberal.[16] Their Christian conflict is not against the newly arrived, but against an alien world of personal sin and destructive forces. They are often marked by high energy against a common enemy, the devil.

In his "Letter from Birmingham Jail," responding to religious leaders who protested the militancy of the civil rights movement, Dr. King wrote, "I confess that I am not afraid of tension. I have earnestly worked and preached against violent tension, but there is a type of constructive tension that is essential for growth."[17] In that same letter, Dr. King acknowledged his debt to the model of the early church: "Whenever the early Christians entered a town, the people in power became disturbed and immediately sought to convict the Christians for being 'disturbers of the peace' and 'outside agitators.' But the Christians pressed on in the conviction that they were a 'colony of heaven,' called to obey God rather than man."[18] In this cause King energized a gathering of diversity—black and white, rich and poor, power brokers and political pawns—who sang and prayed together, held hands and broke bread together, camped along the roadside and confronted "powers and principalities" together. He called them "a special army, with no supplies but its sincerity, no uniform but its determination, no arsenal except its faith, no currency but its conscience. . . . It was an army whose allegiance was to God and whose strategy and intelligence were the eloquently simple dictates of conscience."[19] He sought not to create tension but to surface the tensions already present. King explained, "I am not afraid of the words 'crisis' and 'tension.' I deeply oppose violence, but constructive crisis and tension are necessary for growth. Innate in all life and growth is tension."[20] With King as its "Drum Major for Justice," the army marched on.

Clarifies Identity

There is a clear correlation between congregational identity and institutional strength. Churches with a dramatic sense of their place in history are more likely to have an impact upon the society: some generate membership growth, and some are sustained by avid adherents. In neighborhoods of changing populations, as noted above, congregations with clear identity in their heritage, ministry, and mission are more apt to grow despite the demographic trends in their communities. The choice of enemies is one way to clarify identity.

However, the capacity to mobilize energy by identifying an "enemy" can be manipulated by demagogues. Some churches may choose their enemies as a way of attracting allies and gaining support. Coser notes that some movements may in fact search out an enemy or sustain the opposition for the sake of group cohesion. "Struggle groups may actually search for enemies with the deliberate purpose or unwitting result of maintaining unity and internal cohesion."[21]

To defend against the manipulation of emotions by ambitious, unprincipled leaders, the early church identified basic values which defined their ambitions and guided their involvement. They took the relatively neutral word *eirēnē* (absence of conflict) and filled it with the powerful social content of the Hebrew shalom. Their identity with issues became a means to *eirēnē*, to right relationships. Their conflicts first with the scribes and Pharisees and Sadducees, then with local wealth and political power, and finally with the evils of Rome—all were grounded and guided by the blessing with which they greeted one another: *Eirēnē* (peace) be with you! Such a salutation was more than well-wishing. It was a social and therefore political vision which stamped their Christian identity, provided criteria for participation, and offered some protection against corrupting the energy generated by naming the enemy.

In the contemporary setting, many congregations have used "peace" as a reason to repress conflict within the church and avoid conflict in the world, as if conflict itself were contrary to the faith. It is ironic that *eirēnē*, which was initially a guideline for defining and expressing social concern, has become a barrier to contemporary participation.

Some Christian groups become involved in social issues that seem to lose sight of *eirēnē* and the guidelines it suggests. They have so depersonalized their enemies that they are willing to do violence in the name of their cause. People who physically attack divorce counselors and bomb abortion clinics have become so committed to their ideology that they can rationalize their violence toward individuals as an act essential to the defense of their embattled faith. Such radical commitments are not easily resolved, since even *eirēnē* (shalom) does not give absolute guidelines for all situations—as the ambiguities of the Christian doctrine of a just war suggests.[22]

Most congregations identify their understanding of *eirēnē* by their ministries: counseling and education, food pantries and soup kitchens, temporary shelters for the homeless, residences for the elderly, alternate schools for nonconforming and restless youth, and employment services for the unemployed. These programs are usually motivated by a desire to serve, but actively avoid any issues that might create conflict in policy or administration. For most churches, *eirēnē* means service, yes; conflict, no!

For maintaining the commitment of a Christian "army," Dr. King used the energy of combat, but the clarity of purpose:

> We are on the move now. The burnings of our churches will not deter us. We are on the move now. The bombing of our homes will not dissuade us. We are on the move now. The beatings and killings of our clergy and young people will not divert us. We are on the move now. . . . We march

on segregated housing, . . . on segregated schools, . . . poverty, . . . ballot boxes. My People, listen! The battle is in our hands.[23]

In the specific conflict with the Montgomery bus company, he said, "Our concern would not be to put the bus company out of business, but put justice in business."[24] In each new setting, conflict provides energy to move Christians toward the purpose of God's kingdom, eirēnē.[25]

Defines Opposition

More than by its friends, "a church is known by the enemies it keeps." The Confessing church that wrote the Barmen Declaration under the shadow of the Nazi rise to power has become a contemporary symbol of witness to the gospel in the midst of conflict. A less well known but equally emphatic protest against the evils of the Third Reich was acted out in the little French town of Le Chambon, where the church and community united to smuggle hundreds, perhaps thousands, to safety. They were guided by local pastors who identified the enemy: "Theis and Trocmé preached resistance against the hatred, betrayal, and naked destruction that Nazi Germany stood for [since] a nation, like an individual, must do all it can to resist le mal (evil, harmdoing). They felt that while evil was being loosed upon the world, neutrality was complicity in that evil."[26]

The reader might wish to stop and make a list of "favorite enemies" and the "evil causes" they represent. Such a suggestion may seem "un-Christian" in this culture where strong aggression is acceptable only in recreation (e.g., sports, television, movies) and military adventures. It may take a moment to let our enemies come to the surface in our consciousness, but most of us can do it. We may discover our feelings about a government agency, cab drivers, heads of state we fear, teams we like to see lose, arrogant academics, intolerant anybodies, and so on. Such an exercise, in the context of our commitment to eirēnē, allows individuals and the church to examine the depths of our commitments. We may disagree with the particular names and issues raised by others, but not with naming the enemy. It is as biblical as the psalmist who hates the enemies of God "with a perfect hatred" (Ps. 139:22), and as Christian as the resistance to Nazi Germany or as the civil rights movement.

In biblical accounts naming the enemy is acceptable but personal hatred is not. The gospel provides one familiar protection against the abuse of conflict: Christians are admonished to "Love your enemies" (Matt. 5:44; Luke 6:27). But they remain "enemies" because they define what the church is against. The church recognized and sustained its enemies and as a result they contributed energy to the life of the Christian movement. It would have been "un-Christian" to witness without naming enemies. But the church did not hate its enemies. By loving, the church personalized the ideologies it resisted and tried to win them over. Thus Matthew continues, "Pray for those who persecute you, so that you may be sons of your Father who is in heaven" (5:44, 45a). Luke expands the admonition: "Bless those who curse you. To him who strikes you on the cheek, offer the other also; and from him who takes away your cloak, do not withhold your coat as well" (6:28b, 29).

Dr. King modeled the combination of naming without hating his enemies. In the struggle for mobilizing feelings in Birmingham, Alabama, for example, King found the symbol of evil in the actions of the Commissioner of Public Safety, Eugene "Bull" Connor. In his rhetoric, King developed a cadence beginning with, "In Bull Connor's Birmingham . . ."[27] until the name of the man was synonymous with fear and repression, with segregation and white supremacy. King achieved this symbolism not only within his own movement but also through nationwide television. Never betraying hatred for the person of Bull Connor, he nonetheless used his name (and his public behavior) to personify the evil King hated and to energize the forces of change. King could say, "While abhorring segregation, we shall love the segregationist. It is the only way to create the beloved community."[28] In a more political and less theological analysis of the confrontation, President John F. Kennedy observed, "The civil rights movement owes Bull Connor as much as it owes Abraham Lincoln."[29] Enemies are to be loved, but they remain enemies.

Produces Leadership

A community in conflict demands and usually produces stronger leadership. External threat precipitates a concentration of leadership in the hands of trusted individuals whom the group empowers.[30] In this way a conflict or sense of crisis often brings out charismatic qualities of leadership. The amount of authority given to such leadership provides an index to the degree of threat perceived by the community.

Conflict in the community, like cognitive dissonance, provides a basis for pastoral leadership. Thus, in the New Testament, it is at those points of sharpest conflict with outside opponents that the authority of Jesus and the apostles is often most clearly asserted. For example, to "some of the scribes" who attack him Jesus asserts his "authority on earth to forgive sins" (Matt. 9:3, 6). When his disciples are denounced for plucking grain on the Sabbath, his answer is to declare, "The Son of man is lord of the sabbath" (Matt. 12:8).[31] Similarly, as noted previously, in Matthew's collection of sayings intended to prepare Christian preachers for persecution, Jesus' authority is expressed in terms of his closeness with his Father (Matt. 10:32–33, 37–40).

Acts offers a similar pattern—the strongest assertion of apostolic authority emerges in the wake of the first severe persecution (Acts 8:1–17). After Philip, along with other leaders, had fled Jerusalem, he preached the gospel with success in Samaria. Even so, before his converts could receive the Holy Spirit, accredited apostles from Jerusalem were needed to come, pray, and lay their hands on them. Here, for the only time in the New Testament, such exclusive apostolic authority in regard to the Spirit is asserted.[32]

In contemporary times, persons willing to lead in crises and conflict are often granted greater latitude in defining issues and more authority in organizational decisions. At the same time they are more vulnerable to attack for personal reasons.[33] Such mixed signals from the community may contribute to the difficulty that many clergy experience in conflict situations and issue-oriented ministries. We should anticipate the trade-off: in crisis situations where power is granted, the personal purity and motivation of the leaders will also be subject to question.

Clearly this ambivalence was the experience of Martin Luther King, Jr. As leader of a controversial cause, he was as much attacked as he was honored. He was subject to bodily injury and personal abuse. He was harassed for minor offenses and imprisoned for challenging social norms and breaking local laws. He was called "communist" by some who disagreed with him, "Uncle Tom" by others who thought he moved too slowly, and "egomaniac" by some who doubted his motivation. Through it all he affirmed life not in its honors but in its sacrifice for a greater purpose. In the familiar words spoken just prior to his death, when he reflected on his possible eulogy, King suggested, "I'd like someone to mention that day that Martin Luther King, Jr., tried to give his life serving others . . . tried to love somebody . . . to feed the hungry . . . to clothe those who were naked . . . visit those who were in prison . . . to love and serve humanity."[34] In the face of increasing death threats at about the same time, he said to Ralph Abernathy, "I cannot live in fear. . . . If a man has not found something worth giving his life for, he is not fit to live."[35] King did not survive the threats, but his sense of Christian conflict changed the profile of the nation and left a legacy of leaders in every sector of our society. Like King, they are leaders "refined by fire" of conflict.

Since charismatic leadership is by definition a gift of God made valid by community recognition, seminaries cannot create charismatic leaders. But seminaries, pastors, and church leaders can appreciate the need for charismatic leaders and urge gifted people to be ready for the *kairos*—when the moment is ripe. There is no single charismatic leadership style, except the willingness to respond to the Spirit at work: to name the evil without hating the individuals and to energize and unify the community in commitment to *eirēnē*, the shalom of God.

Christ and Culture

Although the gospel is in tension with the world, there is no one biblical pattern of relationship between the church and the world. In *Christ and Culture*, H. Richard Niebuhr[36] offered what is widely regarded as a classic statement of typical relationships between faith-communities and the flow of history. In his typology Niebuhr expands the conflict model of counterculture and establishment church from a single dichotomy to five distinctive ways in which the church has treated the tension between the gospel and the world: (1) sectarian—Christ-against-Culture, which withdraws from the world to create its own environment; (2) cultural—Christ-of-Culture, in which the distinction between gospel and history is largely eliminated; (3) churchly—Christ-above-Culture, in which the faith is seen to be above but not completely distinct from its environment; (4) dualist—Christ-and-Culture-in-Paradox, in which the two worlds remain interactive in tension; (5) conversionist—Christ-transforming-Culture, in which the church actively seeks to change culture in the name of the gospel.

Niebuhr's five categories reflect the resolutions of the conflict between the gospel and the world as expressed in major religious institutions, especially in the nineteenth century: sectarian, civil, Catholic, Lutheran, and Reformed. These categories are particularly useful in expressing the conflict model in five distinctive institutional patterns. Pastors, congregations, and church traditions can identify their style and "claim their turf" in dialogues around issues of the church in the world.

At the same time, since Niebuhr's categories are grounded in historic theologies and religious institutions, they are ill-equipped to interpret new confrontational religious movements which have swept through North America in ever-increasing numbers in the twentieth century: for example, Moral Majority and the Metropolitan Community Churches (gay rights), pro-life groups and religious feminists, charismatic renewal and antinuclear coalitions. These groups see their mission, at least in part, as informing and transforming public policies through theological foundations that are significantly different from the Niebuhr typology. Further, a range of liberationist theologians from Roman Catholics to those of the free church tradition also have found Niebuhr too restrictive.[37] Yet like Niebuhr's typology, these movements claim roots in the Christian faith. They all use conflict between the faith and the world to define their mission and recruit their members.

The uses (and abuses) of external conflict for religious purposes are well established in both religious institutions and religious movements. Those who cannot use conflict lose their distinctiveness and soon find the faith carried only by the weaker vehicles of tradition, organization, and personal affection. These weaker carriers of faith can be undermined by internal conflict.

CONSTRUCTIVE USE OF INTERNAL CONFLICT

Using conflict within the community is more delicate and perhaps more dangerous. Such conflict inevitably involves both the intimacy of personal relationships and the escalation of ideological differences. Internal conflict found expression in a variety of forms among early Christians: (1) the clash of personal feelings; (2) the difficulties of resolving ethnic differences between Jews and Gentiles; (3) the emerging problems of wealth in the Christian community. As the church took form, we also note (4) the struggle to develop structure within a counterculture faith, and, in the longer view, (5) the tensions that were embraced in bringing together the variety of materials contained in the New Testament canon.

The Management of Personal Feelings

The earliest conflicts in the Jesus movement are, of course, obscured to some degree by the layers of Gospel material. If the church wanted (and needed?) to remember a very human side of the disciples, the "brethren" sayings of Jesus in Matthew supplied such a source. These are, indeed, the problems of every community in every age: anger, insult, and reconciliation (Matt. 5:21–24); criticism of others and inability to see one's own shortcomings (Matt. 7:3); and willingness to forgive (Matt. 18:21–22).

Further, "conflict management" in the church may be seen embedded in Matt. 18:15–18, where a detailed procedure is outlined for cases where "your brother sins against you." If a one-on-one discussion is fruitless, "one or two others" should be included in the negotiations. If this proves unsuccessful, the next step is to "tell it to the church; and if he refuses to listen even to the church, let him be to you as a Gentile and a tax collector." These appear to be guidelines for settled congregations, more management-oriented than the charismatically led Jesus movement.

Conflicts internal to the Pauline church were apparent especially at Corinth. The issues there had a theological dimension involving some type of "spiritualized" understanding of the gospel (1 Cor. 2:1–16) and exhibited themselves in such matters as the rightful place of ecstatic experience in the congregation (1 Corinthians 12—14). But the evidence is ample that much of the problem also derived from social and economic tensions, accompanied by a spirit of religious elitism ("I belong to Paul," "I belong to Apollos," "I belong to Cephas" [1 Cor. 1:12; 3:4]).[38] Paul's consistent approach to these problems was to reorient the Corinthians' priorities by reminding them of their mission, and therefore to maintain peace and unity within the congregation while recognizing the great diversity in origin, talent, status, and means from which it was compounded.

Ethnic Differences Remain

Although the conflicts in Corinth appear to reflect differences in class and status indigenous to the local community, the Christian movement clearly struggled to expand its boundaries and absorb people of vastly different backgrounds. The conflicts of race, faith, and politics that we observed in the Jerusalem community inevitably made their impact on Christian congregations abroad. This is particularly apparent in the account Paul gives of his confrontation with Peter at Antioch. At first Peter had accepted table fellowship with gentile Christians there, but when "certain men came from James . . . he drew back and separated himself, fearing the circumcision party. And with him the rest of the Jews acted insincerely, so that even Barnabas was carried away by their insincerity" (Gal. 2:12–13). That Peter and other leading Christians should have made such an about-face must reflect inordinate pressure that went beyond theological issues. It doubtless involved the status of Christian congregations within and without Palestine vis-à-vis the mounting political tensions within Judaism, of which many, at least, still considered themselves a part.

These tensions extended, of course, throughout the whole missionary career of Paul, as testified in his own epistles by his continuing struggle to free gentile Christians from circumcision and other legal demands. That in one form or another these problems were still at issue after Paul's time is evident both from the struggle with Christian Judaizers reflected in the Epistle to the Colossians and from the role similar groups play throughout the Book of Acts. There Luke is repeatedly at pains to point out how accord was effected between Paul and the Jerusalem leadership (Acts 15:19–20, 28–29; 21:25), an agreement which, in light of Galatians 2, may not have been consistently observed.

Wealth and the Counterculture Church

In James we have an energy-packed epistle written to structure yet maintain the counterculture movement of the early church. While we cannot know precisely the time or circumstances under which James was written, it is clear that the believers to whom the epistle was addressed found themselves under pressure at several points and that these pressures from outside produced conflict within. Thus when a man who is apparently not one of the community enters the Christians' assembly, they are not to fall over themselves in such a way as to discriminate against the poor in the congregation (James 2:1–4). Such admonition would not have been given if there had not been some kind of intervention by wealthy non-Christians in the affairs of the church.[39] Further, there are "wars" and "fightings" among the members, and these James attributes to covetousness. He declares, "You fight and wage war" (James 4:2), but his strongest words are reserved for the rich, who have "kept back by fraud . . . the wages of the laborers who mowed your fields" (James 5:4). In the face of such injustice, Christians are to "be patient . . . until the coming of the Lord" (James 5:7).

It is clear that the Christians to whom James addressed his letter were under pressure from wealthy outsiders who both overawed and oppressed them. In either case these pressures raised economic conflict within the congregations. While James bitterly denounces the wealthy who oppress Christians, his concern is not primarily with them but with Christians who allow these pressures to produce havoc within their own ranks. Here we see the influence of wealth and social class on the young church struggling to maintain its countercultural integrity.

Structuring the Counterculture

Particularly instructive evidences of the struggle between those who strove for acceptance and those who yearned for the old counterculture ideals are provided by a comparison of the pastoral epistles (1 and 2 Timothy and Titus) with the apocryphal *Acts of Paul*.

We have already seen in chapter 1 how these pastoral epistles, which are in the nature of primitive church manuals or books of order, reflect a high degree of structure and concern for orderliness and public respect. This relates not only to the organization of the community but also to the personal life style of its members. Radicalism is condemned. Marriage is strongly advised (1 Tim. 5:14, 15); people "who forbid marriage and enjoin abstinence from foods which God created to be received with thanksgiving by those who believe and know the truth" (1 Tim. 4:3) are characterized as having departed from the faith "by giving heed to deceitful spirits and doctrines of demons" (1 Tim. 4:1). Similarly, total abstinence from wine is put in question: "No longer drink only water, but use a little wine for the sake of your stomach and your frequent ailments" (1 Tim. 5:23). Many of the stipulations set down in 1 Timothy are found also in Titus.

The image of Christian society presented by the *Acts of Paul* stands in sharp contrast to that in the pastoral epistles. Although in its present form this book comes from about A.D. 190, in a detailed structural analysis of the work Dennis MacDonald has found much evidence to indicate that a long heritage of oral tradition lies behind it. Thus we can reasonably carry the counterculture type of Christianity reflected by the stories in the *Acts of Paul* back to a point contemporary with the pastoral epistles.[40] It is probable that the Pastorals were written with the express intention of counteracting a radical life style such as that portrayed in the *Acts*. At many points the stipulations set forth in the former are the exact opposite of the kind of living lauded in the latter.[41]

The *Acts of Paul* tells the story of Thecla, who, as she is about to be married, is converted by Paul who preaches a set of beatitudes that emphasize celibacy and renunciation of the world. As a result she refuses marriage and instead determines to cut her hair and enter on a wandering life style in the company of her new-found mentor. They experience a series of miracle-filled adventures reminiscent of Hellenistic romances. At one point they, together with a family of believers, live in a tomb, where for food "they had five loaves, and vegetables, and water, and they were joyful over the holy works of Christ" (3:26). At another time, when a prominent man of Antioch makes advances to her, Thecla "ripped his cloak, took off the crown from his head, and made him a laughing-stock" (3:26). During her wanderings, she dresses in men's clothing. When Thecla finally decides to return to her home town of Iconium, Paul commissions her, "Go and teach the word of God!" (3:41). The story ends with the words, "After enlightening many with the word of God she slept with a noble sleep" (3:43).[42]

When we compare the *Acts of Paul* with the admonitions of the pastoral epistles, a number of contrasts are evident that cover a range of social and other life style issues in regard to diet, attitude toward public authority, marriage, women's dress and deportment, and women as preachers and teachers of the gospel. Behind all of this lie sharply differing attitudes about the importance of public acceptability.

What we have just observed throws into the sharpest contrast yet a basic dichotomy in early Christianity that we have seen developing from the middle of the first century onward. Initially a movement speaking out in word and way of life against the normative culture of its time, within a few decades Christianity showed evidences of concern for public respectability combined with movements toward institutionalization.[43] As these tendencies brought the Christian communities ever nearer to being a church in the technical sense, the counterculture ideals of the primitive movement always remained and repeatedly cropped up. This is particularly observable in what may be thought of as the third and subsequent generations.

But as charisma becomes more and more routinized in a movement, as institutionalization hardens, there are always those too young to have known the realities of the earliest years, who in reaction against the developments of their own time long for and seek to recreate "the good old days" of pristine purity. The urge to "get back to the blueprint" supposedly laid out by the pioneers of the movement is strong. We have seen how during the last third of the first century the Gospels evoke the traditions of the Jesus movement and seek to relate them to the life of the communities of that time. At the end of the century similar or even more pronounced tendencies toward social and economic radicalism appear in Revelation aimed apparently at maintaining the church militant against the intrusion of the world. About the same time or a little later they reach a yet greater extreme in the style of life mirrored in the stories ultimately incorporated in the *Acts of Paul,* focused primarily on radical life style within the Christian community. Revelation was incorporated into the canon but the *Acts of Paul* was not; yet both reflect concerns to revitalize the energy of the early church.

In these trends we see a summary of the basic nature of conflict in the New Testament era. From both a theological and sociological viewpoint, the controlling tension in early Christianity throughout the period we are studying was between counterculture and acceptability.[44] At the outset this relates to the restlessness of the early Christians versus the later, settled communities. The public issue that marked the Jesus movement was its counterculture stance. When Christianity became urban the tension between counterculture and public acceptability became more acute. For example, the law took new orientations: in Palestine and in other areas under the influence of the James Party, many clung to their Jewish traditions; in the Pauline churches, where the environment was Hellenistic, the trend was away from them.[45] As Christian communities encountered various kinds of pressures, they reacted in different ways: the urge for "equable respectability"[46] moved many toward institutionalization (a kind of organizational legalism!), while in other instances the old counterculture ideals repeatedly arose to restore those things they felt were essential for rekindling their commitments. This oscillation of prayer and activity, of resting and working, of institutional structuring and spiritual renewal, has been the rhythmic breathing of the church since the beginning.

Embracing Tension in the Canon

A crowning example of a positive outcome of internal conflict is found in the formation of the New Testament canon during the latter half of the second century. Here the process was strikingly different from what we have observed in the Acts of the Apostles. There is no evidence of a formalized decision, but rather of a gradual consensus. The "scriptures" of the earliest Christians were, of course, the Law, the Prophets and the Writings (cf. Luke 24:44) of the Jewish biblical canon. Christian literature only gradually assumed a place of authority alongside that of the Old Testament. In the writings of the Christian Fathers of the first half of the second century there is little evidence of a set body of authoritative Christian writings ranking with the Old Testament as Scripture.

What did emerge, however, during the middle years of the second century was a growing sense of the need for such Scripture and a consensus as to the writings that made it up. Three major controversies raised Christian consciousness regarding the importance of a canon: those precipitated by the Gnostics, by the Montanists, and by Marcion. Each of those movements was rejected, but in the conflict they influenced and strengthened the vitality and stability of the church.

Although Gnosticism has long been recognized for its literary productivity, since the discovery and publication of the contents of the Gnostic library at Nag Hammadi we have had concrete evidence of the extent of this activity. While Gnostics made wide use of other Christian writings, including many of those ultimately incorporated into the New Testament, the presence of their own writings side by side with these had the effect of widening the scope of the Christian literature for which claims of authority were increasingly being made.

Montanism was concerned over the general routinization of charisma within the institutionalized structure and the attendant "worldliness" of nominal Christians. Montanus and his followers proclaimed a new and final outpouring of the Holy Spirit, with himself and two of his women followers as recipients of the gift of prophecy. Their ecstatic messages sought to recall Christians to pristine piety and simplicity of life. As we have seen, such movements have both a social and a theological dimension. Montanism threatened the established, institutionalized church by its promotion of a new, nonroutinized source of authority which was spontaneous and unpredictable, and could not be contained and controlled within the now-established structures of church life and governance.[47] The church was challenged with the urgency of renewal to define the sources of its continuing authority through the development of a widely acceptable canon. Both Gnosticism and Montanism, then, raised for the church the issue of abiding authority, Gnosticism through new writings, Montanism through a new manifestation of prophecy.

The issues raised by Marcion, however, most directly precipitated the establishment of a wide consensus throughout the church in regard to a canon of Christian Scripture. Troubled by the contrasts he found between the "God of the law" in the Old Testament and the "good God," the Father of Jesus Christ, Marcion concluded that they could not be the same and that only the latter could truly be the God of Christianity. Accordingly he rejected the Old Testament and edited the Christian books most commonly used to form a canon of his own. This consisted of his own expurgated edition of the Gospel of Luke, from which he had sought to rid all evidences of Judaism, and a similar revision of the epistles of Paul whom he considered to be the true exponent of the Gospel. To this he added a composition of his own, the *Antitheses*.

Marcion was particularly significant for the development of the Christian canon because unlike the Gnostics and Montanus he established a canon of his own which forced the church to further define its own list of books enjoying the status of Scripture. In his case the dynamics went in the opposite direction from those unleashed by Gnosticism and Montanism: whereas they broadened the base of authority, Marcion sought to narrow it. But in both instances, the conflict that ensued worked, by the end of the second century, to produce a generally recognized canon of Scripture. The church came to know who it was by recognizing who it was not.

In the formation of the canon, we see two major contributions to the development of the church. First, the church established, from several sources and under several pressures, an authoritative body of written documents, while at the same time relegating to the margin and ultimately excluding those who found themselves unable to compromise. Second, the church included in the canon a wide breadth of materials as authoritative. Taking as a general norm the criterion of "apostolicity," which they naturally applied in a fashion consonant with their concepts rather than with those of modern historical criticism, their response to the conflicts of the second century was to establish boundaries. In so doing they accepted into the canon a rich spectrum of viewpoints on sociopolitical stance, life style, and theological understanding.

Indeed, it is not too much to say that most subsequent heresies in Christian history have been able to find in the New Testament some basis for their belief. Their difficulty has not been in their lack of at least a biblical toehold. There is good reason to conclude, in fact, that in the early centuries the ultimate identification of a group as heretical or orthodox repeatedly depended on whether the movement for other reasons succeeded or failed to survive.[48]

The broad sweep of New Testament material is an affirmation of using conflict constructively. A canon that could include such varying interpretations of Christian faith and life as the Synoptic Gospels and John, as the pastoral epistles and 1 Peter on the one hand and the Revelation on the other, stands as an example of Coser's thesis, roughly stated, that conflicts when seen in the context of the larger cause have in the end promoted stability and unity.

IMPLICATIONS OF INTERNAL CONFLICT

Internal conflict is among Christians rather than between Christians and the world. The energy of internal conflict may be even greater because it combines both intimacy and ideology in the same social space. Therefore, internal conflict is usually more sensitive and often more explosive. We explore three areas in which New Testament dynamics of internal conflict have implications for contemporary congregations: (1) in the procedures for resolving conflict; (2) in the sources of authority; and (3) in leadership development.

Procedures for Resolving Internal Conflict

In an effort to absorb the disruptive emotions of internal conflict, the early church seems to have developed an "organizational process" which channeled the emotions of conflict into specific actions. According to the guidelines given in Matthew (5:21–24; 7:3; 18:15–22) for the resolution of conflict, church members were to work their way through in progressively larger groups for sharing: one-on-one, with one or two others, with the whole church, until the issue was resolved, or "if he refuses to listen even to the church, let him be to you as a Gentile and tax collector" (Matt. 18:15–18).

Such a procedure would personalize the conflict and increase communication through direct contact among the members. Although couched in the language of judgment and sin, these passages permit members to admit their feelings and do something specific toward reconciliation with others, before God. These procedures are remarkably similar to most conflict management approaches in the contemporary church:[49] the recognition of conflict, communication among members, respect for differences, and appeal to a higher unity.

Another and perhaps even earlier organizational approach may be seen in the story of the appointment of the Seven (Acts 6:1–6). Within the primitive Jerusalem congregation, a "murmuring" arose between the "Hellenists" and the "Hebrews" (probably those of Diaspora versus those of Palestinian origin) because the Hellenists' "widows were neglected in the daily distribution." A solution was achieved in the appointment of the Seven "to serve tables" which "pleased the whole multitude," and the community was stronger not only because of the satisfactory solution but also because the conflict had produced a new level of group trust. In a similar way, the "Council of Jerusalem" (Acts 15) while dealing with a much broader and more fundamental issue, that of the obligations of gentile Christians, is portrayed as reaching a decision that "seemed good to the Holy Spirit and to us" (the apostles and elders of Jerusalem). When this decision was communicated to the gentile Christians at Antioch, Luke reports that "they rejoiced at the exhortation" (Acts 15:28, 31). The early church remembered that they dealt with internal conflict by sharing their differences, recognizing a common calling, and rejoicing in the unity they experienced in the Holy Spirit.

Paul's own first-hand and less idealized account of the same or a similar conflict with the leaders at Jerusalem (Gal. 2:11–16) demonstrates that the church was able to arrive at an agreement on the admission of Gentiles using a more objective "constitutional" basis to establish their rightful place within Christianity. By contrast, in Corinth Paul approaches the conflict by identifying those individuals who stood as symbols for particular factions ("I belong to Paul," "I belong to Apollos," "I belong to Cephas" [1 Cor. 1:12; 3:4]). Yet the general approach is similar, as Paul urges the community to see the conflict in a larger, theological context (1 Cor. 2:1–16). Subsequently Paul portrays the issue as part of the worship life of the entire community (1 Corinthians 12—14) with even larger implications for the continuing conflict of the church against the "world" beyond.

In these incidents we see three dimensions in the way the New Testament handles internal conflict: (1) differences are personalized and shared, (2) issues are tested against a sense of mission, and (3) the community rejoices, celebrates its common convictions, and demonstrates them in subsequent actions. Throughout the process, the organization of the church remained minimal and pragmatic—as little and as local as necessary to get the job done. Conflict provides our earliest glimpse into the primitive organizational life of the early church.

In contemporary times, the way a church resolves conflict often stamps the identity of that church. Note the number of denominations whose names reflect their governance: Episcopal, Presbyterian, Brethren, Congregational, and so on. Further, many local congregations take on the character of their decision-making style.[50] Healthy congregations are characterized by mutual respect and open communication, clear standards for their decisions, and the expectation of living up to their agreements—procedures much like those of the early Christian communities. This is evident throughout the decision making of the church, from the office procedures to the church school materials they use, from the process of repairing the roof to that of calling and receiving a pastor: in the crunch of conflict, congregations (like individuals) develop a process-style that reflects their character.

Second, the New Testament church personalized the process. Knowing people personally is the unique dimension of internal conflict. Matthew expects the "brethren" to talk face to face. Paul names names in recounting his tensions with other Christian leaders (Cephas, "certain men" who "came from James" [Gal. 2:11–12]). Within the community, conflict is associated with particular persons. Resolving internal conflict requires a sensitivity to the needs of individuals, to the "political" dimensions of group life, and to the larger ideological issues that the conflict reflects. The personal dimension is, however, so complex and exhausting that it can defeat many efforts to use conflict constructively.

Within the family of the church there can be no "enemies." Enemies is a word of alienation, used primarily for those who have been depersonalized and have become symbols of the evil they represent—in the way Dr. King used "Bull" Connor. Within the community, conflicts are never only an idea, never only a personal perspective: they are always both. Personalizing and organizational process work in tandem with each other. Each can be used to bring out the best in the other so that people can humanize the idea, and ideas can transcend personal differences to unify the group. Unfortunately, each can also work at cross-purposes, so the organization can box people in, and troubled people can bring chaos to group process.

Thus in the parish, for example, in conflict over a choice of evangelistic approaches, the issues are always a mixture of "theological positions" and "personal opinions." When a person speaks, we always hear both theology and personality. In the parish the issues become dangerously explosive when we reduce the person simply to an ideology (by stereotyping as a "fuzzy liberal" or "frozen fundy") or when we deny that the person has any ideology (by making the issue into a personality quirk, "He's always like that—just like his father!"). The challenge of parish leadership is the weaving of both the personal and the ideological into larger patterns of commitment in which the church celebrates the participation of the Holy Spirit.

Third, internal conflict never happens in sterile isolation, but external pressures always intrude on internal decisions. Sometimes external conflict helps to unify an internally divided community. Thus, in Paul's letter to Corinth, perhaps our earliest fragment of conflict management in the New Testament, we see (a) the identification of individuals with each faction, (b) the recommendation of a more objective process, and especially (c) an appeal to all sides to be united in a larger, common cause. This third element might be called an inspirational or charismatic appeal to rise above differences and find harmony in something beyond all differences. In this sense, external conflict is often used to resolve or reduce internal conflict not only in the early church, but in the leadership of contemporary congregations.

A dramatic difference between the early and contemporary church can be seen in their approaches to conflict. Most of the biblical memories redirect conflict by a commitment to a higher, common cause. They harness energy of human differences to reach toward the vision of a new world. Most of our contemporary literature is concerned to resolve conflict within the congregation. It offers guidance for the management of personality differences among members within the church. In responding to conflict, the early church focused primarily on God's activity in the world, while the contemporary church seems preoccupied with itself.

Sources of Authority

In the formation of the New Testament, as we have noted, the church demonstrated the positive use of conflict in both the process of its decisions and the product of its efforts in the formation of the canon. The tension is particularly dramatic in the differences discernible between the institutional continuity of the pastoral epistles and the disruptive-renewal quality of the counterculture in Revelation.

Through succeeding centuries, the canon, with its gathering of early church tensions, has remained the central authority for belief and action. We have been blessed by its diversity, for it offers normative guidance for both institutional stability and creative renewal. In this unity and diversity, each new generation has found a resource for articulating the faith. Every branch of Christianity has found its own means to interpret the common Bible—through bishops and councils, through pastors and study groups, through assemblies and scholars, through counseling and prayers, through liturgy and social action. The rich diversity of New Testament tensions embedded in the text gives the Bible an authority that reflects both the earthiness of experience and the transcendence of inspiration.

The New Testament is best used when the diversity of its viewpoints and social dynamics are appreciated and applied as a resource in each new cultural setting and for each new social issue. The voices of the church in creeds and confessions, resolutions and programs, are both statements and symbols of the mission they proclaim. Like the development of the canon, these statements are hammered out in conflictual settings and, like the Bible, they often incorporate diverse perspectives on a common theme. Further, the conflictual process of reaching resolution is often as significant as the statements that result. Churches rarely recognize that they are often more united by experiencing the tensions of decision making than by the programs or statements that result. The prayers and debates of the struggle may be more binding than creeds and proclamations which they produce. Despite continuing differences, the urgency of mission may bring the church together now, as it did among first-century Christians—that is the genius of New Testament tensions.

The contemporary church often represses the very conflict that the early church found energizing. For example, a denominational gathering that seeks to resolve an issue of faith or determine a priority among pressing choices of ministry can come closer together even as they voice their disagreements; but many church leaders would lament the "fight." A local church fussing with building plans or arguing over the expansion of their community ministry finds unity not despite the expression of their differences but because their cause is large enough to embrace their diversity. Many contemporary churches would suppress such conflict. In certain experiences of the early church we see a more constructive use of conflict through a process characterized by open communication, mutual respect, coherence with the church's mission, and celebration of the Holy Spirit.

Thus the development of the canon may be complete. But the dynamic process by which it was formed and the diversity that it sustains remain as a witness and model of the church's positive use of internal conflict.

Leadership

Throughout our discussion we have identified three leadership roles: organizational management, associational caring, and spiritual charisma. These each assume particular functions in response to situations of internal conflict.

As organizational managers, congregational leaders are responsible for fairness of process. Although most literature defines the dimensions of congregational conflict in a rational way, the Epistle of James may be more accurate in calling the experience "waging war" within the church. Too often leaders think of themselves as referees or even coaches in a contest of wills. More often churches need sportscasters to "announce" the event and help the congregation maintain the process of open communication, mutual respect, coherence with mission, and celebration of the spirit.

For associational leaders, caring for the "players" is an exhausting experience. Leaders are often pushed to take sides, to represent a particular position, not only because it is "right" but even more because of the personal relationships involved. But many leaders are neutralized for fear of alienating others who might disagree. Leaders bear a special burden of keeping communication open and honest. Leaders also must clarify the issues (always more than one) and suggest their relationship to a larger vision of Christian commitment. In internal conflict, leaders are inevitably in the middle in their feelings, as well as in the process.

Yet relationships can be used to help resolve issues, although not strictly by the organizational process. Rather, relational leaders can provide a personal "switchboard" that connects particular caring people with the issue they care most about without the complications of the "democratic process." Caring pastors and knowledgeable lay leaders can resolve some problems simply by the intimacy of their congregational awareness. Sometimes, for example, the organ can be repaired more effectively by quietly approaching a more wealthy member of the congregation than by working the issue through a hostile committee. Sometimes the congregation will join in a controversial community ministry because an involved and trusted member of the church invites others, even though the board does not want to be pushed. Although the democratic process is standard operating procedure, it is not the only or always the best way to resolve conflict.

It is difficult for many congregational leaders to take on the role of charismatic-spiritual leader when they are busy managing the organizational process and are exhausted by the emotional demands of personal relationships. When they see themselves as carriers of charisma, congregational leaders challenge the church to think beyond the assumptions and passions of the moment, to find creative and mutually satisfying alternative solutions. In his discussion of religious leadership, Robert Greenleaf[51] calls this "contingency thinking," leadership by imagining alternatives to conditions as we find them. He says it is the peculiar responsibility of leaders not to become embroiled in a limited perspective but to offer alternative options and to inspire confidence in a new direction. In consulting with secular corporations, Terrence Deal and Allen Kennedy have used a more dramatic term to describe the same kind of leader—corporate "outlaw"[52]—not because they have broken codes but because they think beyond the assumptions that restrain others. In this sense, like the religious in more primitive cultures, the pastor-leader is expected to be different, that he might help others become whole.

SUMMARY

Based on the work of Lewis Coser, we have looked for the positive use of conflict while recognizing that conflict also has "a dark side of the force." We have distinguished between two kinds of conflict. (1) Conflict between the church and the "world" is essential to the gospel. Such external conflict takes on the character of a counterculture movement and mobilizes energy that transcends cultural differences to bring unity in purpose to a church. (2) Internal conflict is a dynamic process within the church which can be useful to develop structure, define mission, and embrace a wide diversity of members.

Unfortunately the confusion between internal and external conflict seems to be a frequent reason why congregations avoid controversy and suppress dissent. Too often patterns of external conflict infiltrate the church and "brothers" or "sisters" become alienated from one another as "enemies," the depersonalized symbols of the issues they advocate. The New Testament demonstrates how these styles are different, and how each can be useful in its own distinctive way.

In the external conflict of the church with the world, the early church was committed to *eirēnē*, God's shalom. They identified the opposition, but they refused to hate their enemies. Internally the church disagreed vigorously within the family. Such internal conflict affirmed their sense of community when they demonstrated that members can disagree while still being held together by an even higher purpose. Thus, recognition of the difference between the gospel and the world contributed to community building. The threats outside reduced the tensions within.

In the contemporary church, the reverse priority seems to prevail: the internal tensions and dissensions often reduce the will of the congregation to become involved in conflicts with the world. In light of the experience of early Christians, it is apparent that many of the tensions in our churches would be reduced if congregations were more committed to the world mission of the church and more involved in the tensions of local ministry.

We are not suggesting that the church seek conflict but that it more openly admit the tension that exists between the *eirēnē* of God and the conditions of the world. A church without internal conflict is not recognizing its humanity. A church without external conflict is not Christian.

FIVE

RITUALS OF
STRUCTURE AND
MYSTERY

Ritual may seem the opposite of conflict but it can serve the same purpose in different ways: to sustain and strengthen commitment to God through the church. The positive function of conflict is to clarify and energize Christian commitment, as we noted in chapter 4. But these dramatic challenges of faith do not change the nature of the church until they become absorbed into the life and natural rhythm of the community. Ritual is the evidence that a particular element of faith has been accepted ("naturalized") into the culture of the congregation. Issues that have been made evident in conflict are incorporated into the church through ritual, thus serving the same end using a radically different social process.

SETTING

Despite or perhaps because of conflict, the early Christian movement was successful—that is a fact of history. It made converts, it spread throughout the empire. At least by the time Luke wrote in the last quarter of the first century, he could use extravagant statements such as that of Tertullus to Felix against Paul (Acts 24:5): "We have found this man a pestilent fellow, an agitator among all the Jews throughout the world." Similarly the last words of Matthew could be taken seriously: "Go ye into all the world . . . " (Matt. 28:19). Sometime around the turn of the first century the *First Epistle of Clement* could remind the Corinthians that their founder Paul had "taught righteousness to the whole world, having traveled to the limits of the west" (*1 Clement* 5:6).[1]

We have no way of knowing how far Christianity had spread by the end of the first century but it was almost certainly grounded in many towns around the perimeter of the Mediterranean. Granted the impulse to proclaim the gospel that characterized the early Christians and the availability of relatively easy travel in the Roman world, it seems likely that within the first century there were Christians also in the farther reaches of the empire which by this time extended north to Britain and to the Rhine and Danube as well as east to Parthia and possibly farther.[2] The fact that we have no literary or archaeological remains of such expansion this early does not rule it out; there is no certain archaeological evidence of Christianity anywhere in the first century and almost no literary remains outside the books preserved in the canon.[3] From the viewpoint of a Roman governor in Pontus on the southern coast of the Black Sea about A.D. 112, we have Pliny's report that Christianity there had penetrated to the villages as well as the cities, but he offers his opinion that it could still be stopped.[4]

However there is little evidence that Christianity was ever in serious danger of being stopped by persecution. Such external conflict, as we have suggested, strengthened the commitment of the early Christians. The great dangers Christianity faced almost from the beginning were numerical growth and social acceptance.

Church growth was a threat to the unity of the church: how could a single movement be maintained among so many congregations located in distant places and drawn from populations which differed in language, culture, and nationality? Even in the twentieth century, with the marvels of modern communication and transportation, the church is divided by class, race, language, nationality, and denominational shading of theological differences. Unity in the midst of radical diversity was a major challenge to the young church in its widely scattered congregations.

Social acceptance was a second threat. This counterculture movement had a revolutionary vision of the social order, where all people worshiped one God, where differences were transcended in the miracle of Jesus Christ. The early Christians needed to interact freely with their surrounding communities without losing their distinctive identity as a community or their revolutionary dream of the kingdom of God. When we see how closely many people interweave their religious faith, their cultural identity, and their national loyalty, we recognize the dilemma that faced the first-century church. Of their many responses, we note how the church protected and perpetuated the faith through worship.

RITUAL AS A SOURCE OF STABILITY

The Protestant churches have inherited an ambivalence about ritual that is apparent at the very beginning of Christianity. Wayne A. Meeks[5] points out that early Christianity lacked most of the characteristics of a Greco-Roman religion. Christians saw themselves as an alternative faith: no temples, statues, sacrifices, public festivals, dances, pilgrimages, and apparently no inscriptions. Much of this separation from recognized accouterments of religion appears to have remained late into the second century, when we first find Christian inscriptions and art in the catacombs. In some instances it was not until the legalization of Christianity that the familiar trappings of a religion became evident (e.g., any extensive church building). Christians developed a religion while refusing many of the symbols of religion familiar to the world in which they lived.

At the same time they developed new rituals of their own. Mary Douglas has pointed out, "It is impossible to have social relations without symbolic acts."[6] Words of greeting, a handshake, a slap on the back, stereotyped words of farewell, and many other set phrases and actions bind us together as social beings. The fact that they are fixed in usage, rather than detracting from their power, is a source of their dynamic. While in saying "How do you do?" and extending our hand we are not usually conscious of actually asking a question and scarcely aware of the reflex of our arm, the significance of such actions can be appreciated by the fact that if we did not do them, we would signal a discourteous sense of rejection.[7] John Gager has declared that the "single, overriding *internal* factor" in the triumph of Christianity was "the radical sense of Christian community."[8] It is understandable, then, that in constructing a distinctive community, Christians needed to develop their own characteristic rituals. The emergence of ritual in Christian life was thus a natural phenomenon. The surprise would have been if it had not happened. It was a response both to an internal need in constructing social relationships and to the sociopolitical need for recognizable but distinctive accouterments of religion.

While to Greco-Roman eyes Christianity must at times scarcely have looked like a religion, it nevertheless drew heavily on its Jewish roots in developing its own rituals. Certainly with a sense of historical continuity, early Christians built on the traditions of Jewish religious meals in celebrating the Lord's Supper. And while the earliest descriptions of the proceedings of Christian worship services come only in the second century from the Roman governor Pliny and the Christian apologist Justin Martyr,[9] these accounts both reflect foundations in more ancient ritual. Justin's description in particular clearly shows the influence of the common synagogue service. It is difficult to escape the conclusion that Christian worship from the beginning was grounded and sustained by ritual. Etienne Trocmé has, in fact, argued strongly for understanding the Passion Story, the kind of narrative we noted in chapter 1, as our earliest Christian liturgy.[10]

The first-century church developed patterns of worship—rituals— that unified the movement while providing flexibility for local variations and for historical change. It rejected some rituals characteristic of its Jewish heritage, since new rituals needed to cross social and economic barriers (language, culture, nationality, and class) and to symbolize a meeting of the *ekklēsia* wherever Christians gathered. For the early church, worship ritual provided continuity, critique, and the opportunity for appropriate change.[11]

In developing these worship rituals, the church succeeded in balancing particular, local, and personal expressions with a common, universal faith. These patterns of behavior (more than theology or organization) provided a framework of stability even when expressions of faith were amended to meet different conditions or historical changes. Rituals defined the role of leadership while leaving specific place for congregational participation. In the context of worship, they provided stability of leadership while protecting liturgical space for the believer to experience the divine.

At the same time the early church, which found its identity as counterculture community, needed to reject openly many of the recognizable religious rituals of the time. The Gospels portray Jesus and his disciples as actively contesting certain observances that were deeply ingrained in Judaism, particularly those having to do with ritual purity (Mark 7:3–4, 19). This rejection doubtless reflects a sense of the dissolution of barriers between Jew and Gentile.[12] As the horizons of Christianity expanded beyond the limits of Judaism, such controlling mechanisms were thrown off. These actions served to affirm new openness to the gentile world and, at the same time, to heighten a sense of identity.

Today many Christians, especially Protestants, cling to the denial of ritual as a symbol of spiritual spontaneity and institutional purity. They imagine that in worship we can always begin new and on our own. In the heritage of a counterculture faith there is indeed consistency in rejecting established religious symbols as a way of avoiding being further coopted through assimilation by the world.

In contemporary churches some rejection of rituals of the religious establishment cleanses the faith and binds the community. Much of the rejection we generate and absorb, however, is the negation of symbols precious to other Christians. The sacramentalists are attacked for "pushing beads," the fundamentalists for "pounding the Bible," the liberals for their "bleeding hearts." Whatever good this may do for building support within our own communities must be measured against the damage it does to the larger mission of our Christian commitment. Beyond rejection, the early church proceeded to build community in very difficult circumstances in part through the development of rituals they held in common.

We shall consider rituals under two headings: Rituals of Structure, which provided continuity and a sense of community among the scattered congregations of the growing church, and Rituals of Mystery, which gave believers direct access to the intervention of the divine. Although in most cases we cannot be certain precisely when, where, or how they were practiced in the early communities, their amazing durability is seen in their familiarity to us today. As we look at each, we should wonder about the choice of that ritual (what are the alternatives, theirs and ours?), about the way it was practiced to achieve their goals, and about its implications for dealing with similar problems in our own time.

RITUALS OF STRUCTURE

Rituals of structure may be seen particularly in settings of exhortation and instruction. But they are not limited simply to the words spoken on such occasions; they express themselves also in the structures within which such exhortation and instruction take place. Meeks has written of "minor rituals"—"gestures, formulas and patterns of speaking" through which believers discover and express "their identity as 'brothers and sisters in Christ.' "[13] While such rituals can be identified in the early generations of the church, we are at many points in semidarkness as to details. But we can identify enough for helpful comparisons with some church practices in our time.

Exclamations, Hymns, and Creeds

Primitive Christians developed rituals of structure to stabilize their worship and community life. As far as we can tell, in the early years their performance was fairly fluid. It is, in fact, a striking feature of the New Testament documents that aside from the sequence of taking bread, blessing, breaking, and giving it along with the cup in the Eucharist, and the Lord's Prayer, nowhere is specific instruction offered concerning the time, place, or form of worship. The fact that such matters are not discussed seems to suggest that the earliest structures of worship were flexible and loosely applied. When, where, and how Christians worshiped probably was determined by a variety of contextual factors. Paul appears to have allowed for such latitude.

Granted that worship services in Corinth may have been more spontaneous than in many other places, he nevertheless assumes the presence of certain structural elements: "When you come together, each one has a hymn, a lesson, a revelation, a tongue, or an interpretation" (1 Cor. 14:26). His chief concern in this situation was that "all things be done for edification, . . . decently and in order" (1 Cor. 14:26, 40).

The most primitive of early Christian rituals reflected a high level of congregational participation; perhaps the earliest were brief exclamations of feeling and affirmation which in time became stylized in Christian worship. Such exclamations though spontaneously uttered may nevertheless take on a ritual character and serve the same binding function as longer credal expressions. Several of these are apparent in the New Testament, such as "Amen" (Rom. 1:25; 1 Cor. 14:16; Heb. 13:21), "Hallelujah" (Rev. 19:1), "Hosanna" (Mark 11:9), "Maranatha" (1 Cor. 16:22), and "Abba" (Rom. 8:15). Though these appear in the Greek text, the fact that they all are Hebrew or Aramaic expressions testifies to their having arisen in Christianity at an early period; several of them, in fact, were taken over from Jewish practice.

Those who have experienced Pentecostal, revival, or traditional black worship are familiar with such expressions. The "Amen" from the congregation assumes a kind of dialogue with the rhythm of the preaching and music to continue and expand the participation of the congregation. Numerous short words and brief phrases in such energetic worship recall the excitement of previous services and may escalate the experience to a level of emotion that is difficult to control. But such recognizable words can also provide a more or less socially acceptable outlet while controlling the level of response. By contrast, in more institutionalized traditions we would still expect to find the word "Amen" printed at the conclusion of a hymn, prayer, or litany.

Hymns and creeds provide an even more institutionalized form of congregational participation by expressing the values and commitments of believers. Credal statements and hymns used by early Christians have been identified in a number of passages in the New Testament. What is probably our earliest ritual confession of faith is repeated by Paul in 1 Cor. 15:3–5, a declaration that he says he had "received" and "delivered" to his converts. The terms translated "received" and "delivered" reflect Jewish language for the transmission of authoritative tradition. This, together with the fact that other linguistic features of this passage point to a Semitic background, suggests that Paul is repeating here in Greek a primitive creed used by Aramaic-speaking Christians in Palestine at a very early period. Paul likely "received," that is, was taught it in one of his first contacts with the apostles or other Christian teachers (cf. Gal. 1:18). Thus in 1 Cor. 15:3–5 we probably have a fragment of ritual that carries us back to within a few years of Easter.[14]

Also very early, although probably not as old, is our first known Christian hymn, the verses preserved in Phil. 2:5–11. Here again Paul almost certainly is quoting an already familiar composition. That Christians were using hymns in their worship is clear from 1 Cor. 14:26, Eph. 5:19; and Col. 3:16; and the "Christ hymn" we have here is doubtless one of them.[15] Somewhat later hymns and confessions of faith—it is not always easy to distinguish between the two—are found in such passages as 1 Tim. 3:16; 2 Tim. 2:11–13; and Rev. 4:11; 5:9–10; 11:17–18.

Such hymns and creeds provided a double service for the early church: they bound the community together and propagated the faith. Just as in our own time, so then—theologians may articulate their faith in careful and sophisticated statements, but the faith of most church members is carried in relatively simple hymns with familiar music and memorable rhymes. Creeds can summarize in a few words what a community has experienced and believes. They crystallize the particular faith of individuals and unify it with that of others in a shared expression of experience and commitment.

Prayers

Prayers played a key role in the ritual of synagogue worship and in Jewish private devotions. The practice of prayer before meals was carried over by Christians (Matt. 15:36; Acts 27:34; 1 Cor. 10:30), as was the assumption of certain bodily positions in prayer: standing (Mark 11:25), kneeling (Eph. 3:5), and raising the hands (1 Tim. 2:8). Equally suggestive, however, are those aspects of Jewish prayer practice that are not mentioned in the New Testament as a part of Christian ritual: the use of phylacteries, prayer shawls, and turning toward Jerusalem (cf. Matt. 23:5; John 4:20). These were doubtless not adopted because of the same counterculture consciousness that prompted the rejection of laws of ritual purity.

As with other aspects of early Christian ritual, so with prayer: form and active participation united the congregation at least as much as content. Even in the case of the model prayer of Jesus, the Lord's Prayer, we have two clearly different traditions as to its exact wording and content (Matt. 6:9–13; Luke 11:2–4). These were used independently of each other in different areas of the early Christian world. While they are the same prayer in the sense that they clearly have a common origin that drew heavily on Jewish prayers, the fact that two separate forms could develop and be equally acceptable is important. The tradition of a "Lord's Prayer," which, as Tertullian said, is "a summary of the whole Gospel," contributed significantly to Christian identity structure and at the same time allowed for diversity.

The unifying power of liturgy can be seen in the shock waves which are generated by efforts to "modernize" it. Anglicans, who embrace a worldwide spectrum of theological and political perspectives "all held together by the Book of Common Prayer," were shocked by a sense of loss when the new liturgy was offered in the early 1970s. Roman Catholics had a similar experience when they "modernized" the mass by celebrating it in the vernacular. Resistance to such changes does not arise from a desire to remain ignorant or obscure, but in the old familiar forms, members and congregations which are otherwise widely separated see themselves before the altar together "in Christ our Lord. Amen."

Preaching

In the evangelical enthusiasm of the early church, preaching served a ritual function. It too developed common forms through which a variety of theological concepts could be spoken. The Christian sermon developed ritual structure which was recognizable even when the content changed. While it can no longer be maintained that the *earliest* Christian preaching necessarily followed the "kerygmatic" outline[16] inherent in the missionary sermons of Acts, it remains clear that these sermons though composed later do follow common patterns.[17] While their origin and background are complex,[18] it is reasonable to think that they reflect styles of preaching current among Christians in at least the later first century.

In preaching, as we have noted in the case of prayer, it is possible to discern diversity within unity. The sermons in Acts fall into two clearly distinguishable types: those directed to Jews and those directed to Gentiles.[19] While the gospel they proclaim is essentially the same, the form of argument they use is distinctly different. Even within those sermons addressed to Jewish audiences, we may also find differences in theological conception within the bounds of a common kerygmatic outline; thus the Christology of the sermon in Acts 3 reflects what appears to be an earlier understanding of Jesus than does that in Acts 2.[20]

As for the sermon in contemporary churches, no first-century ritual remains so significant in Protestant worship and yet can provide a vehicle for so many different styles and messages. Early in the Christian era, preaching became, and has remained, the showcase of the Word. At a time when some church leaders are suggesting that preaching is dead, others are using the marvels of modern communication to develop dimensions of preaching never imagined by former generations of believers. In form the sermon remains, but the medium of communication, style of presentation, and relevant content of the message must be molded to this era as it has been through the centuries.

Offerings

Offerings served to unify the church, not only locally but more widely throughout the early Christian world. They affirm the commitment of believers, the quality of caring within one congregation, and mutual dependency among several congregations.

Little is said of fund raising in the New Testament, as if it were assumed. We have one prime example in Paul's campaign among the churches of western Asia Minor and Greece on behalf of the community at Jerusalem (Rom. 15:25–27; 1 Cor. 16:1–4; 2 Cor. 8:1–7; 9:1–5; cf. Acts 24:17). Paul clearly sensed the group-binding force of this offering for both the community in which the funds were raised and the larger church which shared in the project. Speaking of the churches of Macedonia, he said:

> For in a severe test of affliction, their abundance of joy and their extreme poverty have overflowed in a wealth of liberality on their part. For they gave according to their means, as I can testify, and beyond their means, of their own free will, begging us earnestly for the favor of taking part in the relief of the saints (2 Cor. 8:2–4).

Using a skill that would have brought a knowing smile to any contemporary fund-raiser, Paul proceeded to challenge the pride of Christians in Corinth with the efforts of the Macedonians:

> Now it is superfluous for me to write to you about the offering for the saints, for I know your readiness, of which I boast about you . . . But I am sending the brethren so that our boasting about you may not prove vain in this case, so that you may be ready, as I said you would be; lest if some Macedonians come with me and find that you are not ready, we be humiliated—to say nothing of you—for being so confident (2 Cor. 9:1–4).

After suggesting both theological and social rationale, Paul recognized the importance of individual commitment in each person who is making a donation: "Each one must do as he has made up his mind, not reluctantly or under compulsion, for God loves a cheerful giver" (2 Cor. 9:7).

The details of the dynamics behind Paul's effort appear to have been complex. It is evident that while he was following a familiar Jewish practice in which funds were collected among the communities of the Diaspora to be sent to Jerusalem, this undertaking was of great importance to him because of the legitimation of the gentile mission that it implied. If the Jewish-Christian community at Jerusalem was willing to accept offerings from uncircumcised gentile Christians, to recognize them, so to speak, as their Diaspora, Paul's mission was vindicated and the unity of the church was strengthened.[21]

In Paul's earnest pursuit of this fund-raising campaign we see a startling combination of strong-arm psychology and a sensitive appreciation of the significance that the ritual of financial giving has for the individual believer, for the local congregation, and for the interrelationships which unite congregations into the larger church.

In contemporary congregations, the offering has been called the most solemn moment of the liturgy—with good reason. As James Luther Adams has pointed out, the offering is the ritual by which congregations reaffirm their independence from state support, members reaffirm their autonomous act of commitment, and the congregation senses itself to be a part of a larger movement.[22] Religious television has recognized the untapped power in the ritual of the offering, but many congregations have avoided (or debased) its potential. Fund raising is a basic ritual for developing unity within and beyond the congregation, allowing money to go where the donor cannot.

The Lord's Day

The Lord's day represents a ritual of time which few contemporary Christians appreciate. Many people in our day do not understand its potency.

Though Sunday may have been observed earlier, evidence of it as a recognized day of particular significance for Christians initially emerges around the end of the first century or in the early decades of the second.[23] A number of writers almost certainly refer to it (Rev.1:10;[24] Ignatius *Magnesians* 9;[25] *Didache* 14:1[26]) and the *Epistle of Barnabas* 15 clearly does. Most of these references speak of "the Lord's day," a name that Sunday may well have had from the beginning of its observance.[27]

What Christians intended by denominating their weekly day of worship as "the Lord's day" is best understood in the context of other aspects of worship in the New Testament. As we have seen, in the Lucan tradition the Jerusalem community's appropriation of the temple as their place of worship seems to be related to their sense that Jesus had declared the temple to be "my house." In discussing the Lord's Supper, Paul refers to it as "the Lord's table" (*kyriakon deipnon*, 1 Cor. 11:20). In both of these instances, there is an underlying sense of community united by its relationship to its Lord. He is the one to whom the space in which they come together belongs. Similarly, then, as the Lord's Table provided the physical setting for community worship, so the Lord's Day came to provide the temporal setting for the same community experience.

We should not underestimate the binding power of worship at a set time for all congregations. The adoption of the Lord's Day not only affirmed a common center of faith, but brought to congregations in distant places the sense that they were worshiping "together" at the same time. Like the offering, the Lord's Day transcended the parochialism of particular congregations and made possible to the early church a sense of unity in time despite their scattered location and diversity in language, culture, and experience.

The rituals of structure we have discussed had deep roots in the participatory character of the early church, as suggested by their exclamations, creeds, and hymns. In prayers and sermons, rituals offered unifying forms with flexibility of content. They served both to unite the group and to proclaim the gospel. In offerings and in the Lord's day, these rituals specifically reached across barriers of nationality, race, and culture to unify the early Christian movement. In all these manifestations they provided patterned behavior by which the worship and community life of the church could be recognized and which the traveler might anticipate from one congregation to another.

The amazing strength of these rituals is evidenced by their familiarity to us today. Although we may treat them as almost optional congregational activities, their power is best tested in the experience of those who have tried to change them or to create a new movement by rejecting the rituals of the past. The Quakers, for example, who rejected traditional rituals of worship and introduced the institution of silence, made silence a ritual and restored the most primitive forms of exclamation and confession—the cycle begins again.

We have noted how rituals have strengthened the inner life of the church, at times perhaps too much. Some have suggested that we need rituals to encourage the outreach of the church, such as foot washing as a ritual of humility and service. Others emphasize the need to recover from the first century the power of ritual to balance the local, particular expression of community with a larger, more universal commitment in Jesus Christ. For many contemporary congregations, the primary issue is to recognize the rituals they have inherited and to use them more intentionally.

RITUALS OF MYSTERY

Rituals of mystery are characterized by their capacity to acknowledge and share the ultimately inexplicable experiences of birth and separation, of danger and security, of denial and success, of personal consciousness and community. These rituals are grounded in the same experiences of faith and doubt that prompt cognitive dissonance, liminality, and moments of illumination. In mysteries of faith, the early Christian community did not try to rationalize its profoundest experiences, but rather made the unknown and unexplained character of life a part of the more intimate relationship within the community between the believer and the transcendent God. Here God's presence and human community are joined in the experience of the believers.

To the objective observer, there is nothing intrinsic in the materials, activities, or leadership of any ritual that gives it power—except the faith of the community. But once the community has invested the ritual with essential meaning, repetition of the ritual interprets and empowers the believing community. Further, the whole can be found in any fragment of the experience,[28] like the last of the baby blanket or the shred of a flag to a military command. The mystery sustains a commitment beyond language or explanation.

Two rituals of mystery have been generally accepted as indigenous to the New Testament church: baptism and the Lord's Supper. These have remarkable similarities to two kinds of communal rites which are widely recognized as basic to community life. Arnold van Gennep first noted the use of ritual in transitional experiences, which he called "rites of passage,"[29] while Elliot D. Chapple and Carlton S. Coon have emphasized the use of ritual in community-affirming experiences which they call "rites of intensification."[30]

Rites of passage are shared in those patterns of behavior that emphasize transition—birth, entry into adulthood, marriage, acceptance in social groups, and separation through declining authority and death. Rites at such transitional moments are important not only to the individual but to the community as well. *Rites of intensification* rehearse and affirm the meaning of belonging—celebrations such as Christmas and Easter in the church, July 4th and Thanksgiving Day in the United States, birthdays and special anniversaries in the family. In rituals of intensification, social history and basic values of belonging are remembered and reshaped to fit the needs of the current situation.

One function of ritual is to act out experience that goes beyond words of explanation. In one of the best-known scenes in *Faust*, Goethe portrays the doctor, in his search for revelation, as throwing open his New Testament at the Gospel of John and starting to translate it into his "beloved German":

> 'Tis written: "In the Beginning was the *Word*."
> Here am I balked: who, now can help afford?
> The *Word?*—impossible so high to rate it,
> If by the Spirit I am truly taught.
> Then thus: "In the Beginning was the *Thought*."
> This first line let me weight completely,
> Lest my impatient pen proceed too fleetly.
> Is it the *Thought* which works, creates, indeed?
> "In the Beginning was the *Power*," I read.
> Yet, as I write, a warning is suggested,
> That I the sense may not have fairly tested.
> The Spirit aids me: now I see the light!
> "In the Beginning was the *Act*," I write.[31]

These lines, which portray so succinctly Goethe's philosophy of life-in-action, may also be applied to our understanding of ritual, particularly "rituals of mystery." In such moments the deed precedes both word and thought. As John Burkhart remarks,

Anyone who has ever tried to master the intricacies of chess knows that playing it, however clumsily, is far more illuminating than talking about it. And every lover knows that all the poems and treatises about lovemaking are simply tedious facts or dancing shadows compared with making love. For embodied creatures, reality lives, it works and plays, in enactment.[32]

We shall consider baptism and eucharist as the two major rituals of Christian mystery. While the term *mystērion* was not applied to these rituals until after the period we are studying, many of the dimensions of the word were already inherent in them: understandings available only to those within the community of faith, a sense of the presence of the transcendent, eschatologically oriented faith. With remarkable consistency baptism and eucharist, even more than the rituals of structure, have maintained their central role in Christian life and practice for two thousand years across a world of cultures and despite the spectrum of interpretations to which they have been subjected. The integrity of the act has transcended varieties of interpretation and encouraged constant renewal of faith within the community. Celebrating both divine presence and communal unity, it strengthens the believing community by its unique combination of the sacred and the mundane.

Baptism: Borrowed and Transformed

Baptism provided the boundary marker for community acceptance in the early church, the gate (marker) which acknowledged the shared experience in Christ through which the believer must pass to be accepted as a member of the community. In the New Testament church, (1) the ritual drew from Judaism both its use of water and its grounding in a relationship with God, rather than the magic of the act itself. (2) In the memory of the church baptism was attached to a powerfully charismatic figure, John the Baptist, while its practice is downplayed in the early Jesus movement. (3) Paul's insight that baptism is related to dynamic union with Christ was enhanced by Luke's understanding that it involves action by the Holy Spirit. (4) Eventually baptism was regularized and institutionalized as essential for order and a means of control.

More Than Magic: A Relationship With God

Rituals of washing with water were common enough in the religions of the Greco-Roman world. They were characteristic, for instance, of both the Eleusinian and the Isiac mysteries and constituted a central element in Jewish piety. Neither Gentiles nor Jews, on coming in contact with Christianity, would have found a ritual such as baptism surprising. Especially in Judaism, there was much that constituted a background for the Christian rite. The laws of the Pentateuch dealing with ritual purity constantly employ water as the means by which impurity is to be removed. In the Judaism of the first century, this, as with much of the Torah, had been extended to include many details of life, so that the observant Jew was continually engaged in ritual washings both at home and in the *miqweh*, a ritual pool or tank in which one could immerse oneself (cf. Mark 7:1–4). In the Mishnah an entire tractate is devoted to the laws regarding such washings (*Miqwaoth*).

A special case of such ablution was that of a person who became a proselyte. In addition to the requirements of circumcision and the offering of a sacrifice, the convert was expected also to undergo an immersion in water (b. *Yebamoth* 46a–47b).[33] This rite thus provided a parallel to Christian baptism in the sense of a lustral use of water at the point of entry into a new religious community and way of life.

It is a mistake to think of the rituals of Israel as "purely symbolic" on the one hand, or as some kind of magical rite on the other. They were an acting out of the covenant relationship with Yahweh; but in washing with water, as with other rituals, Israelites were not only dramatizing their covenant relationship, they were actually doing something that made the covenant effective for themselves as a community. For this reason, the observance of such rituals could be a matter of life or death (e.g., Num. 19:13, 20).

In the Qumran community, washings with water were important, as is reflected especially in the *Manual of Discipline*, a document that sets forth the system of rules that governed the community's life. Of particular importance for Christian baptism is the ethical dimension they assumed. The *Manual of Discipline* understands that the quality of human action is determined by two spirits, the spirit of truth or "spirit of holiness" (*rwh qdwšh*) and the spirit of falsehood. Speaking of an evil man, the *Manual* declares:

> He shall be cleansed from all his sins by the spirit of holiness uniting him to His truth. . . . And when his flesh is sprinkled with purifying water and sanctified by cleansing water, it shall be made clean by the humble submission of his soul to all the precepts of God (III. 7–9).[34]

Similarly, the *Manual* warns:

> They ["the men of falsehood who walk in the way of wickedness"] shall not enter the water to partake of the pure Meal of the saints, for they shall not be cleansed unless they turn from their wickedness: for all who transgress His word are unclean (V. 13–14).[35]

Here the rituals of washing are impotent unless accompanied by the action of the "spirit of holiness," by repentance,[36] and by a reformation of life. In this we can sense the dynamic understanding of ritual which Christians received from Judaism, in which the effectiveness of the rite depends on a relationship with the deity. This stands in marked contrast to magic, where the ritual is a means by which one constrains the god to perform a desired action.

John the Baptist: Judgment, Repentance and New Beginnings

In their early tradition concerning the origin of baptism, Christians focused their memories on John, a charismatic figure whom they designated, significantly, as the "Baptist." John became a symbol of judgment and repentance and justice, standing between the old world and new beginnings.

All we know directly of the baptism preached and practiced by John comes to us from Christian sources, which, on the one hand, see it as an intentional forerunner of the Christian rite and, on the other, are at pains to distinguish the uniqueness of the Christian practice. This evidence suggests that the prime characteristic of John's rite was that it was "a baptism of repentance for the forgiveness of sins" (Mark 1:4). In this it stood close to the washings practiced at Qumran. At the same time, John's baptism exhibits marked contrasts with the rite as performed and understood there. At Qumran, as with Jewish lustrations in general, it was performed repeatedly, and there is no clear evidence that it was an initiatory rite; all indications are that John's baptism was performed but once and signaled the beginning of a new orientation of life, which, in contrast to Qumran, carried with it the forgiveness of past sins.[37] While at least the Christian perspective on John depicts him in terms of Isa. 40:3, a passage that the Qumran community also used to describe itself (*Manual of Discipline* VIII. 13–14), it is not clear that John's wide-ranging invitation to baptism ("all the country of Judea," "all the people of Jerusalem," [Mark 1:5]; tax collectors, soldiers [Luke 3:12–14]) was understood as a call to enter a community. Rather than functioning as an element in community formation or maintenance, the baptism of John seems to have involved an individualized experience of ethical reorientation and a sense of freedom from sin.[38] This may also relate to the fact that while the washing rituals at Qumran were an "arcane discipline," a rite conducted within the intimacy of the community, baptism as practiced by John was a public act. It implied not withdrawal from the world but, according to Luke's account, a new rectitude of life within it (Luke 3:10–14).

Significantly we have even less information about baptism practiced by the Jesus movement than we do regarding that of John the Baptist. The synoptic tradition knows nothing of it; only the Gospel of John mentions that Jesus and his disciples baptized (3:22, 26), and then specifies that "Jesus himself did not baptize, but only his disciples" (4:2). The latter remark is probably motivated by the Fourth Evangelist's evident concern to distinguish Jesus and his movement clearly from John's (e.g., John 1:19–34; 3:27–30) so that Jesus is not seen as another Baptist. At the same time, by portraying Jesus' disciples as baptizing (and indeed more successfully than John!), the Jesus movement is shown as in no way falling short of that which the Baptist offered. If indeed Jesus or his disciples did practice baptism, the rite was hardly central to their mission. It probably was understood to involve repentance and forgiveness (as with John) in view of the imminence of the kingdom. Rather, the early church held on to the symbolic memory of John the Baptist as the untamed voice from the wilderness, announcing judgment and calling to repentance.

Earliest Vision Reinforced by Gift
of the Spirit

Christian baptism emerges clearly with the post-Easter community. Paul's personal practice as an evangelist exhibited ambivalence regarding baptism (1 Cor. 1:14–16), evidently because of political dynamics within his situation (as with Jesus?). But clearly he supported the rite and understood its implications both for freedom from sin and for unity of believers with Christ in hope of the resurrection: "All of us who have been baptized into Christ Jesus were baptized into his death. . . . For if we have been united with him in a death like his, we shall certainly be united with him in a resurrection like his. We know that our old self was crucified with him so that . . . we might no longer be enslaved to sin" (Rom. 6:3, 5–6).

The vision of Christian solidarity in baptism is made explicit by another, unknown Christian writing in Paul's shadow. Reflecting a liturgical practice of divesting oneself of one's old clothing and donning a new garment at baptism, he declares: "You have put off the old nature with its practices and have put on the new nature, which is being renewed in knowledge after the image of its creator. Here there cannot be Greek and Jew, circumcised and uncircumcised, barbarian, Scythian, slave, free man, but Christ is all, and in all" (Col. 3:9–11). The new life in Christ, signaled by baptism, transcends all racial, social, and economic barriers. This ritual of mystery (cf. Col. 1:26–27; Eph. 3:2–6), which flew in the face of the then socially acceptable hierarchy of humanity, provided a basis for establishing and maintaining the new community "in Christ."

Luke, whose historical perspective on the Christian community we have noted before, above all others in the New Testament makes baptism focal in the development of the early church. In a new way Luke linked baptism and the gift of the Holy Spirit. Here he stands in contrast to Paul, who in discussing the gifts of the Spirit makes no allusion to baptism. But in Luke's view Christian baptism is proclaimed at the very beginning of the church, at Pentecost, when Peter declares: "Repent, and be baptized everyone of you in the name of Jesus Christ for the forgiveness of your sins; and you shall receive the gift of the Holy Spirit" (Acts 2:38). Obviously for Luke, this is an extension of John the Baptist's promise, "He will baptize you with the Holy Spirit and with fire" (Luke 3:16), which in the case of the apostles has just been fulfilled.

Luke's introduction of baptism at Pentecost helps to explain why, for him at least, there is no recognition of its practice in the Jesus movement. This point of view on baptism is also consonant with the adoptionist Christology of Peter's Pentecost sermon: "Let all the house of Israel therefore know assuredly that God has made him both Lord and Christ, this Jesus whom you crucified" (Acts 2:36). This, in turn, helps us to understand what is unique for Luke in Christian baptism: it is "in the name of Jesus." Like the baptism of John, it is for the forgiveness of sins; in fulfillment of John's prediction, it is accompanied by the gift of the Holy Spirit (which also echoes the faith of Qumran), but now that Jesus has been made "both Lord and Christ" its central characteristic and dynamic lies "in the name of Jesus." This constitutes its distinctively Christian character.

The remainder of the Book of Acts can be seen as the spelling out of the story of the acts of the Spirit under the banner of baptism in the name of Jesus. Luke rings the changes on this theme. The usual pattern seems to have been that converts were baptized and then, with the laying on of hands, received the Holy Spirit; but at the point where the first Gentile is converted, Luke's story reverses the sequence. With evident humor he recounts how to Peter's amazement the Spirit falls on unbaptized Gentiles, which then leaves the apostle with no alternative but to baptize them (Acts 10:44–48; 11:15–18)! Here, as the boundaries of the community expand, the borders of baptism grow with it.

Baptism: Regularizing the Mystery

As the church grew more and more into an institution, it was inevitable that a ritual of such power and significance as baptism should be regularized. This can be understood from the standpoint both of a concern to assure careful handling of a ritual of mystery that controlled entry to the church and of the power it gave those who were qualified to administer it.

The regularizing of baptismal ritual can already be glimpsed in the later books of the New Testament. We have noted the allusion to the removal of old garments before baptism and the donning of new afterward that is implicit in Col. 3:3–11 (and possibly as early as Gal. 3:27). From a liturgical standpoint, the earliest elaboration of the primitive baptism "in the name of Jesus" appears at the end of the Gospel of Matthew where the Risen Lord is portrayed as instructing his disciples to baptize their converts "in the name of the Father and of the Son and of the Holy Spirit" (Matt. 28:19). This represents a development at least as early as the eighties. The same formula appears in what apparently is one of the earlier sections of the *Didache*, probably written in the East during the early years of the second century. Included with it are the following instructions:

Now concerning baptism. Baptize as follows, when you have rehearsed the aforesaid teaching: Baptize in the name of the Father and of the Son and of the Holy Spirit, in running water. But if you do not have running water, use warm. But if you have neither, pour water on the head three times—in the name of Father, Son and Holy Spirit. And prior to baptism, both he who is baptizing and he who is being baptized should fast, along with any others who can. And be sure that the one who is to be baptized fasts for one or two days beforehand (7:1–4).[39]

Writing from Rome at the middle of the second century, Justin Martyr gives essentially the same description of Christian baptismal practice (*First Apology* 61).[40] What is striking in both the *Didache* and Justin is the degree to which the ritual had become standardized over a wide area, together with the tone of authority with which the stipulations for its performance are laid down in the *Didache*. We can sense that a ritual of mystery was becoming institutionalized within the structure of the church.

A further aspect of this development has to do with the authority for administering the rite. In the New Testament there is no rule as to who is qualified to baptize. The earliest Christian writer to discuss the question is Ignatius, writing about A.D. 110 to the Christians of Smyrna in Asia Minor. He declares, "It is not right either to baptize or to celebrate the agape apart from the bishop; but whatever he approves is also pleasing to God—so that everything you do may be secure and valid" (*Smyrnaeans* 8:2).[41]

Admittedly not all Christian communities had reached as extreme a view of the authority of the bishop as that reflected by Ignatius in the early second century. Nevertheless the trend toward regularizing and controlling the mystery so dramatically reflected by him was predictable in terms of the social dynamics of a developing institution. A ritual that at the same time stood as the recognized door to the church and to the salvation it offered yet was fraught with such weight of symbolism could not be allowed to run at will. Discipline in the administration of the ritual was important. By the same token, those in whose hands the authority for its administration was lodged found themselves in possession of massive leverage. Control of the mystery was essential to the governance of the institutionalized church.

Baptism as Boundary and Transition

Two interwoven understandings of baptism can be discerned: first, baptism as boundary in the early church, the barrier against the world within which worldly differences could be transcended and all sorts of people could live together in harmony (e.g., Col. 3:9–11); second, baptism as a rite of passage in which the believer acknowledged within the community a new perspective gained by new experience shared with the Lord (e.g., Acts 9:17–19). In the contemporary church we see these issues confused and obscured: (1) baptism as the entry of new members, from babes in arms to members of the teen-age "confirmation class" to mature adults who have had a life-changing experience; and (2) baptism as a rite of passage which may have even broader implications through the church's sacramental affirmation of significant transitions in people's lives. Furthermore, the elements of baptism—washing, charismatic source, new community, confirmation of the Spirit, order without interference—have been preserved in unique and sometimes compelling ways.

Baptism as Membership. Rediscovery of the historic meaning and power of baptism in the New Testament causes some embarrassment in most mainline churches. With the advent of infant baptism, the boundaries of the counterculture church were softened. The foundations of Christian commitment shifted from an adult decision to the education of children who were already "in." This cultural compromise of Christian commitment prompted Karl Barth to suggest that baptism and confirmation amounted to two "half sacraments."[42]

Many churches have attempted to distinguish different kinds of entry. The moment of infant baptism retains peculiar power in most congregations, a time when parents are open to change and members lean forward with a smile and a memory. In a child the congregation sees the joy of the family, and the promise of covenant continuity. In the confirmation of youth, the congregation celebrates the generations of faith within community and a milestone on the road toward responsible adult decisions. In the baptism and acceptance of adults, members of the congregation may feel their faith confirmed (as in cognitive dissonance) and the Christian body enlarged, stretched, and sometimes challenged. All of these moments may be included in "baptism," but they have greatest impact when they are treated as different experiences: for the infant, presentation; for the youth, a challenge; for the adult, initiation into an affirming and challenging community.

Such a distinction allows the congregation to celebrate each in a distinctive way. The arrival of a child, particularly the first child, may be of more significance than the rituals of marriage in a contemporary culture where the boundaries between courtship and nesting have been blurred. Rituals that surround the advent of the first child—correspondence, social gatherings, classes, announcements, relationships with doctors and medical institutions, and the subsequent presence of the child in a variety of social settings—all suggest a new status for parents and even grandparents. Though the actions are focused on the child, the effect is to socialize all the participants into their new estate. Often at the time of "presenting" their child, parents are more willing to explore their own relationships to God, to each other, to the church, and to the larger community. In the baptism of a child, the focus of transition is on the parents, and often "a little child shall lead them" to a richer, more durable faith.

The confirmation of youth provides an opportunity for teen-agers to explore the traditions of the church, including the challenge of its countercultural expectations. This is not the "second half" of infant baptism, but like the commencement rituals teen-agers also experience it is the beginning of even larger demands for commitments as adults. But confirmation can be a terminal event, the completion of the religious journey, unless it is coupled with recognition of more adult "initiation" into the church. Some Roman Catholic congregations have attempted to recover the fourth-century rites of initiation, and some Protestant churches have developed a series of recognition and "re-confirmation" events for significant times in the lives of adults in the Christian community.[43] The implications of this are clear: the efficacy of infant baptism depends on celebrations (rituals) in which it is reaffirmed not only in confirmation (as a teen-ager) but even more in the transitional events of more adult life experiences. Without communal recognition of adult passages, the half sacraments of baptism-confirmation become terminal. The entry may be once, but the "baptismal" affirmations continue as many milestones in faith.

Baptism as Rite of Passage. The contemporary church retains a wide variety of rites of passage in celebrating marriage, ordaining officers, installing pastors, and even in the more mundane acts of greeting visitors and "passing the peace" among those who share worship. In each of these activities, basic commitments of the congregation are articulated in the rubrics and acted out by the participants. Such activities say far more about the congregation than an exterior sign which says, Welcome, or a printed bulletin which proclaims a church as friendly.

Death in the congregation may rehearse the most compelling rites of passage, when the family and friends who share the loss are supported by the larger community of which they are a part. More than just the funeral, the actions of the congregation express their feelings and reweave the bond that holds them as community. Touching, standing or sitting together, flowers, brief notes, music, especially shared silence are often far more powerful than the spoken word of Christian doctrine. Families and communities develop rituals to carry them across the threshold from one relationship to another.

In congregational life the departure of significant families or the arrival of a new pastor often provide for new rites of passage to be acted in ways that expose the values of the church to review and recommitment. Such transitional moments are often disturbing and sometimes threatening to the stability of a congregation. In times of crisis and decision Martin Luther found reassurance in performing baptism. In the same way some congregations use such threshold events to reassess and affirm the deepest commitments that hold them together "in Christ." Sometimes the articulation is extraneous. People need an action in which they can participate physically. They need what baptism provides: a worshipful way to let go of the past and affirm the presence of God as they move into the future.

Preservation of the Elements

The rites of baptism are not automatically associated with every transitional event, but we can recognize the presence of the Spirit when the elements of baptismal *mystērion* are remembered and encouraged. Baptism includes water—at least the symbolic washing of the past, the letting go of evil ambitions and destructive relationships. As with the mentor, John the Baptist, the efficacy of baptism does not depend on particular actions of official leaders. But it is marked by new relationship with God and therefore ignores or denies the power of worldly status, class, race, nationality, and gender. Baptism is experienced in the healing power of the Holy Spirit to make a person whole, sometimes symbolized by the laying on of hands but always by identification with God's poor, the *ptōchoi*, the renewal of faith, *pistis*, and the commitment to peace, *eirēnē*.

Eucharist: Sacred Space

Since the beginning of Christianity, spiritual nourishment for the journey of individuals and the community has been provided by the sacrament of the Eucharist. Called Eucharist (Thanksgiving) in some traditions and the Lord's Supper or the Lord's Table in others, this sacrament of intensification has a variety of names which reflect both the intimacy it engenders and the power it holds for believers. Antecedents of this sacrament existed in both Jewish and Hellenistic Roman culture, but its most profound contribution to the building of Christian community derived from the conviction that Christ was uniquely present in the celebration. In the New Testament memory of the Lord's Supper, we see how mystery becomes both a stabilizing and a prophetic force in shaping the early church. Thus we note (1) historical sources for the eucharist, (2) the dimensions of conflict in its celebration in Corinth, (3) the use of mystery as sacred space to exclude Christian enemies and confirm Christian community, and (4) the role of sacrament in the maintenance of the counterculture community.

Historical Sources of the Eucharist

Communal meals with religious import were familiar to both Jews and Gentiles. In developing the eucharistic celebration, early Christians drew consciously and unconsciously on a wealth of precedents in both Jewish and pagan religions. These help us to appreciate the richness of the heritage of meaning embodied in the Lord's Supper and to evaluate its role in the social dynamics of early Christianity.

The celebration of communal meals as a religious act lay deep in the history of Israelite piety. We think, of course, in the first instance of the Passover; it was, however, only the chief among several ritual feasts. These were celebrated as times of joy, or peace and well-being (shalom), and as memorials to the dead (e.g., Jer. 16:5–7; Ezek. 24:17, 22). In the last-mentioned case especially, bread and wine are mentioned as central to the memorial meal.

In early Christian times we read in rabbinic literature of Haburoth, organizations of Pharisees who met together regularly for religiously oriented meals which also included memorial meals for the dead.[44] Of particular interest, however, are the sacred meals at Qumran. In the Dead Sea Scrolls stipulations are laid down for their ritual celebration: "And when the table has been prepared for eating, and the new wine for drinking, the Priest shall be the first to stretch out his hand to bless the firstfruits of the bread and new wine" (Manual of Discipline VI. 4–5).[45]

Furthermore, the meals at Qumran were focused eschatologically, for they were understood as anticipatory celebrations of a future banquet when the Messiah would feast with his people.[46] In a document beginning with the words, "This is the rule for all the congregation of Israel in the last days," the following regulations are laid down, which are virtually identical with those regularly observed by the Qumran community, except that now the Messiah is present. After the priest has blessed the bread and wine, "The Messiah of Israel shall extend his hand over the bread, [and] all the Congregation of the Community [shall utter a] blessing, [each man in the order] of his dignity" (The Messianic Rule II.17–22).[47]

It is clear, then, that most of the themes embodied in the Lord's

Supper as described in the New Testament (Matt. 26:26–30; Mark 14:22–26; Luke 22:15–19; 1 Cor. 11:23–26) are found in one context or another in Jewish religious meals: (a) the blessing, the breaking and eating of bread, (b) the drinking of wine, (c) the covenantal basis of the ritual, (d) its performance within the bounds of the community, (e) its function as a memorial for one who had died, and (f) the fact that it is anticipatory of a meal with the Messiah in the kingdom to come. All these were thematic of Jewish meals before the emergence of Christianity; they were in the air of early Christianity. In celebrating the Eucharist, the first Christians followed familiar patterns of action and thought.

A Uniquely Christian Supper

The central element unique to Christianity in the Eucharist is the figure of Jesus; viewed looking back, he is the offering for the remission of sin, embodied in the bread and wine; looking forward, he is the Messiah to come with whom his people will drink the wine "new" in his kingdom.[48] The presence of Jesus means that the ritual embraces the entirety of the New Covenant.

The social impact of ritual meals in the early Christian communities is particularly evident in the congregation at Corinth. In Paul's correspondence with that church he gives the fullest discussion of his understanding of the Lord's Supper. While he does not appeal to the exclusiveness of the congregation in the way we find it at Qumran, he is sharply aware of the sacred nature of the meal; for him the rite itself has an exclusivity that cannot be transgressed without mortal danger. The elements come to have, as Gerd Theissen remarks, a "numinous quality."[49] Paul asks the Corinthians, "The cup of blessing which we bless, is it not a participation in the blood of Christ? The bread which we break, is it not a participation in the body of Christ? Because there is one bread, we who are many are one body, for we all partake of the one bread" (1 Cor. 10:16–17). Having then discussed issues that threaten to fracture the community, he concludes: "Whoever, therefore, eats the bread or drinks the cup of the Lord in an unworthy manner will be guilty of profaning the body and blood of the Lord. . . . For anyone who eats and drinks without discerning the body eats and drinks judgment upon himself. That is why many of you are weak and ill, and some have died" (1 Cor. 11:27, 29–30). The eucharist thus has come to lie in "a taboo zone, where violating the norm brings with it incalculable disaster."[50] This taboo zone, which depends upon theological expectation and social imagination, provides the basis of our discussion.

Conflict in Corinth

The dynamic quality of mystery evidenced here is couched in a situation of social conflict. Mystical as Paul's argument may be, it was no abstract speculation but was grounded in the social realities of the Corinthian congregation. As every pastor and church leader will recognize, this was a "good fight" in the Corinthian church. Since he is writing to the participants in the conflict, Paul has no need to spell out its exact nature, and we are thus left in at least semidarkness as to what was really at the root of their difficulties. Paul describes the phenomena of the situation. The congregation is divided in several ways but particularly over matters of food. Some count it a sin to eat meat offered previously in a pagan temple to a god; others, considering themselves "strong," do not. Furthermore, in the ritual meals of the congregation, which combined agape and eucharist, the communal element is being eroded and the spirit of agape lost, so that, as Paul says, "When you meet together, it is not the Lord's supper that you eat" (1 Cor. 11:20). Rather than waiting to eat together, each one eats when he or she desires. The well-to-do bring large amounts of food and gorge themselves, while the poor go hungry. Christian unity in social diversity is being sorely tested.

What lay behind these abuses has been assessed in different ways. From the perspective of the history of religions, Bo Reicke has seen the problem surrounding the meals as arising from the teachings of "docetic, libertinistic Gnostics who were at the same time Judaistic";[51] taking the Old Testament prophecies of the glories of the Messianic kingdom literally, they celebrated its fulfillment by indulging in sumptuous feasts (cf. Isa. 25:6–8). Docetically rejecting a suffering redeemer, they gave ebullient expression to their joy in a glorified one. Their gnostic inclinations led them to emphasize individual religious experience and salvation at the expense of a concern for the community. Reicke cites the later Cerinthians and Ebionites as groups that exhibited comparable characteristics.[52]

More recently Gerd Theissen has approached this problem from a socioeconomic standpoint and has arrived at a different analysis. He understands the basic cleavage in the Corinthian congregation to have been between the well-to-do and the poor. Only those who were at least relatively affluent could have afforded to buy meat, so the strong who felt themselves free to eat meat offered to idols must have been from among this group. The tensions that developed within the communal meals reflect the same division. In pagan contexts at least it was common for poorer guests to be served more sparsely than wealthy ones at the same feast, and such practices apparently had penetrated the Christian agape-eucharist. As the congregations met in private homes, only those members who could afford houses large enough to contain the congregation would have been in the position of host; the more wealthy were thus to some degree in charge of arrangements, and their attitudes set the pace of the proceedings.[53]

Both theological and sociological factors, as described by Reicke and Theissen, may have been disruptive in the Corinthian congregation. While it is difficult to be specific in identifying the doctrinal views of the troublesome elements there as "gnostic" or "docetic," since clear evidence of such groups in the church comes to light only at a later time, these tendencies may have been already in the air. Paul seems to feel the church is being corrupted by materialistic eschatological expectations coupled with a highly individualistic concept of salvation seen in the behavior of more affluent members in the church who felt themselves strong in thinking and acting for themselves without reference to the viewpoints of others. Something more compelling would be necessary to unite them.

Eucharistic Mystērion: *Sacred Space*

Paul understood the unity of the church to be grounded in a common experience which was clearly distinguishable from its surrounding culture. Stephen C. Barton has recently drawn attention to the anthropology of social boundaries in connection with the disorderliness in the agape-eucharist at Corinth. He notes that social boundaries are often seen as areas of anxiety fraught with danger and that a common way of coping with this danger is through ritual action by which the sacredness of the boundary is maintained. We have already seen how both at Qumran and in the early Christian congregations communal meals served to set a boundary between the community and the world outside. This helps us to understand, then, why Paul was so deeply concerned over the ruptures that were occurring within the very ritual that signaled the community's integrity, and why he saw these as a cause of illness and death.[54] There is an anthropological dimension to Paul's sense of the mystic, numinous nature of the eucharistic rite.

The power of this "mystery" underlies Paul's strategy in countering the developing problems at Corinth. He rightly saw that the root of the difficulty lay in a misapprehension of the sacredness of the ritual meal. The sacred space, the "taboo zone," it occupies, which marks off the boundaries of the community and thus makes possible its unity, was being vitiated; the result was that "there are divisions among you" (1 Cor. 11:18). Paul's response, then, was to emphasize the mystical dimension of the meal: to partake of the wine and the bread which has been blessed is a *koinōnia* of the blood and body of Christ. We should allow the word *koinōnia* here its range of meanings, which include both "fellowship" and "participation." To partake of the meal is to have a fellowship that derives from and is characterized by the offered life of Christ; such a fellowship binds the community. At the same time to partake of the meal is to participate in that life and in Christ's body, the church. This latter sense is particularly apparent here in view of the following verse: "We who are many are one body, for we all partake of one bread" (1 Cor. 10:17). Paul's sense of the numinous nature of the rite is emphasized again in his warning: "For any one who eats and drinks without discerning the body eats and drinks judgment upon himself" (1 Cor. 11:29). The arrogance of affluence and individualism denied identity with the *ptōchoi*—God's poor, and destroyed *eirēnē*—the right relations within the community. To ignore the theological and social unity of the community and yet to participate in the meal is to transgress a sacred boundary. Although angry with their behavior, Paul continued to call them an *ekklēsia* because in the *mystērion* of the ritual there remained the prospect of God's intervening power.

Eucharist and Social Tensions

We are not told of the outcome of Paul's efforts to restore unity to the Corinthian congregation through his assertion of the true nature of the agape-eucharist. It is clear, however, that this ritual meal continued to be an arena where the value of spiritual unity within the church was challenged by pressures from the world outside. We note, then, two developments: the separation of the eucharist from the agape meal, and the enhancement of the sacramental sense of the eucharist along with a tendency toward regularization of its ritual.

In the Epistle of Jude, written perhaps around the turn of the first century, we encounter a scathing warning against "ungodly persons who pervert the grace of our God" (Jude 4) by insinuating themselves into Christian communities, spreading false teaching, and leading licentious lives. Jude mentions the agape-meals in particular as a setting for their nefarious influence within the community: "These are blemishes on your love feasts" (Jude 12). Writing probably at about the same time, the author of the *First Epistle of Clement* (3:1–2), though not mentioning the agape specifically, relates the disorders in the Corinthian church of his time in part to excesses in food and drink. This suggests that the problems of a half-century or more before had not permanently been solved. It seems likely that gluttony and disorder may all too often have infected the communal meals of early Christian congregations,[55] and that this may have been a factor in the ultimate separation of the agape meal from the eucharist in the second century. While agape and Eucharist are still united in the *Didache*, by the middle of the century, at least in Rome, significant changes had taken place. Justin Martyr (*Apology* 1.67) describes the Sunday worship services there: Scripture (the prophets and the "memoirs of the apostles") is read and expounded, there are prayers, and then the eucharist is celebrated. Nothing is said of an agape-meal. This was an important shift; in moving the Eucharist away from the context of the more informal agape and incorporating it into an increasingly fixed liturgical service of worship,[56] we can sense an effort to safeguard it from the excesses to which the former too frequently had become subject.

Of equal importance was the enhancement of the sense of mystery surrounding the Eucharist and an increasing regularization of this ritual. We have seen how Paul, in attempting to stop the abuses current at Corinth in his time, stressed the numinous character of the meal. By the early second century this development became more and more distinct. Thus Ignatius of Antioch in his mystical way could declare: "I desire the bread of God, which is the flesh of Jesus Christ, . . . and for drink I desire his blood, which is imperishable love" (*Epistle to the Romans* 7:3). Similarly, the "one loaf . . . is the medicine of immortality, the antidote which results not in dying but in living forever in Jesus Christ" (*Epistle to the Ephesians* 20:2).[57] The *Didache* (9–10) gives specific instruction for the celebration of the Eucharist and specifies the prayers that are to be offered.

The trends that we have observed in the development of the Eucharist over the first century and a half of Christian history have been deplored by many. The divorce between Eucharist and agape deprived the former of its "homely" setting in the physical and social life of the community and intensified the separation of the sacred from the secular. This move went hand in hand, of course, with an increasing sense of the sacramental nature of the Lord's Supper (in the early second century the *Didache* [14:1–2] can refer to it as "your sacrifice"). While we are still far from later attempts to define the nature of the Eucharist in philosophical terms, the increasing sense of mystery is reflected in the figurative language used.

But when these developments are viewed from the standpoint of the social dynamics involved, we can appreciate them as responses to the pressures and threats with which the early church had to contend. It is impossible to second-guess what would have been the outcome had

Christian communities reacted differently to dangers within and without. What is clear is that the developments that took place in Baptism and the Eucharist, the rituals of mystery, were successful in the sense that they served to solidify and maintain the church as a spiritual institution in history.

Eucharist: Nourishing the Christian Vision

Celebration of the Lord's Supper provides the classic expression of the rites of intensification.[58] Across successive centuries of diverse national cultures and contradictory theological expressions, the story of faith has been acted out in ritual through which believers could participate. Although language has changed and emphases have shifted, from the perspective of social dynamics in the church, enacting the *mystērion* has had its own renewing effect. Those rituals of structure, hymns, creeds, prayers, offerings, and preaching, which surround the rituals of mystery, Baptism and Eucharist, have remained remarkably intact. This is doubtless due to the centrality of the latter as bearers of "mystery" and as rituals of transition (Baptism) and intensification (Eucharist). We note (1) the power of mystery carried in ritual, (2) the sacramental reinforcement of personal faith, community identity, and eschatological hope, and (3) the impact of acting out faith as a living sacrifice (sacrament).

Power of Mystery

Mystērion still sustains the power of the eucharist. The direct relationship between God and the believer remains the binding force that preserves the revolutionary nature of the Christian community. Within its "sacred boundaries" all social distinctions can disappear and all secular authority is seen in the perspective of God's expectations.

Even where some form of the agape meal or love feast continues it is clearly distinguished from the mystery of the Eucharist. Most congregations have annual community events in which the table is central, such as the Mother's Day breakfast or the fall Harvest Festival. In such events faith is strengthened and story is retold through the program and the speaker, and even more through rituals of sharing food and telling stories. Such "church family suppers" remain important reminders of both the love feast in the early church and the example for the eucharist. But most congregations do not try to reunite the Lord's Supper and the Love Feast except for unusual, "experimental" events. Instinctively we seek to avoid experiences like those reported in 1 Corinthians and Jude by protecting the Lord's Table; contemporary church suppers are too informal and the Eucharist is too sacred.

Communal Consciousness

Compared with the way Paul drew on the Eucharist to develop communal consciousness among the Christians at Corinth, many contemporary Communion practices and meditations appear to reinforce the affluent individualism that he deplored. His response to the Corinthian church shows us that in our time we have overemphasized the individual dimensions of Communion, and misunderstood the power of the *mystērion* in both sacraments of Baptism and the Lord's Supper.

More broadly, however, and based on a sense of community similar to Paul's at Corinth, many contemporary congregations have expanded the affirmation (intensification) of faith beyond traditional Christian holidays such as Christmas and Easter (and the larger Christian calendar) to include special celebrations on national holidays like Thanksgiving and Independence Day, and personal holidays, like birthdays and anniversaries. In these events they reflect the *ekklēsia* with its combination of public concern and Christian distinctiveness. In protecting their sacred space, both history and anticipation are important: they remember how God moved them from beyond time and place. In the *mystērion* of common thanksgiving (Eucharist) they become the body of Christ in the world.

When the church sees itself as the body of Christ and sees the Eucharist as its memory and hope, it acts out its ministry through its behavior in the world. Thus Avery Dulles suggests:

> The church becomes an actual event of grace when it appears most concretely as a sacrament—that is, in the actions of the church as such whereby men are bound together in grace by a visible expression. The more widely and intensely the faithful participate in this corporate action of the Church, the more the Church achieves itself.[59]

Eucharist as Unity of Sacrifice

In more than any other single setting, in the Eucharist the threads of the Christian symbolic universe are woven into a single design. God's invitation to the table requires the sacrifice of our worldly wealth so we may identify with those God loves and has invited with us to the table, God's poor, the *ptōchoi*. At the table of our Lord we sacrifice our worldly perception and see the world through eyes of faith, *pistis*. Gathered in God's keeping we turn our backs on worldly status and share those right relations through which God reigns in peace, *eirēnē*. Each act is a sacrifice of an old perspective and a gain of both new insight and conviction. To the believer within the Christian community, such sacrifice brings reward.

Thus one member of a Christian community recorded her impressions as she experienced her church moving toward deeper commitment. In this case, the congregation struggled with the question whether it should become a "sanctuary church" to provide protection for a Christian family of refugees from a war-torn country in Central America. After describing the difficulty of making a decision because of external conflict with government policy and internal conflict among members, she wrote:

> To a large extent the community as a whole really did experience something of a conversion. People did things they had never done before. We raised money from nowhere, found food for a family of six for many weeks. An apartment materialized (through much work) from the church's gym, when we had never before been able to clean it up! We did a lot we never dreamed we could do. People within the church met others they had not known before. The next two membership classes were triple the normal size with people joining because of the sanctuary project. We were amazed! For many it was the first time ideals and ethics were focused and verbalized and questioned and reconfirmed. It was a very powerful time and it felt good. I remember one Sunday morning walking in as people gathered around the altar for communion, which was our custom. The celebrant was talking about how our cup "runneth over" and as he spoke, he poured the cup full allowing it to run over (into a larger container!). It was a simple symbolic act, and yet the presence of the Holy Spirit and the love of the people gathered was so tangible that the atmosphere was almost overwhelming. That gesture reduced me to tears, but they were tears of joy. For a moment I experienced what the eucharist was about.[60]

Such sacred space has preserved the church through the centuries. These rites of initiation and intensification provide protected contact between the believer and the divine, and a sacred boundary to preserve the revolutionary vision of Christian community in the world. Through the centuries they have made available an area for the spiritual encounter of individuals and the prophetic renewal of the church.

FULL CYCLE

We have now come full cycle from our discussion in chapter 1. There the point was made that new members must be socialized into and shaped by the language and vision of a church community. In this final chapter we have noted the opposite dynamic: the language and vision of the congregation must be shaped by the transcendent relationship with God in Jesus Christ. In chapter 1 individuals share the vocabulary and values of the church, while in chapter 5 the church community and its members individually in the *mystērion* renew their commitment through a relationship with God.

We have suggested five broad areas of tension that were significant in shaping the early church, and remain as elemental forces in the development of contemporary congregations. In the *ekklēsia* we have tensions of language and vision, of the intimate community and the structural society. By a commitment to God's poor, the *ptōchoi*, we reject the values of the world and confirm the love of God in action. In faith, *pistis*, we cross over the threshold of cognitive dissonance with such energy that we want to bring others with us. Our search for shalom, *eirēnē*, makes conflict with the world both essential and constructive. In rituals of structure and *mystērion* we maintain the order while renewing the spiritual life of the church. These do not occur in isolation, but each reinforces the others and needs the others for the full development of community. Taken together, these are constructive tensions in the social dynamic of Christian experience, then and now.

ABBREVIATIONS

AB	Anchor Bible
BR	*Biblical Research*
BTB	*Biblical Theology Bulletin*
CBQMS	Catholic Biblical Quarterly Monograph Series
HNT	Handbuch zum Neuen Testament
HUCA	*Hebrew Union College Annual*
JBL	*Journal of Biblical Literature*
JTS	*Journal of Theological Studies*
LCL	Loeb Classical Library
NovTSup	Novem Testamentum, Supplements
NTS	New Testament Studies
RelSRev	*Religious Studies Review*
SBLMS	Society of Biblical Literature Monograph Series
SBT	Studies in Biblical Theology
TDNT	G. Kittel and G. Friedrich, eds., *Theological Dictionary of the New Testament*
TF	*Theologische Forschung*
ZNTW	*Zeitschrift für die neutestamentliche Wissenschaft*

NOTES

INTRODUCTION

1. See Peter Berger, *The Sacred Canopy* (Garden City, NY: Doubleday 1967), 105, for a more extended discussion of this approach.

2. Examples of this approach are Oscar Cullmann, *Christ and Time* (London: SCM Press, 1951); idem, *Salvation as History* (London: SCM Press, 1967); G. Ernest Wright, *God Who Acts*, SBT 8 (London: SCM Press, 1952); John Bright, *A History of Israel* (Philadelphia: Westminster Press, 1959; 3d ed., 1981); and in a somewhat more secular way, William F. Albright, *From the Stone Age to Christianity*, rev. ed. (Garden City, N.Y.: Doubleday & Co., 1957).

3. G. W. F. Hegel, *Philosophy of History*, trans. J. Sibree (London: George Bell, 1905), 17–82.

4. Rudolf Bultmann, *History and Eschatology* (New York: Harper & Brothers, 1957).

5. See especially A.J. Greimas, *Sémantique structural* (Paris: Larousse, 1966); Daniel Patte, *What Is Structural Exegesis?* (Philadelphia: Fortress Press, 1976); Edgar V. McKnight, *Meaning in Texts* (Philadelphia: Fortress Press, 1978).

6. Jonathan Z. Smith, "The Social Description of Early Christianity," *RelSRev* 1 (1975): 19–25; Abraham J. Malherbe, *Social Aspects of Early Christianity*, 2d ed. (Philadelphia: Fortress Press, 1983); Bruce J. Malina, *The New Testament World: Insights from Cultural Anthropology* (London: SCM Press, 1983); Wayne A. Meeks, *The First Urban Christians* (New Haven: Yale Univ. Press, 1983); Gerd Theissen, *Sociology of Early Palestinian Christianity* (Philadelphia: Fortress Press, 1977); idem, *The Social Setting of Pauline Christianity* (Philadelphia: Fortress Press, 1982). For an extensive bibliography of studies on the early church from a social science perspective, see John H. Elliott, "Social Science Criticism of the New Testament: More on Methods and Models," in *Social-Scientific Criticism of the New Testament and Its Social World*, ed. John H. Elliott, Semeia 35 (Decatur, Georgia: Scholars Press, 1986), 1–2, n. 1.

7. Gerd Theissen discusses this problem at length in "The Sociological Interpretation of Religious Traditions: Its Methodological Problems as Ex-

emplified in Early Christianity," in *The Social Setting of Pauline Christianity*, 175–200.

8. Peter Berger, *The Sacred Canopy* (Garden City, N.Y.: Doubleday & Co., 1967), 180.

9. For further reading on this issue, see Meeks, *First Urban Christians*, 2–7; Berger, *Sacred Canopy*, 179–88.

1. COMMUNITY FORMATION: VISION, INTIMACY, AND ORGANIZATION

1. Philo *Migration of Abraham* 89–91.

2. This intensification of a concern for identity may also be understood in light of new pressures that Christianity doubtless encountered after the Jewish-Roman War of A.D. 70. The temple was gone, Jerusalem could no longer function as the physical and symbolic center of Judaism, and Judaism itself was forced to launch a massive reevaluation of its own identity. Over the ensuing centuries it would radically transform itself from the variegated spectrum it had been into the highly self-conscious, unifocal orthodoxy we know as historic rabbinic Judaism. As this developed, and as at the same time Christianity became more and more a religion of Gentiles, it is understandable that the need for Christian self-definition was ever more keenly felt.

3. James M. Gustafson, *Treasures in Earthen Vessels: the Church as a Human Community* (New York: Harper & Row, 1961), 45. Throughout the book Gustafson presents other ways in which the church is a community "of interpretation," "of memory and understanding," and "of belief and action."

4. George Herbert Mead, *Mind, Self and Society* (Chicago: Univ. of Chicago Press, 1934), 51–75.

5. Ibid., 65.

6. On these concepts, see esp. Peter L. Berger and Thomas Luckmann, *The Social Construction of Reality* (Garden City, N.Y.: Doubleday & Co., 1966), 85–118; and Peter L. Berger, *The Sacred Canopy* (Garden City, N.Y.: Doubleday & Co., 1967) 29–52.

7. Karl Ludwig Schmidt, *"Ekklēsia,"* in *TDNT* 3:501–36.

8. One ancient lexicographer, in fact, defines *ptōchos* as meaning "the beggar, the one who has lost his possessions," Pseudo-Ammonius, *On Similar and Differing Vocabulary*, quoted by Friedrich Hauch, who gives further examples, *"Ptōchos,"* in *TDNT* 6:886.

9. For further study of the meaning of the "poor" in the Old Testament, see Ernst Bammel, *"Ptōchos,"* in *TDNT* 6:888–94; Martin Hengel, *Property and Riches in the Early Church* (Philadelphia: Fortress Press, 1974), 12–22; Carolyn Osiek, *Rich and Poor in the Shepherd of Hermas*, CBQMS 15 (Washington, D.C.: Catholic Biblical Association, 1983), 15–38; Wolfgang Stegemann, *The Gospel and the Poor* (Philadelphia: Fortress Press, 1984), 13–21.

10. 1QM XI.9, 13 (English text in Geza Vermes, *The Dead Sea Scrolls in English*, 2d ed. [New York: Penguin, 1981], 138); 1QM XIII.14 (Vermes, 141); 1QH V.13 (Vermes, 159); 1QpHab XII.3, 6, 10 (Vermes, 242); 4QpPs 37 I.8 (Vermes, 244), II.10 (Vermes, 245).

11. 4QpPs 37 I.8 (Vermes, 244); 1QpHab XII.3 (Vermes, 242).

12. The Septuagint reads at this point: *ek pisteos mou*, which may be understood either as "on the basis of faith in me" or as "on the basis of my

faithfulness." In either instance it makes explicit the sense of relationship to God that is implicit in the equally ambiguous Hebrew text: *bĕˀmûnātô,* "by his [whose?] faithfulness." The Hebrew suggests, in any case, a covenantal relationship.

13. For an extensive discussion of the terms for faith in the Bible, see Rudolf Bultmann and Artur Weiser, *"Pisteuō,"* in *TDNT,* 6:174–228.

14. For further reading on the terms *šālôm, eirēnē,* see Werner Foerster and Gerhard von Rad, *"Eirēnē,"* in *TDNT* 2:400–417; Walter Brueggemann, *Living Toward a Vision: Biblical Reflections on Shalom* (Philadelphia: United Church Press, 1976).

15. Raymond E. Brown, *The Semitic Background of the Term "Mystery" in the New Testament,* Facet Books, Biblical Series 21 (Philadelphia: Fortress Press, 1968), 69.

16. Günther Bornkamm, *"Mystērion,"* in *TDNT* 4:808–10.

17. Berger and Luckmann, *Social Construction of Reality,* 89–91.

18. For an extended description of the many elements that made up the symbolic world of the New Testament, see Luke T. Johnson, *The Writings of the New Testament* (Philadelphia: Fortress Press, 1986), 21–83.

19. Berger and Luckmann, *Social Construction of Reality,* 103.

20. See Hans Conzelmann, *The Theology of St Luke* (New York: Harper & Row, 1961).

21. Berger and Luckmann, *Social Construction of Reality,* 92–103.

22. For a more in-depth study of the difference language makes in cultural perception and commitment, see Thomas Kochman, *Black and White Styles in Conflict* (Chicago: Univ. of Chicago Press, 1981).

23. Denham Grierson, *Transforming a People of God* (Melbourne: Joint Board of Christian Education of Australia and New Zealand, 1984), 70.

24. William McKinney, David A. Roozen, and Jackson W. Carroll, *Religion's Public Presence* (Washington, D.C.: Alban Institute, 1982).

25. This approach to Christian education can be traced to the seminal work by C. Ellis Nelson, *Where Faith Begins* (Atlanta: John Knox Press, 1967).

26. James F. Hopewell, *Congregation: Stories and Structures* (Philadelphia: Fortress Press, 1987). A brief presentation can be found in Jackson W. Carroll et al., *Handbook for Congregational Studies* (Nashville: Abingdon Press, 1986).

27. Gerd Theissen, *Sociology of Early Palestinian Christianity* (Philadelphia: Fortress Press, 1977) ix, passim.

28. Charles Cooley, Robert C. Angell, and Lowell J. Carr, *Introductory Sociology* (New York: Charles Scribner's Sons, 1933), 55.

29. Charles Cooley, *Social Organizations* (New York: Free Press, 1956), 23.

30. For further reading on the group-building uses of humor, see Samuel C. Heilman, *Synagogue Life: A Study in Symbolic Interaction* (Chicago: Univ. of Chicago Press, 1973), esp. chap. 6, "Joking."

31. Jakob Jónsson, *Humor and Irony in the New Testament* (Reykjavík: Bókaútgáfa Meningarsjóds, 1965).

32. For examples of such *chreiai,* see David R. Cartlidge and David L. Dungan, *Documents for the Study of the Gospels* (Philadelphia: Fortress Press, 1980), 141–49; see also the articles in *Pronouncement Stories,* ed. Robert C. Tannehill, Semeia 20 (Chico, Calif.: Scholars Press, 1981).

33. Certainly this story also functioned in the early church theologically

somewhat in the same manner as Paul's dictum that the gospel was "to the Jew first and also to the Greek" (Rom. 1:16), but it can also be seen to have functioned socially in the manner we describe here.

34. Similar humorous references to God in rabbinic literature are noted by Jónsson, *Humor and Irony*, 53–56. One is also reminded of Tevye's conversation with God in *Fiddler on the Roof.*

35. For a discussion of the difference between conflict within the church and conflict between the church and the world, see chap. 4, "Using Conflict Constructively."

36. Eduard Schweizer, *Church Order in the New Testament* (London: SCM Press, 1961), 125–30.

37. See Ronald F. Hock, *The Social Context of Paul's Ministry: Tentmaking and Apostleship* (Philadelphia: Fortress Press, 1980).

38. 1 Cor. 14:33b–35 has been the object of much debate: did Paul write this, or is it an interpolation? See Hans Conzelmann, *1 Corinthians*, Hermeneia (Philadelphia: Fortress Press, 1975), 246; Victor P. Furnish, *The Moral Teaching of Paul* (Nashville: Abingdon Press, 1983), 91–92.

39. Gerd Theissen, *The Social Setting of Pauline Christianity*, ed. John H. Schütz (Philadelphia: Fortress Press, 1982), 40.

40. Paul was, however, conscious in formal terms of the social texture of his congregations. In 1 Cor. 1:26 he analyzes the Christian community at Corinth in categories analogous to those in Aristotle's *Politics*, 6.1.9 (1317 B); see Laurence Welborn, "On the Discord in Corinth," *JBL* 106 (1987), 83–113.

41. Ferdinand Tönnies, *Community and Society (Gemeinschaft und Gesellschaft)*, trans. Charles P. Loomis (East Lansing, Mich.: Michigan State Univ. Press, 1957), 42ff.

42. Tönnies, *Community and Society*, 64ff.

43. Bruce Reed, *Dynamics of Religion* (London: Darton, Longman & Todd, 1978). Reed finds support for such categories in a wide assortment of theological and social analysts, including Sigmund Freud, Charles Rycroft, Bateson, Laing, McKellar, Bion, and others. He notes remarkable similarities in studies from many cultures and disciplines: from the classical philosophies of Confucious—small tranquillity/great similarity, Plato—oligarchic society/ideal republic, and Augustine—city of men/city of God; among early sociologists such as Tönnies—Gesellschaft/Gemeinschaft, Maine—contract society/status society, and Durkheim—organic solidarity/mechanical solidarity; and among more contemporary social analysts such as Redfield—technical order/moral order, Eliade—profane/sacred, and Turner—structure/communitas.

44. G. H. Mueller, "Asceticism and Mysticism," in *International Yearbook for the Sociology of Religion*, 1973, 68–132. Also see "The Protestant and the Catholic Ethic," in *Annual Review of the Social Sciences of Religion*, 1978, 2:143–66.

45. For a more extended application of this distinction in the life of the parish, see Carl S. Dudley, *Affectional and Directional Orientations to Faith* (Washington, D.C.: Alban Institute, 1982).

46. This suggests why some observers reject the "family" as an inadequate reflection of the New Testament church (e.g., Parker Palmer, *The Community of Strangers* [New York: Crossroad, 1981], see esp. chap. 7, "Practicing the

Public Life") while others use it as the primary metaphor for the early Christian community (e.g., Ralph P. Martin, *The Family and the Fellowship: New Testament Images of the Church* [Grand Rapids: Wm. B. Eerdmans, 1979]).

47. Reed, *Dynamics of Religion*, chap. 7, esp. 157–64.

48. E.g., Carl S. Dudley, *Making the Small Church Effective* (Nashville: Abingdon Press, 1978); David R. Ray, *Small Churches Are the Right Size* (New York: Pilgrim Press, 1982); Lyle E. Schaller, *The Small Church Is Different* (Nashville: Abingdon Press, 1982).

49. See, e.g., the comparative treatment of the city and suburban church in the work of Gaylord B. Noyce, *The Responsible Suburban Church* (Philadelphia: Westminster Press, 1970); idem, *Survival and Mission for the City Church* (Philadelphia: Westminster Press, 1975).

50. Michael Novak, *The Rise of the Unmeltable Ethnics* (New York: Macmillan Co., 1971), 56.

51. Ibid., 119.

52. Ibid., 56.

53. Tex Sample, *Blue-Collar Ministry* (Valley Forge, Pa.: Judson Press, 1984), 127–131.

54. See Marlene Wilson, *How to Mobilize Church Volunteers* (Minneapolis: Augsburg Pub. House, 1983), esp. 28–43.

55. *Interaction Process Analysis* (Reading, Mass.: Addison-Wesley, 1949). Revised in *Personality and Interpersonal Behavior* (New York: Holt, Rinehart & Winston, 1970).

56. Robert R. Blake and Jane Srygley Mouton, *Building a Dynamic Corporation Through Grid Organization Development* (Reading, Mass.: Addison-Wesley, 1969).

57. *The Parish Paper* 4 (October, 1974).

2. THE ENERGY OF COUNTERCULTURE CHRISTIANITY

1. Other psychological reactions can be identified, such as avoidance of problems, denial that we are concerned or that we can do anything, etc. Throughout this study we are concerned with the way groups reflect and build on individual responses.

2. Gerd Theissen, *Sociology of Early Palestinian Christianity* (Philadelphia: Fortress Press, 1977), 34–36.

3. It would be a mistake to consider the Jesus movement in every respect as a "sect": the tradition is clear that Jesus never repudiated his identity with Judaism, as is made clear by his action in the temple and is reflected by the superscription on the cross. We are concerned here particularly with the counterculture aspects of early Christianity and the energy generated by such a stance.

4. Ernst Troeltsch, *The Social Teaching of the Christian Churches*, trans. Olive Wyon (New York: Macmillan Co., 1931), 1:331.

5. H. Richard Niebuhr, *The Social Sources of Denominationalism* (Henry Holt, 1929, 1957; New York: New American Library, 1975), 17.

6. Abbreviated from Liston Pope, *Millhands and Preachers,* (New Haven: Yale Univ. Press, 1942), 123–24.

7. See Ronald F. Hock, *The Social Context of Paul's Ministry: Tentmaking and Apostleship* (Philadelphia: Fortress Press, 1980).

8. Philo's discussion of the fifth commandment is helpful at this point; speaking of the laws based on it, he points to those directed "to servants on rendering an affectionate loyalty to their masters, to masters on showing the gentleness and kindness by which inequality is equalized" (Philo *The Decalogue* 167, LCL).

9. Whether or not Paul wrote 2 Cor. 6:14—7:1 is debated. Hans Dieter Betz suggests that the passage is in fact an anti-Pauline insertion "2 Cor. 6:14—7:1: An Anti-Pauline Fragment?" *JBL* 92 (1973): 88–108.

10. Wayne Meeks, *The First Urban Christians* (New Haven: Yale Univ. Press, 1983), 94–96.

11. Geza Vermes, trans., *The Dead Sea Scrolls in English*, 2d ed. (New York: Penguin, 1981), 76.

12. Troeltsch, *Social Teaching*, 1:669: "The sect also maintains the original radicalism of the Christian ideal and its hostility towards the world, and it retains the fundamental demand for personal service, which indeed it is also able to regard as a work of grace. . . . The sect does not live on the miracles of the past, nor on the miraculous nature of the institution, but on the constantly renewed miracle of the Presence of Christ, and on the subjective reality of the individual mastery of life."

13. *From Max Weber: Essays in Sociology*, ed. H. H. Gerth and C. Wright Mills (N.Y.: Oxford Univ. Press, 1958), 328–29: "Wherever prophecies of salvation have created religious communities, the first power with which they have come into conflict has been the natural sib. . . . Prophecy has created a new social community, particularly where it became a soteriological religion of congregations. Thereby the relations of the sib and of matrimony have been, at least relatively, devalued. The magical ties and exclusiveness of the sibs have been shattered, and within the new community the prophetic religion has developed a religious ethic of brotherliness. The ethic has simply taken over the original principles of social and ethical conduct which the 'association of neighbors' had offered, whether it was the community of villagers, members of the sib, the guild, or of partners in seafaring, hunting, and warring expeditions."

14. David L. Balch, *Let Wives Be Submissive*, SBLMS 26, (Chico, Calif.: Scholars Press, 1981), 21–62.

15. Troeltsch, *Social Teaching*, 1:331, identified the countercultural church primarily with "the lower classes, or at least those elements in society which are opposed to the State and Society; they work upwards from below, and not downwards from above."

16. Adolf Deissmann, *Paul: A Study in Social and Religious History*, trans. William E. Wilson (New York: Harper & Brothers, 1957), 48, 51. A related thesis was that of Karl Holl, who in 1921 proposed the view that the Jerusalem community adopted the title of "The Poor" as an expression of an idealization, regardless of their actual economic condition. This thesis was accepted by a number of major scholars (e.g., Ernst Bammel, *"Ptōchos," TDNT* 6:909), but was conclusively demolished by Leander E. Keck ("The Poor Among the Saints in the New Testament," *ZNTW* 56 [1965]: 100–129; "The Poor Among the Saints in Jewish Christianity and Qumran," *ZNTW* 57 [1966]: 54–78), who showed that such an application of the term is unknown in either the Lukan or Matthean traditions and that the Pauline passages are best understood as referring to specific crisis periods.

17. Niebuhr, *Social Sources of Denominationalism*, 31.

18. Meeks, *First Urban Christians*, 54.

19. Ibid., 54–55; note the following evaluation of unrest in the Roman Empire by Clarence L. Lee ("Social Unrest and Primitive Christianity," in *Early Church History: The Roman Empire as the Setting of Primitive Christianity*, ed. Stephen Benko and John J. O'Rourke [London: Oliphants, 1972], 134–35): "In one of the few studies made of the phenomenon of social unrest in the early Empire, Ramsay MacMullen has singled out the subversive activities and attitudes of the aristocracy as the most significant disruptive force in the Empire. All other forms of unrest among the other classes were, in effect, the outer edges of this central core of aristocratic discontent. The basic complaint of the aristocracy was its loss of social and political ascendancy. . . . The unrest of the aristocracy, in short, was a romantic reaction, an attempt to restore a departed social ideal."

20. Meeks, *First Urban Christians*, 55–72; Gerd Theissen, *The Social Setting of Pauline Christianity* (Philadelphia: Fortress Press, 1982), 69–174. Wolfgang Stegemann, *The Gospel and the Poor* (Philadelphia: Fortress Press, 1980), 31–40, concludes, however, that among the early Christians there were no destitute, and, except in Luke, no wealthy. Rather, Christians were from "the little people."

21. For a succinct description of these tensions, see Martin Hengel, *Property and Riches in the Early Church* (Philadelphia: Fortress Press, 1974), 23.

22. Whether Jesus and most, at least, of his immediate disciples came from among the poor has been answered variously; Stegemann, *Gospel and the Poor*, 23–25, argues that they did, while Hengel, *Property and Riches*, 26–27, thinks that Jesus came "from the middle class of Galilee, the skilled workers." While we incline to agree with Hengel, the evidence seems to us too tenuous to warrant a firm conclusion.

23. That Paul was aware of Jesus-sayings is evident in the way they underlie his statements, cf. Biörn Fjärstedt, *Synoptic Tradition in 1 Corinthians* (Uppsala: Teologiska Institutionen, 1974); David L. Dungan, *The Sayings of Jesus in the Churches of Paul* (Philadelphia: Fortress Press, 1971); but that the sayings as such were known and cherished in his congregations in the way they were elsewhere remains doubtful.

24. For a discussion of the dynamics of Paul's collection for "the poor in Jerusalem," see chap. 4.

25. Hengel, *Property and Riches*, 15–22.

26. In the judgment scene in Matt. 25:31–46 the "righteous" are rewarded for having fed the hungry, clothed the naked and visited those in prison, and those who did not do these things are punished. This passage reflects conditions later in the first century when Christians, and especially Christian missionaries, were imprisoned and suffered other deprivations. The persons addressed are from "all the nations" (v. 32), and those they have befriended are "these my brethren" (v. 40), Christians who witness to the gospel and are thus identified with their Lord ("you did it to me," v. 40; cf. Matt. 10:40–42). In its Matthean setting this passage is therefore not to be understood as expressing general concern for the poor, but rather primarily for itinerant and other needy and persecuted preachers of the gospel.

27. See the short but excellent discussion of this by Joseph Fitzmyer, S.J., *The Gospel According to Luke (I–IX)*, AB (Garden City, N.Y.: Doubleday & Co., 1981), 1:247–51.

28. The expression "poor in spirit" appears, in its Hebrew form, also in the Dead Sea Scrolls (1QM 14:7), where those so designated are paralleled with "the perfect of way" through whom God will work for the destruction of "all the nations of wickedness" (Vermes, *Dead Sea Scrolls*, 142; cf. Herbert Braun, *Qumran und das Neue Testament* [Tübingen: J.C.B. Mohr, 1966], 1.13); for Matthew their reward is likewise eschatological, "the kingdom of heaven."

29. Hengel, *Property and Riches*, 17: "We shall look in vain for direct praise of the poor or of poverty in Jewish literature; it is first to be found in the gospel (Luke 6:30)," cf. 25.

30. This double perspective of physical and spiritual salvation combined in Jesus' words and actions is notable especially in the miracle stories; cf. Luke 8:48; 18:42, where the verb *sōzō*, "to save," implies both healing and salvation.

31. See esp. *The Shepherd of Hermas*, Vision 3.9; Mandate 2; Similitude 2; cf. Carolyn Osiek, *Rich and Poor in the Shepherd of Hermas*, CBQMS 15 (Washington, D.C.: Catholic Biblical Society, 1983).

32. *Didache* 1:6; Robert A. Kraft, trans., *The Apostolic Fathers* (New York: Nelson, 1965), 141.

33. *Didache* 11:4–6; 12:3–5; Kraft, *Apostolic Fathers*, 3:170, 172.

34. *The Epistle to Diognetus* 5:1–9; trans. James A. Kleist, in *Ancient Christian Writers* (Westminster, Md.: Newman Press, 1961), 6:138–39.

35. For a summary of similar questions from a sociological perspective, see Allan W. Eister, "H. Richard Niebuhr and the Paradox of Religious Organization: A Radical Critique," in *Beyond the Classics? Essays in the Scientific Study of Religion*, ed. Charles Y. Glock and Phillip E. Hammond (New York: Harper & Row, 1973).

36. "The Growth of Religious Reformed Movements," in *The Annals of the American Academy of Political and Social Science*, vol. 480, July, 1985.

37. Martin E. Marty, *The Public Church* (New York: Crossroads, 1981).

38. David A. Roozen, William McKinney, and Jackson C. Carroll, *Varieties of Religious Presence* (New York: Pilgrim Press, 1984), 34.

39. Dean R. Hoge, "A Test of Theories of Denominational Growth and Decline," in *Understanding Church Growth and Decline*, ed. Dean R. Hoge and David A. Roozen (New York: Pilgrim Press, 1979).

40. Gary Schwartz, *Sect Ideologies and Social Status* (Chicago: Univ. of Chicago Press, 1970), chaps. 2, 3.

41. Charles Glock and Rodney Stark have developed a list of five such relative deprivations and identified the kinds of social movement associated with each: Economic deprivation tends toward political revolution or separatist sects. Deprivation of social status finds expression in political realignment or churchlike religious movements. Threats to physical health tend to produce healing movements. Ethical conflict generates social and political reform movements. Psychological loss of identity leads toward religious cults. Cf. Glock and Stark, *Religion and Society in Tension* (Chicago: Rand McNally & Co., 1965), 265ff.; and C. Y. Glock, B. B. Ringer and E. R. Babbie, *To Comfort and To Challenge* (Berkeley and Los Angeles: Univ. of California Press, 1967). See also Hoge and Roozen, *Understanding Church Growth and Decline*, 49ff.; and Bryan Wilson, *Religion in Sociological Perspective* (New York: Oxford Univ. Press, 1982), which discuss significant questions about the character of church participation based on relative deprivation.

42. Dieter Hessel, *Social Ministry* (Philadelphia: Westminster Press, 1982); David S. King, *No Church Is an Island* (New York: Pilgrim Press, 1980);

Gibson Winter, *The Suburban Captivity of the Churches* (Garden City, N.Y.: Doubleday & Co., 1961).

43. Robert McAfee Brown, *Theology in a New Key* (Philadelphia: Westminster Press, 1978), 52. Bonhoeffer, *Letters from Prison*, is quoted by Brown, 50.

44. José Miguez Bonino, *Doing Theology in a Revolutionary Situation* (Philadelphia: Fortress Press, 1975), 112.

45. For usable case histories and guidelines that challenge the church, see Robert A. Evans and Alice Frazer Evans, *Human Rights, A Dialogue Between the First and Third Worlds* (Maryknoll, N.Y.: Orbis Books, 1983).

46. Max Weber, *On Charisma and Institution Building*, ed. S. N. Eisenstadt, (Chicago: Univ. of Chicago Press, 1968). Weber, Troeltsch, and Tönnies were contemporaries and colleagues. Weber put a greater emphasis on process, and so used *Vergemeinschaftung* and *Vergesellschaftung*, rather than *Gemeinschaft* and *Gesellschaft*.

47. Ibid., 46.

48. Ibid., 46.

49. Ibid., 20.

50. *From Max Weber*, ed. Gerth and Mills, 246–47.

51. Ibid., 248.

52. From the viewpoint of a Sandinista, as quoted by Connor Cruise O'Brien, "God and Man in Nicaragua," *The Atlantic*, 258 (August, 1986): 71.

53. *From Max Weber*, 250.

54. Ibid., 253.

55. Bruce Malina has challeged the "received view" that Jesus' leadership was "charismatic," and has offered an alternative "reputational, legitimate" model of Jesus' leadership based on his understanding of first-century Mediterranean political conditions ("Jesus as Charismatic Leader?" *BTB* 14 [1984]: 55–62). We agree with his effort to remove from Jesus an overly dramatic, "Germanic" cultural bias implicit in Weber's definition of charisma. However, his alternative argument would be more convincing if he had explored the layers of New Testament material in the Gospels (which he appears to treat almost as on-site descriptions of Jesus). Malina's lifting our cross-cultural consciousness is important, but a more modest definition of "charisma" remains supported by first-century data and is helpful in working with contemporary congregations.

56. Luke's portrayal of Philip's own situation is ambiguous in terms of our categories and illustrates the mixed character of these types in the early communities: he is called an "evangelist," a preacher of the gospel (Acts 21:8), he performs miracles and baptizes converts (Acts 8:6, 13, 38), and he can be rapt away by the Spirit to a distant place (Acts 8:39–40), but he is not qualified to mediate that Spirit to his converts; this must be done by the accredited apostles themselves (Acts 8:14–17).

57. Hegesippus (ca. A.D. 180) as cited by Eusebius *Ecclesiastical History* 2.23.3–19.

58. Oscar Cullmann, *Peter: Disciple, Apostle, Martyr* (London: SCM Press, 1962), 71–157; Raymond E. Brown and John P. Meier, *Antioch and Rome* (New York: Paulist Press, 1983), 97–104.

59. James D. Anderson and Ezra Earl Jones, *The Management of Ministry* (New York: Harper & Row, 1978), 78–79.

60. For an excellent discussion of the "corporate characters" in industry,

see Terrance E. Deal and Allan A. Kennedy, *Corporate Cultures: The Rites and Rituals of Corporate Life* (Reading, Mass.: Addison-Wesley Publ. Co., 1982).
  61. Cf. Anderson and Jones, *Management of Ministry*, chaps. 5, 10, and passim.
  62. Urban T. Holmes, *The Priest in Community* (New York: Seabury Press, 1978), 79ff.
  63. Robert Greenleaf, *The Religious Leader as Servant* (Peterborough, N.H.: Windy Row Press, 1982), 15–23, 46ff.

3. FAITH CRISIS AND CHRISTIAN WITNESS

  1. *1 Clement* 23:3 (*The Apostolic Fathers*, vol 2: *First and Second Clement*, ed. Robert M. Grant and Holt H. Graham [New York: Nelson, 1965], 48).
  2. Leon Festinger, *A Theory of Cognitive Dissonance* (Stanford, Calif.: Stanford Univ. Press, 1957); idem, *Conflict, Decision and Dissonance* (Stanford, Calif.: Stanford Univ. Press, 1964).
  3. Leon Festinger, Henry W. Riecken, and Stanley Schachter, *When Prophecy Fails* (New York: Harper & Brothers, 1956), 4, 216.
  4. Ibid., 27.
  5. John Gager, *Kingdom and Community* (Englewood Cliffs, N.J.: Prentice-Hall, 1975), 37–49, notes.
  6. It should be noted that Festinger et al. (*When Prophecy Fails*, 25) avoid such a comparison with a disclaimer concerning the death of Jesus: "Was it or was it not a disconfirmation? We do not know and cannot say. But this one unclarity makes the whole episode inconclusive with respect to our hypothesis." Other scholars resist the application of cognitive dissonance to the behavior of the early church because it can produce patently false conclusions. It is possible, for instance, in laboratory experiments to create conditions in which subjects will accept otherwise obviously erroneous data due to social pressure. They will then try to convince other subjects that their conclusion is, in fact, correct. Such pseudoevangelism under experimental conditions is vigorous but temporary. It is significantly different from the sustained evangelistic energy of the early church, which was maintained by supportive congregations, a common symbolic universe, and a community of "satisfied customers."
  Recently Bruce J. Malina ("Normative Dissonance and Christian Origins," in *Social Scientific Criticism of the New Testament and Its Social World*, ed. John H. Elliott [Decatur, Ga.: Scholars Press, 1986] 35–59), has rejected the Festinger-Gager hypothesis of cognitive dissonance and subsequent evangelistic zeal as an explanation for "the survival and spread of the early Jesus movement" (55). He points out that in the Roman world, "cognitive dissonance was normal; life was replete with ambivalence." Therefore, Malina argues, cognitive dissonance experienced by early Christians cannot be expected to have produced the dynamic results Gager suggests. Rather, Malina focuses on "sociological ambivalence." He believes early Christians lived relatively comfortably with this ambivalence, and that their equanimity explains "why earliest Christianity did in fact avoid extremism and survive" (39). In our view Malina has provided a valuable additional insight on the dynamics of ambiguity in early Christianity but not one that displaces Gager's interpretation. There are indeed many lesser ambiguities in the Gospels (as detailed by Malina, 45–47) which seem not to

have concerned early Christians seriously. But the record is clear that in the two cases studied here, the crucifixion and the nonoccurrence of the Parousia, cognitive dissonance that was deeply disturbing did indeed occur.

7. Gager, *Kingdom and Community*, 47.

8. Wayne A. Meeks, *The First Urban Christians* (New Haven: Yale Univ. Press, 1983), 177.

9. The theme of the messianic secret has been much discussed by scholars. From the standpoint of Mark's intention, the classic study is that of William Wrede, *Das Messiasgeheimnis in den Evangelien* (Göttingen: Vandenhoeck & Ruprecht, 1913); *The Messianic Secret*, trans. J.C.G. Greig (Greenwood, S.C.: Attic Press, 1971), who argued that Mark constructed it to counter the problem met by Christian evangelists in proclaiming that Jesus was the Messiah when there was no evidence that he himself had made such a claim. For a similar point of view, see Rudolf Bultmann, *Theology of the New Testament*, trans. Kendrick Grobel (New York: Charles Scribner's Sons, 1951, 1955), 1:32 (1:26–32 provide helpful background reading to our discussion here). A different approach, which understands the secret to be historical in the life of Jesus as his way of avoiding a misunderstanding of his messiahship, has been held by many; an example is Oscar Cullmann, *Die Christologie des Neuen Testaments* (Tübingen: J.C.B. Mohr, 1958), 125–26; *The Christology of the New Testament* (Philadelphia: Westminster Press, 1959), 124–26. Our concern at this point, of course, is not with the life and thinking of the historical Jesus, but with Mark's resolution of cognitive dissonance at a much later time.

10. Gager, *Kingdom and Community*, 45, sees the statement of Mark 9:1 and those of Mark 13 (e.g., 13:10) to relate to two succeeding stages of cognitive dissonance in the early church: that among "the earliest believers" and that which arose when the Parousia did not take place within the first generation. While this is plausible, we see no compelling reason to make such a sharp distinction; in any case, our concern here is with what significance these sayings had for Christians at the time the Gospel of Mark was written; from the fact of their inclusion in that Gospel, it is clear that they remained relevant.

11. Lloyd Gaston, *No Stone on Another*, NovTSup 23 (Leiden: E.J. Brill, 1970), 12.

12. Ernst Lohmeyer, *Das Evangelium des Markus*, Kritisch-exegetischer Kommentar über das Neue Testament, 1.2; 16th ed. (Göttingen: Vandenhoeck & Ruprecht, 1963), 269. Cf. Dan. 9:24; 11:36; 12:7 (LXX).

13. Adolf Schlatter, *Das Evangelium des Matthäus*, Erläuterungen zum Neuen Testament 5 (Calw & Stuttgart: Verlag der Vereinsbuchhandlung, 1900), 160, followed by Alan Hugh M'Neile, *The Gospel According to St. Matthew* (New York: St. Martin's Press, 1965), 142, understood this text to refer not to towns where the disciples preach and are persecuted, but to places where they find shelter: in times of persecution, cities of refuge will not be lacking. In either case the disciples will not have exhausted all the places to preach.

14. David Hill, *The Gospel of Matthew*, New Century Bible Commentary (Grand Rapids: Wm. B. Eerdmans, 1981), 190, comments on this text: "The mission to Israel will not be completed before the Son of man comes."

15. Hans Conzelmann, *The Theology of St Luke* (New York: Harper & Row, 1961), 103–4.

16. All quotations from Clement are taken from *The Apostolic Fathers*, 2.48–53.

17. Cf. C. Peter Wagner, *Your Church Can Grow* (Glendale, Calif.: Regal Books, 1976), esp. chap. 8, pp. 110ff.; also Donald A. McGavran, *Understanding Church Growth* (Grand Rapids: Wm. B. Eerdmans, 1970), 198–215.

18. Dean R. Hoge and David A. Roozen, *Church Membership Growth and Decline, 1950–1978* (New York: Pilgrim Press, 1979).

19. Carl S. Dudley, *Where Have All Our People Gone?* (New York: Pilgrim Press, 1979), 56, 78–79. Churches which establish committees usually are declining already, and are too willing to turn the problem over to a committee to solve. Committees do have an important function, but are no substitute for excitement.

20. Urban T. Holmes, *Priest in Community* (New York: Seabury Press, 1978), 78.

21. Transcript from Beth Hart, November, 1983.

22. Thomas H. Holmes and Richard H. Rahe, "The Social Adjustment Rating Scale," *Journal of Psychosomatic Research* 11 (1967): 213–18.

23. Edward Rauff, *Why People Join the Church* (New York: Pilgrim Press, 1979), see esp. chap. 4.

24. Victor Turner, *The Ritual Process* (Ithaca, N.Y.: Cornell Univ. Press, 1969).

25. Ibid., 111–12.

26. Cf. Bruce Reed, *The Dynamics of Religion*, 71ff., who also employs a concept of "oscillation" as basic to the religious life of individuals and the strength of the religious community.

27. Meeks, *First Urban Christians*, 150–57.

28. See Turner, *Ritual Process*, 111ff. Here we note the similarities of liminality to cognitive dissonance. In chap. 5 we expand on the use of ritual in the context of worship.

29. James Loder, *The Transforming Moment, Understanding Convictional Moments* (New York: Harper & Row, 1981), 69–70.

30. Ibid., 35–36.

31. Ibid., 35.

4. USING CONFLICT CONSTRUCTIVELY

1. Lewis Coser, *Functions of Social Conflict* (New York: Free Press), 1956. Coser was chosen because he advocates an affirmative approach to conflict as potentially but not necessarily useful, based on the earlier work of Georg Simmel.

2. Ibid., 67ff.

3. John Gager, *Kingdom and Community* (Englewood Cliffs, N.J.: Prentice-Hall, 1975), 80.

4. Coser, *Functions of Social Conflict*, 118.

5. Ibid., 74.

6. E.P. Sanders, *Jesus and Judaism* (Philadelphia: Fortress Press, 1985), 61–76, offers a somewhat different explanation: Jesus' invasion of the temple before his death and his threat or prediction of its destruction were not manifestations of antipathy to it and its priesthood, but reflected rather his anticipation of the end of the age and a new temple as part of the imminent restoration of Israel. This absence of antipathy toward the temple would account for the early apostles continuing to worship there. On either interpretation, the shift from Pharisees to Sadducees as chief antagonists is understandable.

7. See the recent discussion by Adela Yarbro Collins, *Crisis and Catharsis* (Philadelphia: Westminster Press, 1984), 54–83.

8. Ibid., 84–110. See also Elisabeth Schüssler Fiorenza, *The Book of Revelation: Justice and Judgment* (Philadelphia: Fortress Press, 1985), 192–203.

9. Collins, *Crisis and Catharsis*, 69–73; Laurence L. Welborn, "On the Date of First Clement," *BR* 29 (1984): 40–44.

10. Collins, *Crisis and Catharsis*, 87–88; see also Schüssler Fiorenza, *Book of Revelation*, 195.

11. Ernst Lohmeyer, *Die Offenbarung des Johannes*, HNT 16 (Tübingen: J.C.B. Mohr, 1953), 31.

12. Collins, *Crisis and Catharsis*, 127–31.

13. In the above discussion of John's political, social, and economic orientation, we are particularly indebted to Collins, *Crisis and Catharsis*, 111–40.

14. Coser, *Functions of Social Conflict*, 87.

15. For a more extended discussion, see Carl S. Dudley, "Neighborhood Churches in Changing Communities," *New Conversations* 3 (Spring, 1978): 4–10.

16. For contrast between clear and fuzzy religious perspectives, see Dean M. Kelley, *Why Conservative Churches Are Growing* (New York: Harper & Row, 1972), esp. chaps. 5 and 6. For further discussion of its implications in racially changing communities, see Carl S. Dudley, "Churches in Changing Communities," in *Metro-Ministries: Ways and Means for the Urban Church*, ed. David Frenchak and Sharrel Keyes (Elgin, Ill.: Cook Pub., 1979).

17. Martin Luther King, Jr., *Why We Can't Wait* (New York: American Book Library, 1963), 79.

18. Ibid., 91.

19. Quoted from the preparation for the Birmingham campaign, ibid., 62.

20. Quoted by John Ansbro, *Martin Luther King, Jr., The Making of a Mind* (Maryknoll, N.Y.: Orbis Books, 1982), 241.

21. Coser, *Functions of Social Conflict*, 110.

22. Cf. Robert McAfee Brown, *Religion and Violence* (Philadelphia: Westminster Press, 1973).

23. *Martin Luther King Jr. 1929–1968* (Chicago: Johnson Pub. Co, 1968), 58.

24. Martin Luther King, Jr., *Stride Toward Freedom* (New York: Harper & Row, 1958), 51.

25. For Dr. King's "pledge" in the civil rights struggle in Birmingham, see *Why We Can't Wait*, 63–64. For a more extended discussion of a similar discipline in contemporary South Africa, see *The Kairos Document* (Springs, South Africa: Kairos Theologians, 1986).

26. Philip P. Hallie, *Lest Innocent Blood Be Shed, The Story of the Village of Le Chambon and How Goodness Happened There* (New York: Harper & Row, 1979), 85.

27. See esp. the chapter on "Bull Connor's Birmingham" in King, *Why We Can't Wait*, 47–58.

28. Martin Luther King, Jr., *Strength to Love* (New York: Harper & Row, 1963), 40.

29. *Martin Luther King, Jr. A Documentary: Montgomery to Memphis*, ed. Flip Shuke (New York: W.W. Norton & Co., 1976), 71.

30. Coser, *Functions of Social Conflict*, 95ff.

31. Whatever the original dictum lying behind this passage may have been, it is clear that for Matthew this is an assertion of Jesus' authority as Son of man.

32. While in light of Coser's model Acts 8:1–17 is highly suggestive of a causative relationship between persecution and the assertion of high apostolic authority, this interpretation of the passage admittedly risks the logical fallacy of seeing such a causative relationship where only a sequential one may exist.

33. William A. Gamson, *Power and Discontent* (Homewood, Ill.: Dorsey Press, 1968) and James Allen Sparks, *Potshots at the Preacher* (Nashville: Abingdon Press, 1977). From very different perspectives, both writers suggest the centrality and vulnerability of leadership in crises and conflict settings.

34. Ebenezer Baptist Church, February, 1968.

35. Reported by William Roger Witherspoon, *Martin Luther King, Jr. . . . To the Mountaintop* (New York: Doubleday & Co., 1985), 214.

36. H. Richard Niebuhr, *Christ and Culture* (New York: Harper & Brothers, 1951).

37. E.g., José Miguez Bonino, *Doing Theology in Revolutionary Situations* (Philadelphia: Fortress Press, 1975), and John Howard Yoder, *The Politics of Jesus* (Grand Rapids: Wm. B. Eerdmans, 1972).

38. Gerd Theissen, *The Social Setting of Pauline Christianity*, 69–174, has developed these insights at length. See also Abraham J. Malherbe, *Social Aspects of Early Christianity*, 2d ed. (Philadelphia: Fortress Press, 1983), 60–91.

39. Bo Reicke, *The Epistles of James, Peter and Jude*, AB (Garden City, N.Y.: Doubleday & Co., 1964), 5, 6, 27, has related the Epistle of James to the reign of Domitian (A.D. 81–96) and interprets the "man with gold rings and fine clothing" (James 2:2) who enters the Christian assembly and is greeted obsequiously as a representative of the nobility which at that time was under pressure from Domitian and sought political allies in the lower classes. Since we have no firm data by which to locate the Epistle of James historically, this must remain a hypothesis. In any case, it is probable that James is warning against some danger from outsiders with prestige which could encourage divisions within the church between economic groups.

40. Dennis R. MacDonald, *The Legend and the Apostle* (Philadelphia: Westminster Press, 1983).

41. That the author of the *Acts of Paul* writes with the Pastorals in mind is evident from his use of characters that appear there: Paul's and Thecla's archenemies are Demas and Hermogenes (cf. 2 Tim. 1:15; 4:10) while one of his closest supporters and host is Onesiphorus together with his family (2 Tim. 1:16; 4:19). Also, Demas and Hermogenes, like Hymenaeus and Philetus in 2 Tim. 2:17–18, are portrayed as teaching the false doctrine that "the resurrection . . . has already taken place." While the Pastorals were probably written in conscious reaction against the *kind* of teaching championed in the *Acts of Paul*, the *Acts* in the form we have them quite clearly are, in turn, also a reaction against the Pastorals.

42. Quotations from the *Acts of Paul* are from the text in Edgar Hennecke, *New Testament Apocrypha*, ed. Wilhelm Schneemelcher, trans. R. McL. Wilson (Philadelphia: Westminster Press, 1964), 2:353–64; another English translation is found in Montague R. James, *The Apocryphal New Testament* (Oxford: Clarendon Press, 1963), 272–81.

43. H. Richard Niebuhr, *Social Sources of Denominationalism* (Henry Holt, 1929; New York: New American Library, 1975), 18–21.

44. Niebuhr, *Social Sources*, 4: "The very essence of Christianity lies in the tension which it presupposes or creates between the worlds of nature and spirit."

45. We have already noted certain similar trends toward a spiritualizing of the law in Hellenistic Judaism; Philo *Migration of Abraham* 86–93.

46. The phrase is from Niebuhr, *Social Sources*, 54.

47. The assessment by Adolf Harnack still merits attention: "There were many who did not *become*, but who *were*, and therefore remained Christians. Then, in addition to this, Christians were already found in all ranks and occupations. . . . Should the Church take the decisive step into the world, conform to its customs, and acknowledge as far as possible its authorities? Or ought she, on the other hand, to remain a society of religious devotees, separated and shut out from the world? . . . It was natural that warning voices should then be raised in the Church against secular tendencies, that the well-known counsels about the imitation of Christ should be held up in their literal strictness before worldly Christians. The Church as a whole, however, under pressure of circumstances rather than by a spontaneous impulse, decided otherwise. She marched through the open door into the Roman state, and settled down there to Christianize the state by imparting to it the word of the Gospel, but at the same time leaving it everything except its gods. On the other hand, she furnished herself with everything of value that could be taken over from the world without overstraining the elastic structure of the organization which she now adopted. With the aid of its philosophy she created her new Christian theology; its polity furnished her with the most exact constitutional forms; its jurisprudence, its trade and commerce, its art and industry, were all taken into her service; and she contrived to borrow some hints even from its religious worship. With this equipment she undertook, and carried through, a world-mission on a grand scale. But believers of the old school protested in the name of the Gospel against this secular Church" ("Montanism," in *Encyclopaedia Britannica*, 11th ed. [New York: Encyclopaedia Britannica, 1911], 18:757).

48. Gager, *Kingdom and Community*, 76–79. In this connection it is also significant that the claim to orthodoxy and the accusation of heresy can shift around. Thus at the time of the Reformation, Protestant "heretics" sought to establish their historic orthodoxy in the *Magdeburg Centuries* by writing a church history that would show their doctrines to have been held by "true believers" in every age, while at the same time they accused the Pope of being apostate and antichrist. The Protestant reinterpretation of apostolic succession to mean "sharing the faith of the apostles" is of a similar nature.

49. Cf. Speed B. Leas, *Leadership and Conflict* (Nashville: Abingdon Press, 1982); G. Douglass Lewis, *Resolving Church Conflicts* (New York: Harper & Row, 1981).

50. Alvin J. Lindgren and Norman Shawchuck, *Let My People Go* (Nashville: Abingdon Press, 1980). See esp. chap. 4 for a lively discussion which gives names to alternative ways of reaching decisions.

51. Robert Greenleaf, *The Religious Leader as Servant* (Peterborough, N.H.: Windy Row Press, 1982), 17ff.

52. Terrence E. Deal and Allan A. Kennedy, *Corporate Cultures, The Rites*

and Rituals of Corporate Life (Reading, Mass.: Addison-Wesley Pub. Co., 1982), 50ff, 88, passim. See also Michael Maccoby, *The Gamesman* (New York: Simon & Schuster, 1976), esp. chap. 7, 172ff.

5. RITUALS OF STRUCTURE
AND MYSTERY

1. *The Apostolic Fathers*, vol. 2, *First and Second Clement*, ed. Robert M. Grant and Holt H. Graham (Camden, N.J.: Thomas Nelson & Sons, 1965), 26.

2. On the significance of travel facilities for the spread of Christianity, see Abraham J. Malherbe, *Social Aspects of Early Christianity*, 2d ed. (Philadelphia: Fortress Press, 1983), 64–67; John E. Stambaugh and David L. Balch, *The New Testament in Its Social Environment* (Philadelphia: Westminster Press, 1986), 37–41.

3. No Christian writing outside the New Testament can be dated to the first century with certainty. *First Clement* and the *Didache* have often been thought to be from as early as the 90s; Clement and some elements in the *Didache* may well be so; but in the case of both documents, dating remains conjectural.

4. Pliny *Letters* 10.96.8–9.

5. Wayne A. Meeks, *The First Urban Christians* (New Haven: Yale Univ. Press, 1983), 140.

6. Mary Douglas, *Natural Symbols: Explorations in Cosmology*, 2d ed. (London: Barrie & Jenkins, 1973), 78, quoted by Meeks, *First Urban Christians*, 141.

7. See the helpful discussion by John E. Burkhart, *Worship* (Philadelphia: Westminster Press, 1982), 23–27.

8. John Gager, *Kingdom and Community* (Englewood Cliffs, N.J.: Prentice-Hall, 1975), 140.

9. Pliny *Epistles* 10.96; Justin Martyr *First Apology* 65–67.

10. Etienne Trocmé, *The Passion as Liturgy: A Study in the Origin of the Passion Narratives in the Four Gospels* (London: SCM Press, 1983).

11. Cf. Clifford Geertz's discussion of ritual as a vehicle for change, in *The Interpretation of Cultures* (New York: Basic Books, 1973), 119ff.

12. Mary Douglas, "Deciphering a Meal," in her *Implicit Meanings: Essays in Anthropology* (London: Routledge & Kegan Paul, 1975), 269, has argued convincingly that the Hebrew dietary and other laws of purity ultimately "point to the hard-won and hard-to-defend territorial boundaries of the Promised Land." We may say then that as Christianity sprung the meaningfulness of territorial, and by extension, national identity, it was appropriate that those rituals by which this identity was symbolized should no longer be observed. Conversely, Judaism, which, though losing its territory literally yet maintained its identity with *Erets Israel*, appropriately retained these rituals. From a Christian perspective, their discontinuance can be accounted for on three levels: the theological (e.g., Paul's arguments in Romans and Galatians); the pragmatic (the evangelization of the Gentiles; cf. Acts 10); and the symbolic (as seen from an anthropological point of view).

13. Meeks, *First Urban Christians*, 142.

14. Cf. Martin Dibelius, *From Tradition to Gospel* (New York: Charles Scribner's Sons, n.d.), 18–20, who thought, however, that the formula in 1 Cor. 15:3–5 was originally composed in Greek; but see R. P. Martin, *Carmen*

Christi: Philippians ii.5–11 in Recent Interpretation and in the Setting of Early Christian Worship (Cambridge: at the University Press, 1967), 299–306, who gives convincing arguments for a Semitic original.

15. As a hymn, see esp. Martin, *Carmen Christi*, 24–41.

16. Charles H. Dodd, *The Apostolic Preaching and Its Developments* (New York: Harper & Brothers, 1936), was a major exponent of this view, which enjoyed wide acceptance. Further research has demonstrated, however, that the sermons in the Book of Acts are literary compositions that cannot be attributed to the apostles of the primitive Jerusalem community; see Ulrich Wilckens, *Die Missionsreden der Apostelgeschichte* (Neukirchen-Vluyn: Neukirchner Verlag, 1963).

17. At this point Dodd's arguments (see n. 16) are valid; see also Dibelius, *From Tradition to Gospel*, 15–18, and Bo Reicke, "A Synopsis of Early Christian Preaching," in Anton Fridrichsen et al., *The Root of the Vine: Essays in Biblical Theology* (London: Dacre Press, 1953), 138–143.

18. See, e.g., Eckhard Plümacher, *Lukas als hellenistischer Schriftsteller* (Göttingen: Vandenhoeck & Ruprecht, 1972), 32–79.

19. Reicke, "Synopsis of Early Christian Preaching," 138–143, has demonstrated this.

20. John A. T. Robinson, "The Most Primitive Christology of All?" *JTS* 7 (1956): 177–89; Richard F. Zehnle, *Peter's Pentecost Discourse. Tradition and Lukan Re-interpretation in Peter's Speeches of Acts 2 and 3*, SBLMS 15 (Nashville: Abingdon Press, 1971).

21. See Dieter Georgi, *Die Geschichte der Kollekte des Paulus für Jerusalem*, TF 38 (Hamburg-Bergstedt: Herbert Reich, 1965), esp. 84–87.

22. James Luther Adams, "The Historical Origins of Voluntarism," in *On Being Human Religiously* (Boston: Beacon Press, 1976), 63–66.

23. Luke tells of Paul preaching at Troas "on the first day of the week, when we were gathered together to break bread" (Acts 20:7). Whether this represents a regular weekly service on Sunday or one occasioned by Paul's visit is unclear; nor is it possible to determine whether the time element in this story is that of an event of the later fifties when Paul would have been at Troas, or whether it reflects a custom of Luke's time that he has woven into his narrative. An even less determinative statement is that in 1 Cor. 16:2, where Paul instructs the Corinthians to put money aside "at home" on the first day of each week, so they will have funds ready for his collection when he comes; nothing is said here of a day for worship; see Meeks, *First Urban Christians*, 143. It is a mistake to think of Sunday as having been introduced as a direct substitute for the Sabbath. The latter was a day of rest, while Sunday, until the fourth century, was not a day of rest, but of celebration (see Gregory Dix, *The Shape of the Liturgy*, 2d ed. [London: Dacre Press, 1949], 336–37). During much of the first century, Christians, other than those who continued to observe the Sabbath, apparently had no fixed day for worship.

24. While most scholars agree that Rev. 1:10 refers to Sunday, two alternative interpretations have been advanced: that the Lord's Day there is Easter (see, e.g., Kenneth A. Strand, "Another Look at the Lord's Day in the Early Church and Rev. 1:10," *NTS* 13 [1967]: 147–81); and that it is equivalent to the Old Testament phrase, "the day of the Lord," that is, the eschaton (see e.g., Samuele Bacchiocchi, *From Sabbath to Sunday* [Rome: Pontifical Gregorian Univ. Press, 1977], 123–31).

25. William R. Schoedel, *Ignatius of Antioch*, Hermeneia (Philadelphia:

Fortress Press, 1985), 123–24; Willy Rordorf, *Sunday* (Philadelphia: Westminster Press, 1968), 205–15.

26. Rordorf, *Sunday*, 209–10.

27. The term in Greek is *kyriakē hēmera* in Rev. 1:10, but simply *kyriakē* ("Lord's") in Ignatius and the *Didache;* the abbreviated form suggests that the name had become widely current by the early second century.

28. Emile Durkheim, *The Elementary Forms of Religious Life* (1915; New York: Free Press, 1965), 228–29.

29. Arnold van Gennep, *Rites of Passage (Les rites de passage,* 1909; Chicago: Univ. of Chicago Press, 1960).

30. E.D. Chapple and C.S. Coon, *Principles of Anthropology* (New York: Henry Holt, 1942).

31. Johann Wolfgang von Goethe, *Faust,* Part 1, Scene 3, trans. Bayard Taylor (New York: Grosset & Dunlap, n.d.), 74.

32. Burkhart, *Worship,* 73.

33. Texts bearing on this ritual are collected in Hermann L. Strack and Paul Billerbeck, *Kommentar zum Neuen Testament aus Talmud und Midrasch* (Munich: C. H. Beck, 1922), 1:101–12. While it cannot be proved that this ritual was practiced as early as John the Baptist and Jesus, it probably was. Some writers have seen it as the major antecedent of Christian baptism (e.g., H. H. Rowley, "Jewish Proselyte Baptism," *HUCA* 15 [1940]: 313–34); a safer view is that if it was current in New Testament times, it was a way of dramatically cleansing the proselyte from all the defilement of the gentile world, and thus making that person fit to enter Judaism.

34. Geza Vermes, *The Dead Sea Scrolls in English,* 2d ed. (New York: Penguin, 1981), 74–75.

35. Ibid., 79.

36. In *Manual of Discipline* V. 14, the phrase translated "turn from their wickedness" is *šbw mrʿtm,* which appears also in Jer. 18:8; 23:14 in reference to corporate and personal repentance.

37. Herbert Braun, *Qumran und das Neue Testament* (Tübingen: J.C.B. Mohr 1966), 2:16, points out that while the forgiveness of sins played a central role at Qumran, it was not imparted through the washings. The latter, connected as they were with obedience to the law and the rules of the sect, had to do with purity.

38. It is true that the Gospels speak of "the disciples of John" (Matt. 11:2–6; Luke 7:18–23; John 1:35; 3:25; 4:1, 2). To what degree they constituted a community we cannot say. As they are repeatedly presented as standing vis-à-vis the disciples of Jesus, for Christian writers the latter may have served as a model according to which John's followers were perceived and described. The existence of sects that have looked to John as their central figure, represented in modern times by the Mandaeans, can tell us little regarding the original relationships among his followers.

39. Robert A. Kraft, trans., *The Apostolic Fathers* (New York: Nelson, 1965), 3:163–64.

40. *The Ante-Nicene Fathers* 1.183.

41. Robert M. Grant, trans., *The Apostolic Fathers* (Camden, N.J.: Thomas Nelson & Sons, 1966), 4:121.

42. Karl Barth, *The Teaching of the Church Regarding Baptism* (London: SCM Press, 1948).

43. Geoffrey Wainwright, *Christian Initiation* (Richmond: John Knox Press,

1969). Robert L. Browning and Roy A. Reed, *The Sacraments in Religious Education as Liturgy: An Ecumenical Model* (Birmingham: Religious Education Press, 1985).

44. Dix, *Shape of the Liturgy*, 50–55; Bo Reicke, *Diakonie, Festfreude und Zelos in Verbindung mit der altchristlichen Agapenfeier* (Uppsala universitets Årsskrift, 1951; Uppsala: Lundequist), 70–71, 114–15.

45. Vermes, *Dead Sea Scrolls in English*, 81; Josephus gives a similar description, *War* 2.129–31 (8.5). Participation in these meals was carefully restricted to the members of the community and thus acted powerfully not only to heighten their sense of community, but also, as a group that saw themselves to be particularly pure, to define their boundaries over against the world outside.

46. Karl Georg Kuhn, "The Lord's Supper and the Communal Meal at Qumran," in Krister Stendahl, ed., *The Scrolls and the New Testament* (New York: Harper & Brothers, 1957), 65–93; Braun, *Qumran und das Neue Testament*, 2:29–43.

47. Vermes, *Dead Sea Scrolls in English*, 121.

48. Braun, *Qumran und das Neue Testament*, 2:39; Douglas, *Implicit Meanings*, 268–69. Note the comment of Alan Hugh M'Neile on Matt. 26:29: "The wine that He would then drink would be 'of a new kind,' *kainon* (see ix. 17), the 'fulfillment' (cf. Lk. xxii. 16) of the wine that He now gave them" (*The Gospel According to St. Matthew* [London: Macmillan & Co., 1965], 383).

49. Gerd Theissen, *The Social Setting of Pauline Christianity*, ed. John H. Schütz (Philadelphia: Fortress Press, 1982), 165.

50. Ibid., 164–65; cf. Meeks, *First Urban Christians*, 159.

51. Reicke, *Diakonie, Festfreude und Zelos*, 287.

52. Ibid., 252–93.

53. Theissen, *Social Setting*, 121–74.

54. Stephen C. Barton, "Paul's Sense of Place: An Anthropological Approach to Community Formation in Corinth," *NTS* 32 (1986): 225–46.

55. Reicke, *Diakonie, Festfreude und Zelos*, 368–93, has argued that the Christian agape celebrations were subject to excesses of gluttony and were hotbeds of political agitation throughout the whole pre-Constantinian period.

56. On this shift, see esp. Hans Lietzmann, *Mass and Lord's Supper* (Leiden: E.J. Brill, 1979), 210–12. He sees it as having been "inevitable as the community grew in numbers and the members could no longer all be included at the common meals, which now gave place to occasional and separate meetings of smaller groups."

57. Grant, trans., *The Apostolic Fathers*, 4:93, 53.

58. Chapple and Coon, *Principles of Anthropology*.

59. Avery Dulles, *Models of the Church* (New York: Doubleday & Co. 1974), 64, 65, 66, 67.

60. Elise Magers, transcript, 9 November 1983.

FOR FURTHER READING: MAJOR SOCIAL SCIENCE SOURCES

Our social science sources have been taken from well-known classics that have particular relevance to the experience of tension in the church. Since many readers are familiar with these authors in other settings, we list them here to provide an orientation to the study as a whole. Beyond this overview of authors, the reader may wish to consult the notes and indexes in the book.

"Community Formation" is based on two major sources. For the development of language and symbolic universe, we have used the concept of "social self" identified with the foundational work of George Herbert Mead, *Mind, Self and Society* (Chicago: Univ. of Chicago Press, 1967), and the more contemporary studies of James M. Gustafson, *Treasures in Earthen Vessels* (Chicago: Univ. of Chicago Press, 1976), and Peter Berger, *The Sacred Canopy* (New York: Doubleday & Co., 1969). For a study of the dynamics of group life, we have used the dialectical concepts of Ferdinand Tönnies, *Community and Society* (New York: Harper & Row, 1977).

"The Energy of Counterculture Christianity" grows from the broader sense of "poverty" in the New Testament, and therefore considers church-sect tensions as seen in contemporary situations. In considering social dynamics, we have built upon the primary work of Ernst Troeltsch, *The Social Teachings of the Christian Churches* (Chicago: Univ. of Chicago Press, 1981), and for concepts of leadership we have drawn on the thinking of *Max Weber On Charisma and Institution Building*, edited by S. N. Eisenstadt (Chicago: Univ. of Chicago Press, 1968).

In "Faith Crisis and Christian Witness" the controversial and, we believe, constructive work of Leon Festinger, *A Theory of Cognitive Dissonance* (Stanford, Calif.: Stanford Univ. Press, 1957), and *When Prophecy Fails* (Minneapolis: Univ. of Minnesota Press, 1956), has been important. It finds parallels in the work of Victor Turner, *The Ritual Process* (Ithaca, N.Y.: Cornell Univ. Press, 1977), and James Loder, *The Transforming Moment* (New York: Harper & Row, 1981).

"Using Conflict Constructively" takes its insights from the classic propositions of Lewis Coser, *The Functions of Social Conflict* (New York: Free Press, 1964), with contemporary support from William Gamson, *Power and Discontent* (Homewood, Ill.: Dorsey Press, 1968).

"Rituals of Structure and Mystery" is based on the foundational study of Arnold van Gennep, *Rites of Passage* (Chicago: Univ. of Chicago Press, 1961), which we believe has been made especially accessible by the contemporary interpretations of Mary Douglas, *Natural Symbols* (New York: Random House, 1972), and Clifford Geertz, *The Interpretation of Cultures* (New York: Basic Books, 1973).

INDEX OF SCRIPTURE PASSAGES

1:16–17—40
1:24–25—82
1:32–34—84
1:34—82
1:43–44—82
2:10—82
3:10–14—150
3:11–12—82
3:17—25
4:11—17
4:36–41—71
4:41—82
6:8–11—40
6:51–52—82
7:1–4—148
7:3–4—138
7:19—138
7:28—26
7:31–37—84
7:36—82
8:14–21—82
8:27—82
8:29—82
8:29–30—82
8:31—82
8:31–33—76
8:34–35—87
8:35—111
9:1—87, 89, 90
9:31—82
9:32—82
10:21—55
10:21–22—57
10:23–25—57
10:28—57
10:31—54
10:32—83
10:35–45—26
11:9—140
11:25—141
11:27–33—26
12:13–34—26
12:15—25
12:37—54, 69
13—87, 92
13:4—87
13:5–9—87
13:7—90
13:10—87, 90, 94
13:14—87
13:24—87, 89
13:26—87
13:30—92
13:30–31—87
13:34—87
14:3—29
14:22–26—158
14:27–28—83
15—83
15:30–31—77
15:40–41—50
16—83
16:7—85

Luke
1:53—55
3:10–11—55
3:10–12—150
3:12–14—150
3:16—151
4:18—56
6:20—56
6:21–22—56
6:23—56
6:24–25—57
6:24–26—56
6:27—116
6:30—58
8:1–3—50
8:2—27
8:3—40, 107
8:9–10—25
8:9–15—90
8:10—17
9:3–5—40
9:27—90
10:1—69
10:1–2—26
10:1–12—40
10:4–12—40
10:16—26, 69
10:38—29
11:2–4—141
12:1—25
12:16–21—25
12:21—25
14:1—56
14:13—56
14:15—56
14:21—56
14:26—27
14:33—57
16:1–9—39
16:13—57
16:13–14—39
16:19–31—56
17:20–21—90
17:21—41
18:1–8—25
18:22–23—57
18:25—57
18:28—57
20:1–8—26
20:20–40—26
21—91
21:8—91
21:12–13—91
21:20—91
21:24—91
21:25–28—91
21:32—91
22:15–19—158
24:6–7—85
24:18–21—76
24:21—84
24:27—31, 84
24:30–31—84
24:32—85
24:35—85
24:44—72, 125
24:44–46—97
24:47—97
24:45–49—84, 85, 86, 90
24:47—97
24:49—30

John
1:1—72
1:10–11—72
1:11–12—86
1:19–34—150
1:29—86
1:42—25
1:49—96
3:22—150
3:26—150
3:27–30—150
4:2—141, 150
4:27—50
5:25—92
5:28–29—92
6:14–15—76
7:46—71
11:1–44—29
11:25–27—71
12:6—50
13:29—50
14:2–3—92
14:16–29—93
14:25–27—16
20:21–23—93

Acts
1—5—71
1:2—86
1:6—77
1:6–8—57
1:8—69
1:14—70
1:15–26—31, 70
1:21–22—70
2—141
2:14–36—19
2:36—152
2:38—151
2:44–45—50, 107
2:46—108
3—141
3:1—108
3:12–26—19
4:10—69
4:13—69
5:12—108
5:20–21—108
5:42—108
6—31
6:1–6—128
7:2–53—19
8:1–17—118
8:14–15—31

INDEX OF SUBJECTS

Christianity as an international movement, 136, 145; and cognitive dissonance, 96–97, 101; in the early church,
50–51; and faith, 96–97, 101; of slaves,
45–47; of wives, 45–47
Eschatology: and the early church, 76–
78; and energy produced by postponed
Parousia, 86–95; and Luke-Acts, 56–
57; and Pauline theology, 54–55; realized, in John, 92–93
Eucharist. *See* Ritual; Sacraments; Sacred space; Status and social standing
Evangelism: and cognitive dissonance,
95–97, 102–3; and the early church,
136; and language, 19–23; and "the
poor," 60, 62–63; and the urban setting, 44–47, 49–51

Faith (*pistis*), 15; and cognitive dissonance, 94–95, 102–3
Family values, 45–47. *See also* Churches
and extended family
Fund raising, 73, 143–44

Gesellschaft/Gemeinschaft, 32–33

Hatred, 116–17
Heritage: in conflict in the early church,
109–11, 121–22; cultural continuity of,
in Luke-Acts, 19; and cultural insecurity, 39–41; of Greco-Roman and Jewish symbols, 137–38; and language,
13–18, 140–41
History, 18–19, 56–57, 84–86, 99; learning from, 3–5
Holy Spirit: and baptism, 151–52; and
the church in history, 85–86; Montanus as the recipient of, 125–26
Humor, 24–26

Identity of the church, 9–11, 21–23, 43–
45, 136–39; in Christian understandings of "the poor," 60–65; and conflict, 114–17, 129; and the crucifixion
and delayed Parousia, 76–78
Institution and organization of the
church: in early church writings, 26–
28; and internal conflict, 120–25, 127–
30; and sacraments, 152–53, 162–63
Intimacy, 23–37, 105

Jesus movement: and appeal to the poor,
54; and cultural insecurity, 40–41; and
the earliest Christians, 124–25; in the
emergence of settled communities, 43–
44
John the Baptist, 149–50

Language: and contemporary use, 19–23;
of the early church, 12–18; of ethnic
churches, 35–36; function of, in community formation, 18–23; and symbolic universe, 18–19

Leadership: charismatic, 67–68; and the
Christ, 71–72; in external conflict,
117–19; New Testament, 68–71; organizational and intimate, 32, 35–36;
pastoral, in times of cognitive dissonance, 97–98; rational and traditional,
65–67; three styles of, in contemporary
churches, 72–75, 132–33
Liberation theology, 60–65
Liminality, 100–101
Lord's Day. *See* Ritual; Worship
Lord's Prayer. *See* Ritual; Worship

Messianic secret, 81–83
Mystery (*mystērion*), 16–17; applied to
rituals, 146–48, 156, 165; and the numinous nature of the eucharist, 160–
61, 163

New Testament writers: James, 57–58,
122; John, 86, 92–93; Luke, 19, 55–
57, 84–86, 90–92, 151–52; Mark, 81–
83, 85–86; Matthew, 83–84, 88–90;
Pastoral Epistles, 26–27, 122–23; Paul,
29–31, 44–47, 54–55, 80–81, 86, 126–
27, 143–44, 158–63; Revelation, 110–
12

Officers of the church, 27–28, 36, 37, 71

Parousia, 87–94
Peace (*eirēnē*), 15–16, 104–5, 115–16,
133—34
Persecution, 136
Poor (*ptōchos*), 14–15, 111–12; four atti-
tudes toward, 51–65
Power and powerlessness. *See* Counter-
culture and power and powerlessness
Primary group, 24–26. *See also* Counter-
culture

Resurrection, 96. *See also* Crucifixion of
Jesus
Rites: of intensification, 146, 163–65; of
passage, 146, 155–56
Ritual, 135–39, 146–56, 156–65

Sacraments: baptism, 101, 148–56, eucharist, 101, 139, 157–65
Sacred space, 157, 160–61, 165
Salvation history, 3, 19
Sect, 41–42. *See also* Counterculture
Slavery, 46–47
Social ministries, 63–65, 96, 145–46
Social sciences: basic approach of, 1–3,
5–7; relation of, to theology, 7–8; resources of, 187–88
Status and social standing, 42–43, 56;
and the early church, 136, 145; as
transcended in baptism, 156; as transcended in eucharist, 164–65; and
transcendence of social differences in
cognitive dissonance, 96–97

Success and wealth, 29, 57–59, 107, 111–
12, 122; and the church in Corinth,
121, 159–63; and cognitive dissonance,
96–97, 101; and the counterculture,
42–43, 51–53, 59–62; among disciples,
26; and "relative deprivation," 63; and
the urban setting, 44–45
Symbolic universe, 18–19, 106; and cognitive dissonance, 78–80, 97

Transforming moment, 101–2

Unity in diversity: of Christians in the
ancient world, 9–11; and cognitive dissonance, 96–97

Urban movement, 44–47, 124–25; and
the early church, 108–9; and Luke,
30–31; and Paul, 29–31; and the Roman Empire, 135–36

Volunteers, 36

Women, 45–47
Worship, 101, 144–46; and hymns and
creeds, 139–41, 145; offering in, as
source of unity, 143–44; and prayers,
139, 141–42; and preaching, 21, 142–
43

INDEX OF ANCIENT
AUTHORS

INDEX OF NAMES

198 Index of Names